IMAGES
*of America*

# SKIING AT LAKE TAHOE

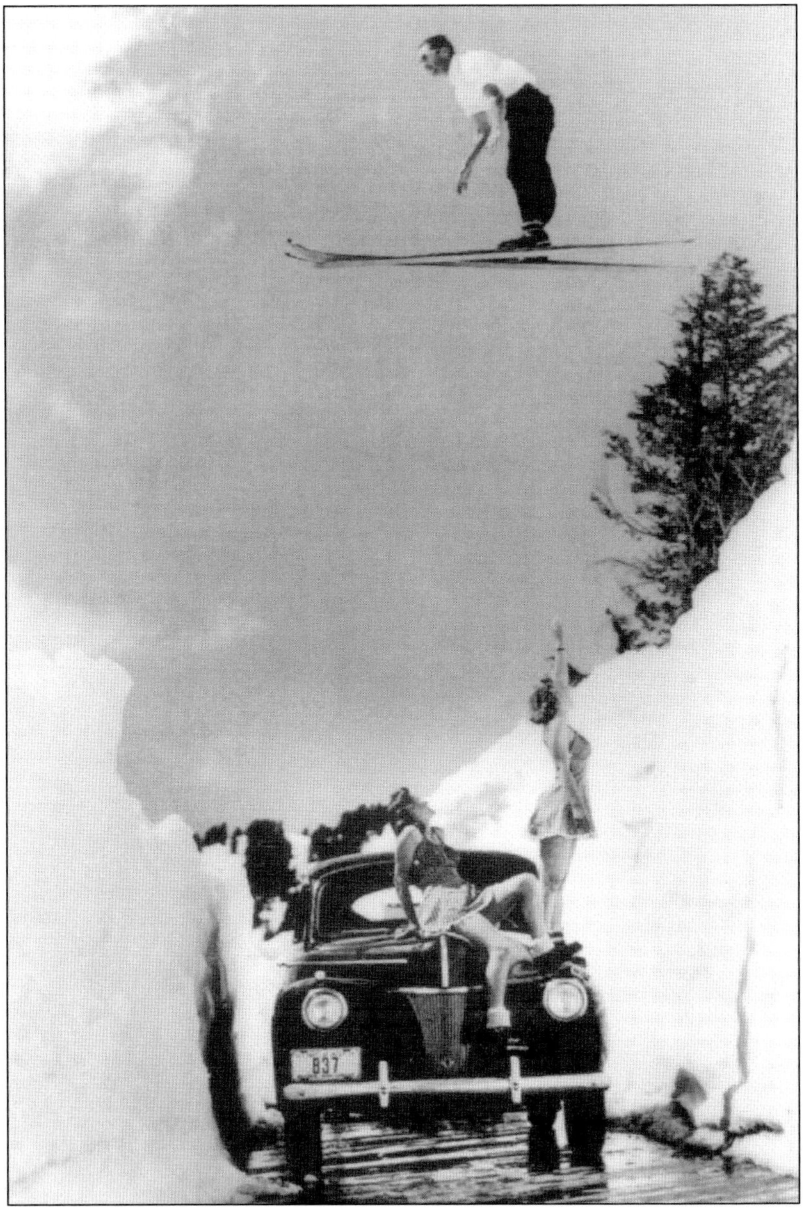

The California Chamber of Commerce began promoting skiing in the Golden State after the International Olympic Committee rejected the state's bid for the 1932 winter games. This promotional photograph by Jervie H. Eastman captures Dick Brown jumping the road to Mount Lassen in 1940. The two women on the car are Artis Tunnison (left) and Beverly Irish. (Courtesy Truckee Donner Historical Society.)

**On the Cover:** Dodge Ridge ski instructors Gordon Soltau (left), Eric Johnson (center), and Wayne Wisauen race side by side in the 1950s. The Lake Tahoe region was already a favorite skiing destination for Californians and Western Nevadans, but after the highly successful 1960 Winter Olympics at Squaw Valley, the whole world took notice. (Courtesy Donner Summit Historical Society/Norm Sayler collection.)

IMAGES
*of America*

# SKIING AT LAKE TAHOE

Mark McLaughlin

ARCADIA PUBLISHING

ISBN 978-0-7385-8906-0

Published by Arcadia Publishing
Charleston, South Carolina

Printed in the United States of America

Library of Congress Control Number: 2011933819

For all general information, please contact Arcadia Publishing:
Telephone 843-853-2070
Fax 843-853-0044
E-mail sales@arcadiapublishing.com
For customer service and orders:
Toll-Free 1-888-313-2665

Visit us on the Internet at www.arcadiapublishing.com

*In memory of Robert "Fro" Frohlich (1955–2010), an award-winning Tahoe ski journalist. A talented writer and hard-charging skier, Frohlich had a bold passion for winter sport and a hearty appetite for the next adventure.*

# Contents


Acknowledgments 6

Introduction 7

1. Fastest Humans in the World 9
2. Truckee Carnivals Launch Winter Sports 17
3. Alpine Skiing Comes of Age (1930s) 29
4. Skiing Ramps Up before World War II 43
5. Downhill Sprouts at Lake Tahoe 55
6. Postwar Boom in Tahoe Skiing 69
7. A Heavenly Valley and Nevada Game On! 91
8. Bring on the Winter Olympics! 103
9. Lake Tahoe's Skiing Then and Now 111

# ACKNOWLEDGMENTS

Very special thanks to Norm Sayler, president of the Donner Summit Historical Society, for sharing his invaluable knowledge regarding regional ski history and for the generous use of images from the society's extensive collection. Much appreciation to the Truckee Donner Historical Society, North Lake Tahoe Historical Society, Western SkiSport Museum, Nevada Historical Society, and South Lake Tahoe Historical Society for the photographs related to the development of Lake Tahoe skiing. This book is better because of the generosity of the following people, who shared background information or historical images from their personal or private collections: Craig Beck, Dana Scanlon, Bill Klein, Vi White, Dick Dorworth, Scott Lawson, Rob Russell, Gary Noy, Tom "Ice Man" Macaulay, the Keston Ramsey family, Frank Titus, David C. Antonucci, David Borges, Bill Oudegeest, Rick and Sue Lundblade, and Rick Brower.

Special thanks to several professional photographers who contributed quality images of modern skiing and snowboarding in the Tahoe region: David E. Caramazzi (www.egidio.com), Keoki Flagg (www.gallerykeoki.com), and Jeff Engerbretson (Diamond Peak). Bill Briner, the official photographer at the 1960 Squaw Valley Olympics, generously contributed images and personal recollections from those Winter Games (www.1960olympicphotos.com). Please visit their websites for more information. A debt of gratitude is owed to my research assistant Meghan Robins for her help in tracking down images and information for this project.

As always, my parents, John and Florence, deserve mention for their ongoing encouragement to pursue my dreams. And finally, thank you to my wife, Nora O'Neill, for her absolute support and understanding as I spent several months focused on this book to meet the publication deadline.

# Introduction

Ski racing in the northern Sierra Nevada harkens back to the 1850s, when grizzled miners rode rusty ore buckets up the mountain and then skied down on short wooden barrel staves mounted with crude leather bindings. Within a decade, racing had morphed into a popular sport in which speed-crazed locals barreled down the mountain on skis up to 15 feet long at speeds approaching 100 miles per hour. These people were the fastest humans on the planet, and the speed records set on those long, heavy boards were not broken until nearly 80 years later.

For these miners, considered the first ski racers in North America, it took a lot of whiskey and serious betting to get them to push the boundaries of physics and good sense. But the boards got longer—and the racers went faster—until the thrill of speed overcame the fear of death.

California skiing got its start not as a sport per se but as a form of transportation over deep snow. Norwegians who arrived during the Gold Rush introduced the concept of skiing on planks of wood as opposed to using web-style snowshoes. It was not long before the adaptive miners were traveling smoothly over the snowbound Sierra, pushing themselves along with one long pole. Doctors were soon skiing for miles to treat injuries or deliver babies. Residents in snow country skied to work and hauled supplies on skis—even at funerals, mourners and pallbearers glided smoothly along.

It was not long before communities throughout the "Lost Sierra" region of Plumas and Sierra Counties had skiers competing for bragging rights. Mining towns sponsored long-board ski teams that raced for cash prizes worth hundreds of dollars. America's first organized ski club was formed when Creed Raymond founded the Alturas Snowshoe Club at La Porte in 1867. (The world's first ski clubs were started in Norway and Australia in 1861.)

The Alturas Snowshoe Club was founded for the physical and mental well-being of the miners, although alcohol-fueled high-speed crashes took their toll. The first downhill racecourse in the western hemisphere was laid out at Johnsville in Plumas County. The course was 1,230 feet long and ran straight down the mountain. There were no chairlifts or rope tows, so the winner of each heat had to hike back up the mountain in order to race again. The boards were long, heavy, and had no side cut to aid in turning. It was all about speed.

By the late 1880s, the mines of the Lost Sierra were tapped out and the longboard-racing era was winding down. Following the construction of the first transcontinental railroad, the town of Truckee, in Nevada County, became the gateway to the central Sierra's winter wonderland. Local businessman Charles F. McGlashan was an intelligent and energetic jack-of-all-trades. In the early 1890s, McGlashan shared his prescient vision of the railroad town of Truckee as a major attraction for winter sports. His persuasive proposal energized Truckee's business community, and they wholeheartedly decided to capitalize on the idea. The cities of Quebec, Canada, and St. Paul, Minnesota, had boosted their local economies with winter carnivals—Truckee could, too.

McGlashan had argued that well-advertised and -promoted ice carnivals and midwinter festivals would spur thousands of people to take the train from the dreary flatlands to Truckee. Before long,

Southern Pacific "Snowball Express" party trains were conveying hundreds of tourists to Truckee so they could enjoy the annual winter carnival the town first established in 1895. Every weekend from early February into March, fun-loving visitors could spend the day sledding, ice skating, and tobogganing before Saturday night dancing and saloon-hopping in Truckee's business district. Hilltop, the small hill with an open slope located across the river from downtown Truckee, provided an excellent place to sled and toboggan. In 1910, an old steam engine from an abandoned lumber mill was hauled in by ox-drawn wagons and converted into a pullback lift. Some ski historians believe this was the first mechanical lift of its kind in the United States.

By 1928, ski jumps were constructed at Hilltop and on Olympic Hill, located near Tahoe City. That year, California applied to host the 1932 Winter Olympic Games in the Truckee-Tahoe region, but the European-dominated International Olympic Committee felt the state lacked both organization and a sufficient sporting background. The decision was also partly influenced by the misperception that all of California basks in a year-round Mediterranean climate.

Despite the IOC's rejection of California to host the 1932 Winter Olympics (the games were awarded to Lake Placid, New York), a victory was secured when Lake Tahoe was voted to host the prestigious National Ski Tournament—the first one held west of the Rockies. The 65-meter ski jump at Olympic Hill (present-day Granlibakken) was the location for this pivotal event, where the beautiful scenery, mild weather, and incredibly deep snow impressed competitors and spectators alike. The winning combination of heavy snowfall, a beautiful lake, and majestic mountains convinced a skeptical media that California really could offer world-class skiing.

The deal was sealed in 1960, when the VIII Olympic Winter Games were held at Squaw Valley, a few miles outside of Tahoe City. Hundreds of Truckee locals turned out for the arrival of the Olympic torch, including a relay of cross-country skiers recruited from Tahoe-Truckee High School. As each person passed the torch, the community's pride at hosting the Olympics soared. On February 15, Dr. Robert Affeldt gave a rousing speech at Truckee's historic Rocking Stone Tower, saying, "Truckee proudly kindles her own Olympic torch from the flame flown from Norway, secure in the knowledge of the great part she has played in the development of winter sports."

In the years since those 1960 Winter Games, the Truckee–Lake Tahoe region has become a mecca for winter sports enthusiasts. Over the past 50 years, more than 15 resorts have been established in the area, with more than 22,000 acres available for lift-served skiing and snowboarding. Large infusions of capital have boosted the capabilities of Lake Tahoe resorts with state-of-the-art technologies and extensive chairlift grids. Today, these modern, crowd-pleasing facilities spread from South Lake Tahoe to the north shore—Truckee and Donner Summit—forming the country's greatest concentration of ski resorts in one area. The challenging mountains and abundant snowfall attract some of the best skiers and snowboarders in the United States, including many who call Lake Tahoe home.

Visitors to the Tahoe Sierra enjoy virtually unlimited choices in recreation. But, when it comes to the social benefits of sport, the 1960 mission statement of the US Olympic Committee is more important than ever: "Instill in the youth of America the qualities of courage, self-reliance, honesty, and tolerance; promote and encourage the physical, moral and cultural education, to the end that their health, patriotism, character and good citizenship may be fully developed."

# *One*

# Fastest Humans in the World

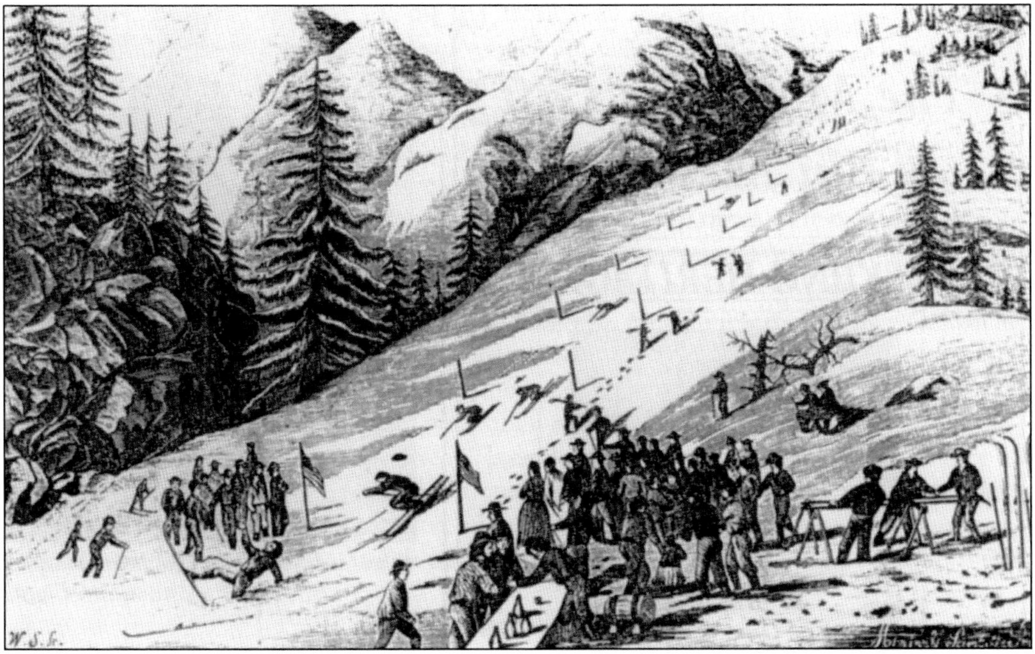

In the 1860s, miners in the northern Sierra Nevada began holding ski races to determine local champions. Early longboard racers rode skis up to 15 feet long, stood four abreast, and shot down the mountain shoulder-to-shoulder on a straight track more than 1,000 feet long—at full speed. Top speeds at the finish line could reach 100 miles per hour. (Courtesy Western SkiSport Museum.)

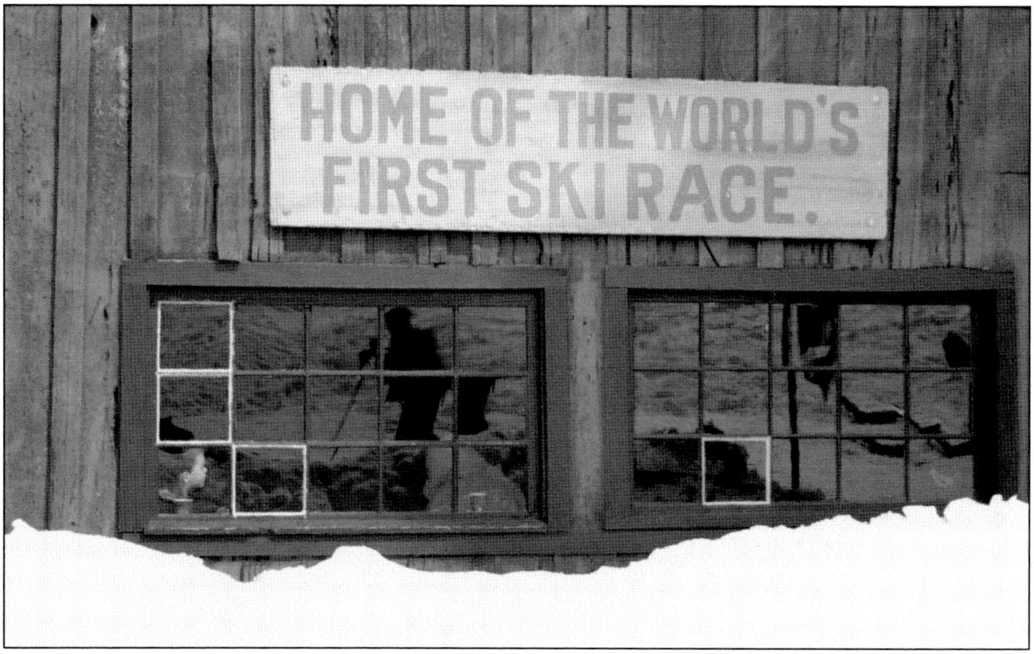

The Plumas Eureka Ski Bowl, located near Eureka Peak in Plumas County, California, is considered by historians to be the site of the world's first consistent, organized alpine ski-racing competitions, which began in the early 1860s. (Courtesy Mark McLaughlin.)

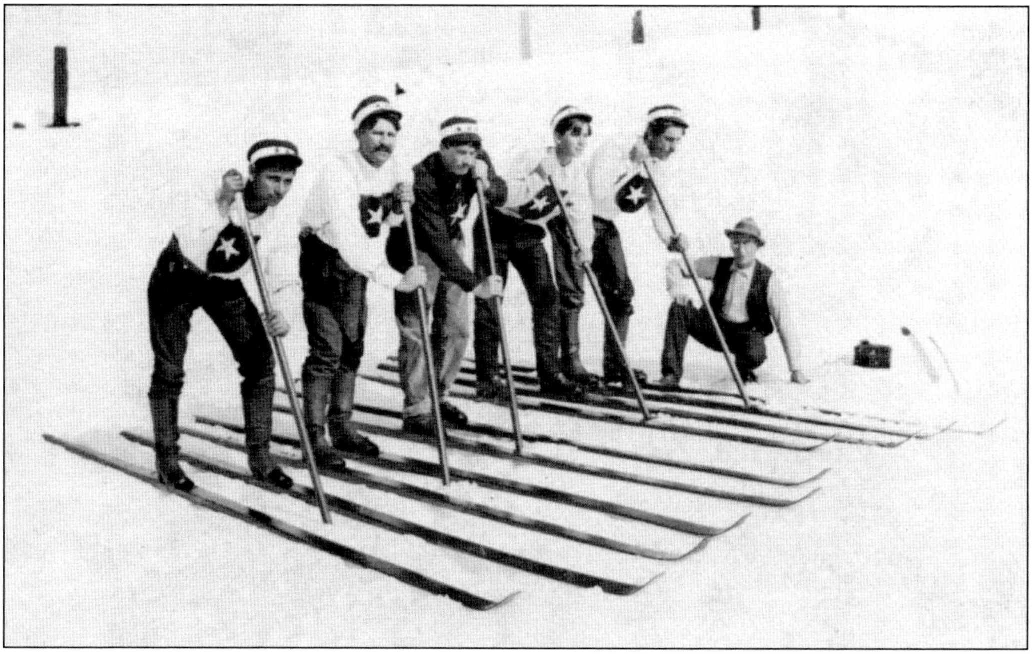
During the longboard-racing era, victory often relied on the "dope" (wax) that skiers applied to the bottom of their boards to improve glide. Dope consisted of ingredients such as whale spermaceti; pine pitch; and oils, as well as rosin and balsam, from trees like cedars, hemlocks, and sugar pines. Mixtures were cooked and then hand rubbed into the base of the skis. Note the "dope maker" and his wax box behind these 1880s-era La Porte racers. (Courtesy Dana Scanlon collection.)

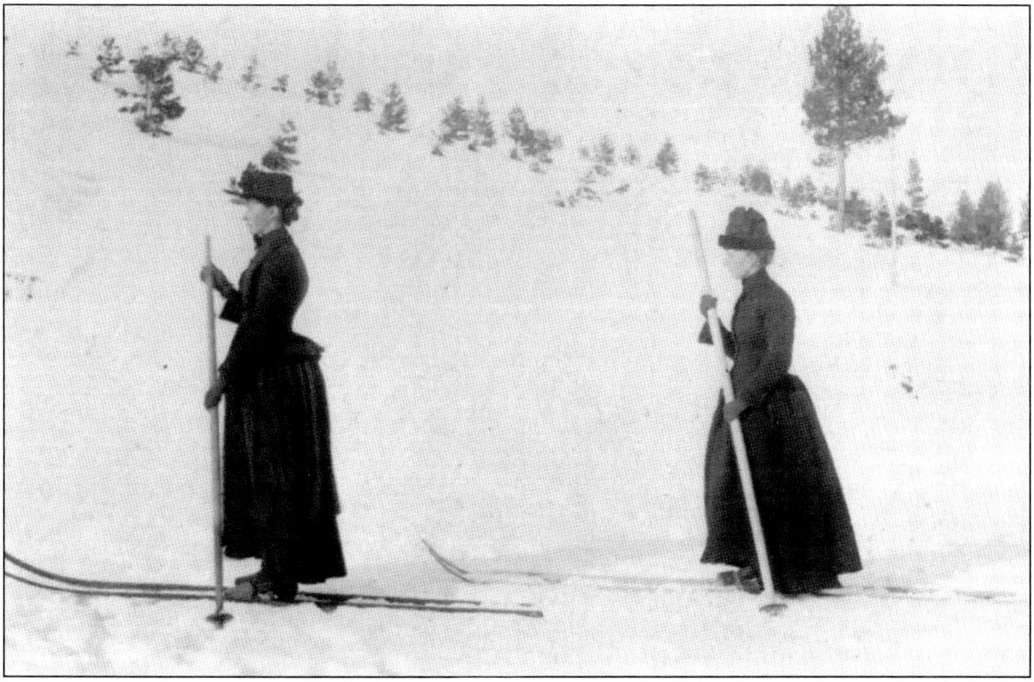

For early pioneer mining communities isolated by the deep mountain snowpack, skis were the only way to travel or transport food, mail, and medicine. However, it did not take long for the drudgery of sliding on snow to morph into the thrill of downhill racing for both men and women. A great tribute to early California ski racing was that women and children were allowed to compete in their own events. During the Victorian era of the 19th century—when women could not vote and were generally disenfranchised socially, politically, and economically—females in the Sierra mining camps were encouraged to grab their skis and hit the hill. In 1867, Lotti Joy (not pictured) flew down La Porte's racecourse at 49 miles per hour to set the earliest women's speed record. The women's races often drew the largest crowds and loudest cheers. (Above, courtesy Truckee Donner Historical Society; below, courtesy Dana Scanlon collection.)

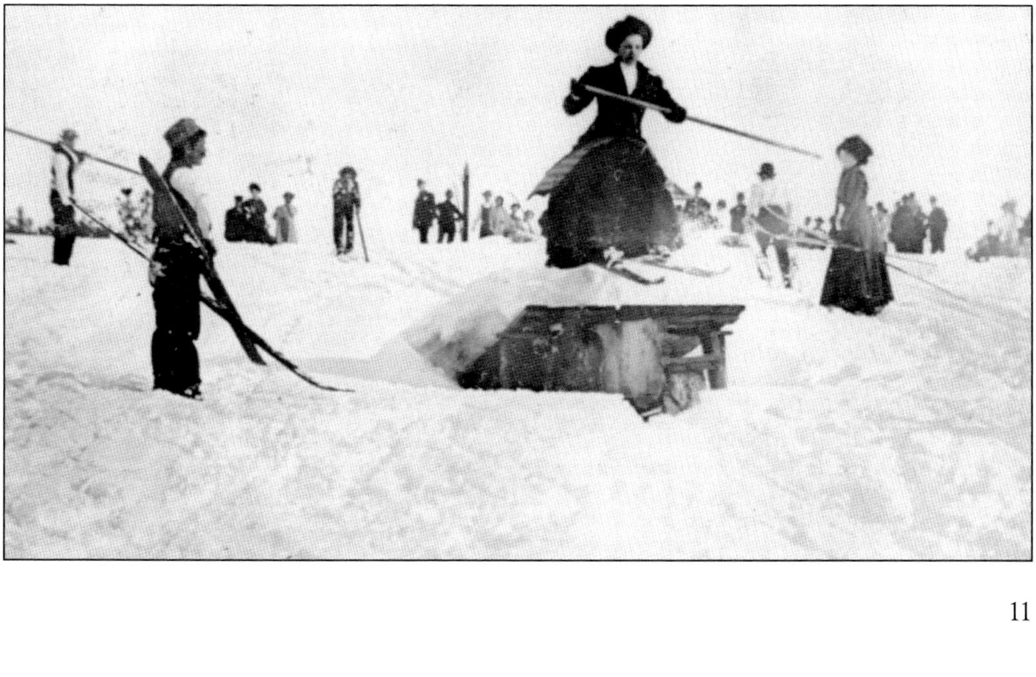

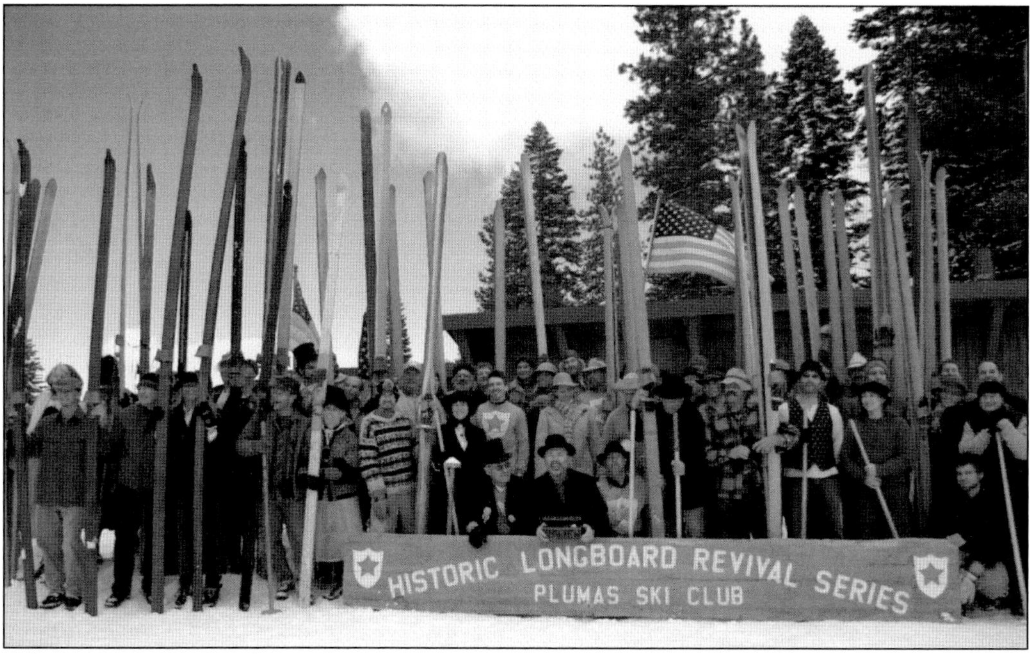


When mining activity diminished in the late 1800s, the organized longboard ski races were slowly abandoned. In the early 1990s, the venerable Plumas Ski Club fired up a revival racing series near Eureka Peak. Competitors are required to wear old-fashioned ski garb or Western wear. These annual winter races attract throngs of spectators to the documented birthplace of organized downhill ski racing in California. (Courtesy Mark McLaughlin.)

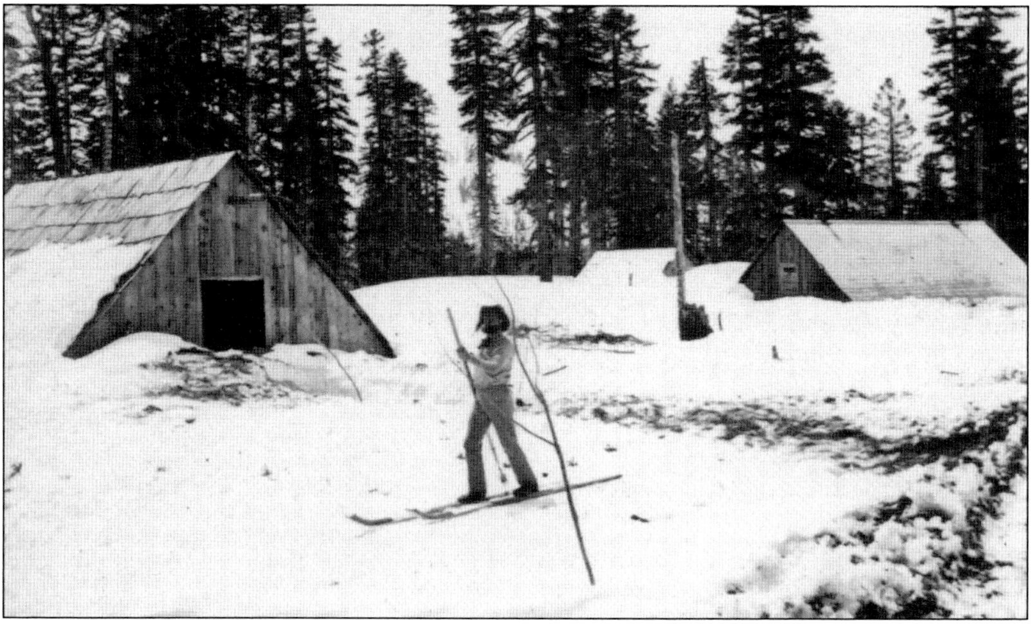

This c. 1864 photograph, one of the earliest known images of a California skier, was taken on the crest of the Sierra Nevada near the Tahoe Basin. Note the black material scattered on the snow (typically wood ash), which was used to accelerate the melting of the spring snowpack. (Courtesy Dana Scanlon collection.)

During his 20-year stint carrying supplies and the US mail over the storm-wracked Sierras during the winter months, John A. "Snowshoe" Thompson earned a well-deserved reputation for extraordinary endurance and heroic bravery. He skied over the mountains through bitter storms with no gun or heavy blankets for protection and only bits of beef jerky for sustenance. To avoid deadly avalanches, he followed the ridgeline wherever he could. This portrait of Thomspon hangs in the Norwegian embassy in Washington, DC. (Courtesy William B. Berry collection.)

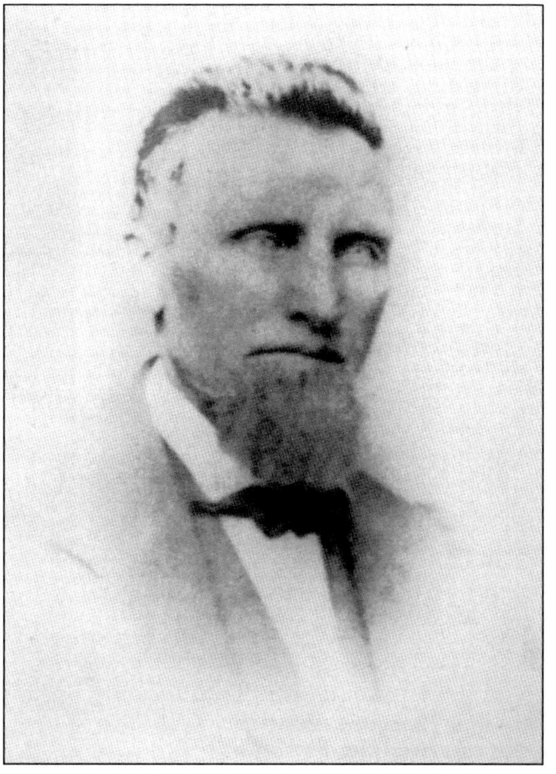

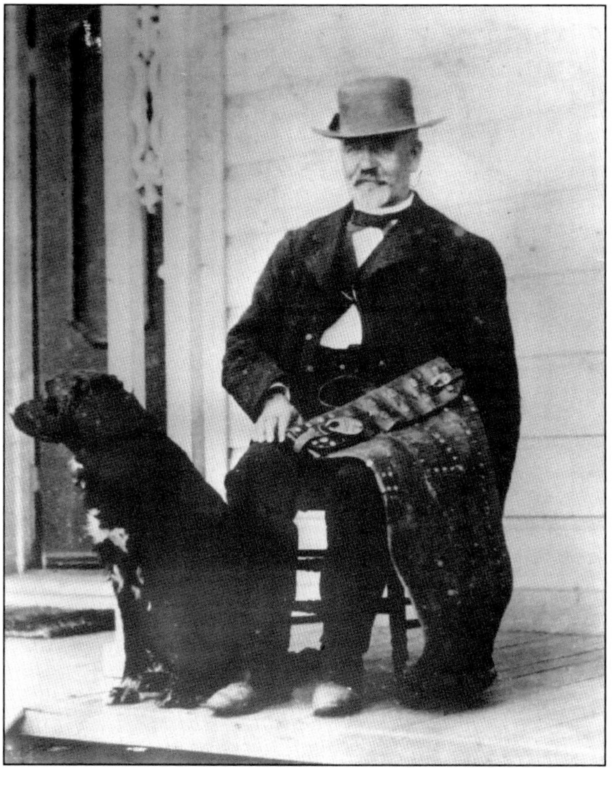

A February 22, 1869, ski meet between John "Snowshoe" Thompson and the racers from Plumas County ended in a rare personal defeat for the famous skiing mailman. "Snowshoe" did not know about waxing skis for maximum glide, and he never had a chance against the pedal-to-the-metal style of the Plumas speedsters. Thompson was soundly beaten on the first day of a five-day competition series and quickly left the festivities to ski back to his home in Alpine County. In this undated photograph, Thompson poses with his mailbag and dog. (Courtesy Western SkiSport Museum.)

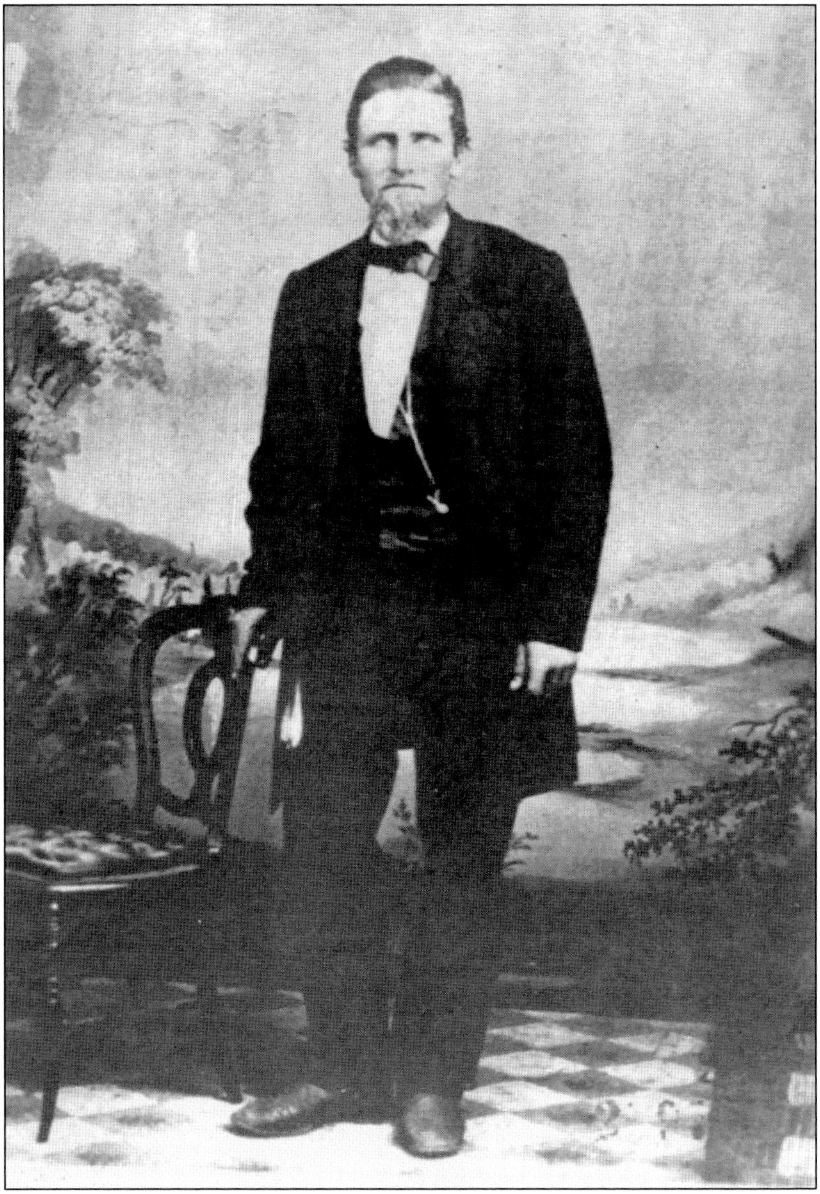

The Norwegian-born John "Snowshoe" Thompson was once described by Sierra ski journalist William B. Berry as the "hardiest and mightiest man that ever shook a leg over the California uplands." But even a hero is human. "I was never frightened but once during all my travels in the mountains," Thompson said. "That was in the winter of 1857. I was crossing Hope Valley [south of Lake Tahoe], when I came upon six great wolves—big timber wolves. They were great, gaunt, shaggy fellows." Thompson managed to ski past the pack of carnivores as they howled a primal warning. The legendary skier also felt the chill of death during the Pyramid Lake Indian War in May 1860. Thompson was in the thick of the battle when his horse was shot out from beneath him. As he ran for his life, he felt hot breath over his shoulder. Expecting hand-to-hand combat with a Paiute brave, he quickly wheeled about and instead discovered a terrified horse, saddled and bridled. He leaped onto the animal and escaped with his life. Until his death, in 1876, Thompson believed that the horse had been heaven-sent. (Courtesy Nevada Historical Society.)

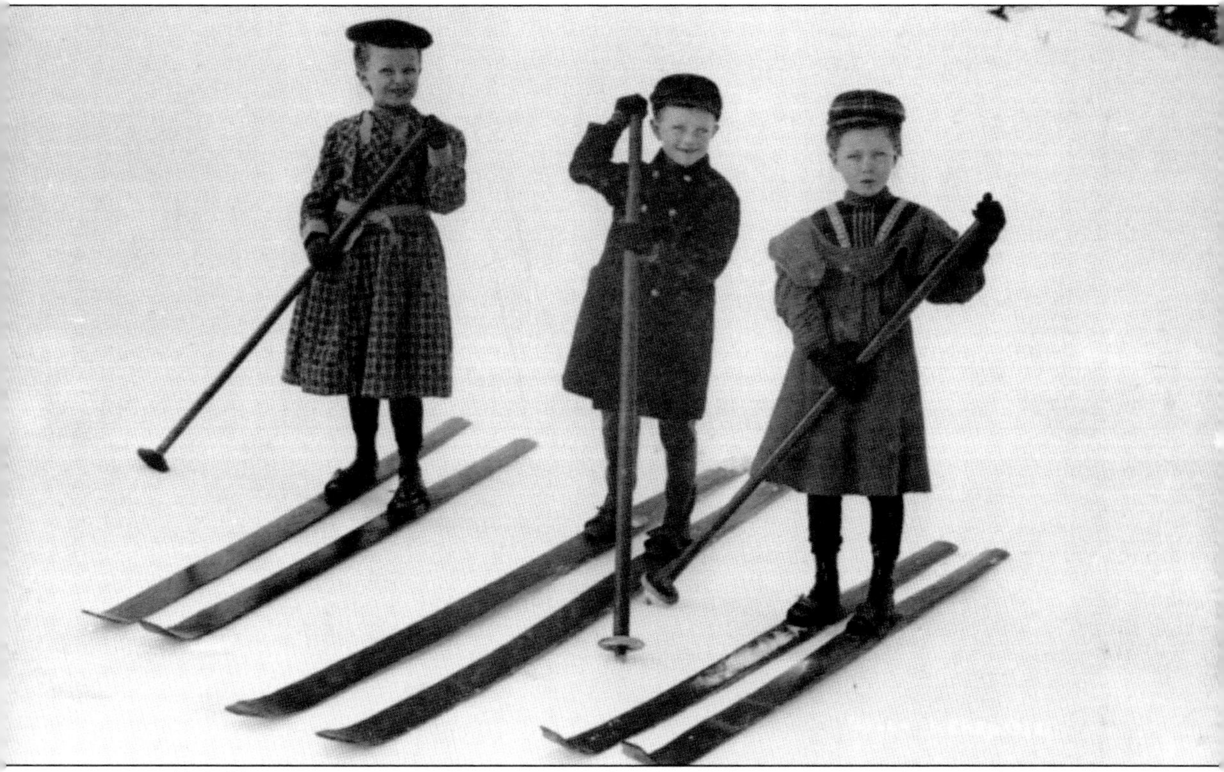

Even small children were encouraged to race on the longboard skis, as shown in this 1879 photograph of, from left to right, Verda Smith, Elmer Schubert and Sylvia Robinson. The only way to stop was to straddle the wooden pole and try to use it as a rudder and brake. One 14-year-old girl zipped down La Porte's steep racecourse in just 21 seconds, while at St. Louis, in Sierra County, a nine-year-old girl schussed through 300 feet of windswept powder in only seven seconds. On February 7, 1861, the *Sacramento Daily Union* reported: "Great big men, extremely small children, and delicate looking females ascend La Porte's Sugar Loaf Mountain, and how they come down! Everyone who has the time to go out in the evening for an hour or two, and every person who can buy or borrow a pair of skis, is out on the mountain, and they appear to enjoy the sport." (Courtesy Truckee Donner Historical Society.)

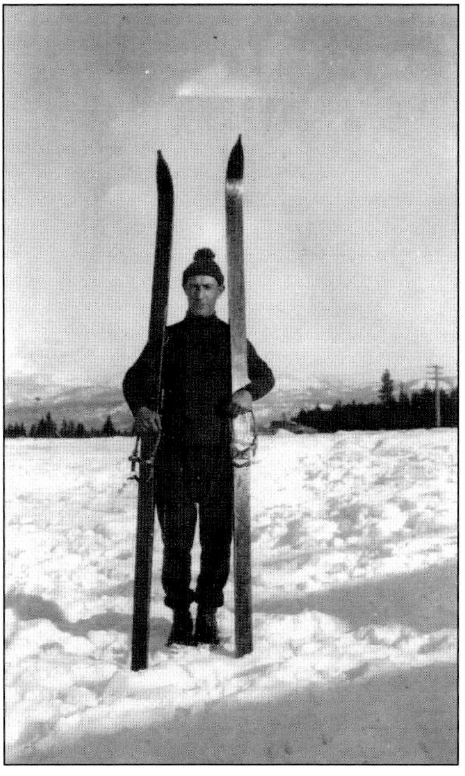

At nearly 15 feet long, racing skis were too heavy and cumbersome for aerial feats. This unidentified enthusiast shows off his shorter, lighter jumping skis, equipped with simple leather bindings that allowed the skier to raise his or her heels while flying through the air. Descent was usually accomplished with a telemark landing, in which one knee bends forward in a genuflection position upon touchdown. (Courtesy Truckee Donner Historical Society.)

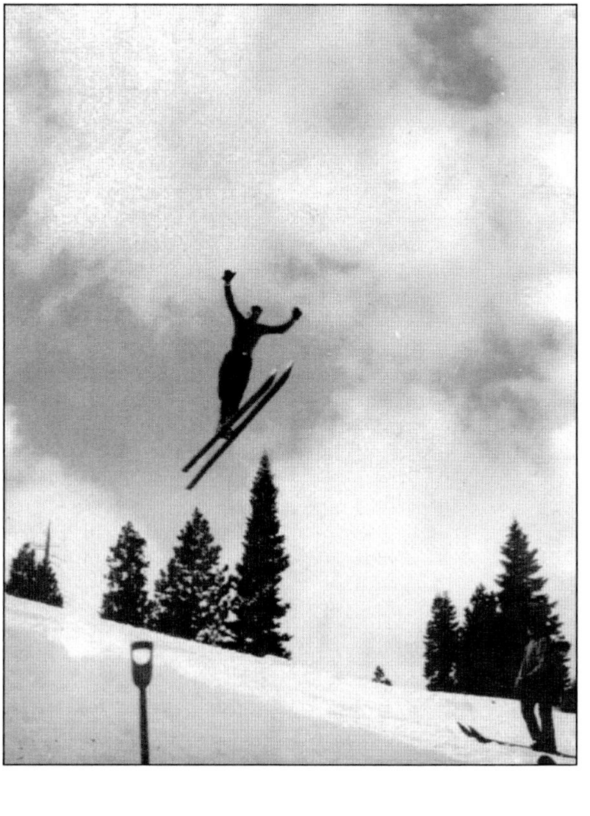

Daredevil skier Johnny Rablin uncorks a nice jump off a hand-shoveled launch at Truckee. In the 1870s and 1880s, Lake Tahoe and Truckee tourism dried up as deep snow blanketed the region, but there was increasing demand for winter sport activities from Californians living in the snowless flatlands. (Courtesy Truckee Donner Historical Society.)

# *Two*

# Truckee Carnivals Launch Winter Sports

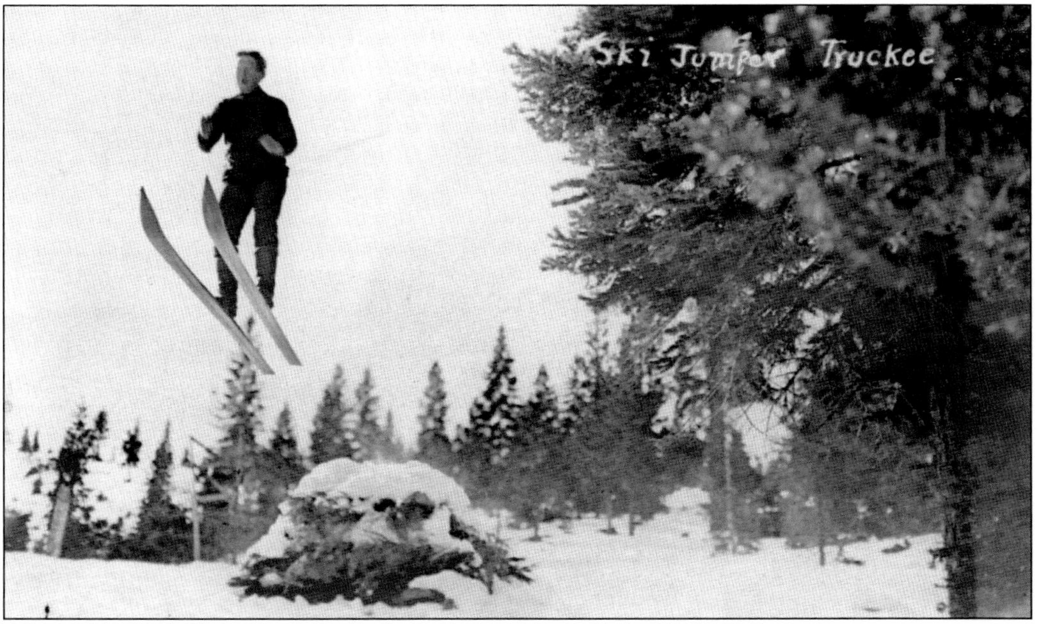


Due to the increasing popularity of winter sports, the Truckee business community got serious about staging winter carnivals and hosting tourists in the 1890s. The resulting crowds were a boon for the local economy. The winter carnivals were well-advertised in San Francisco and attracted celebrities, film directors, and hordes of people willing to spend a weekend patronizing the town's hotels, saloons, or dance hall. (Courtesy Dana Scanlon collection.)

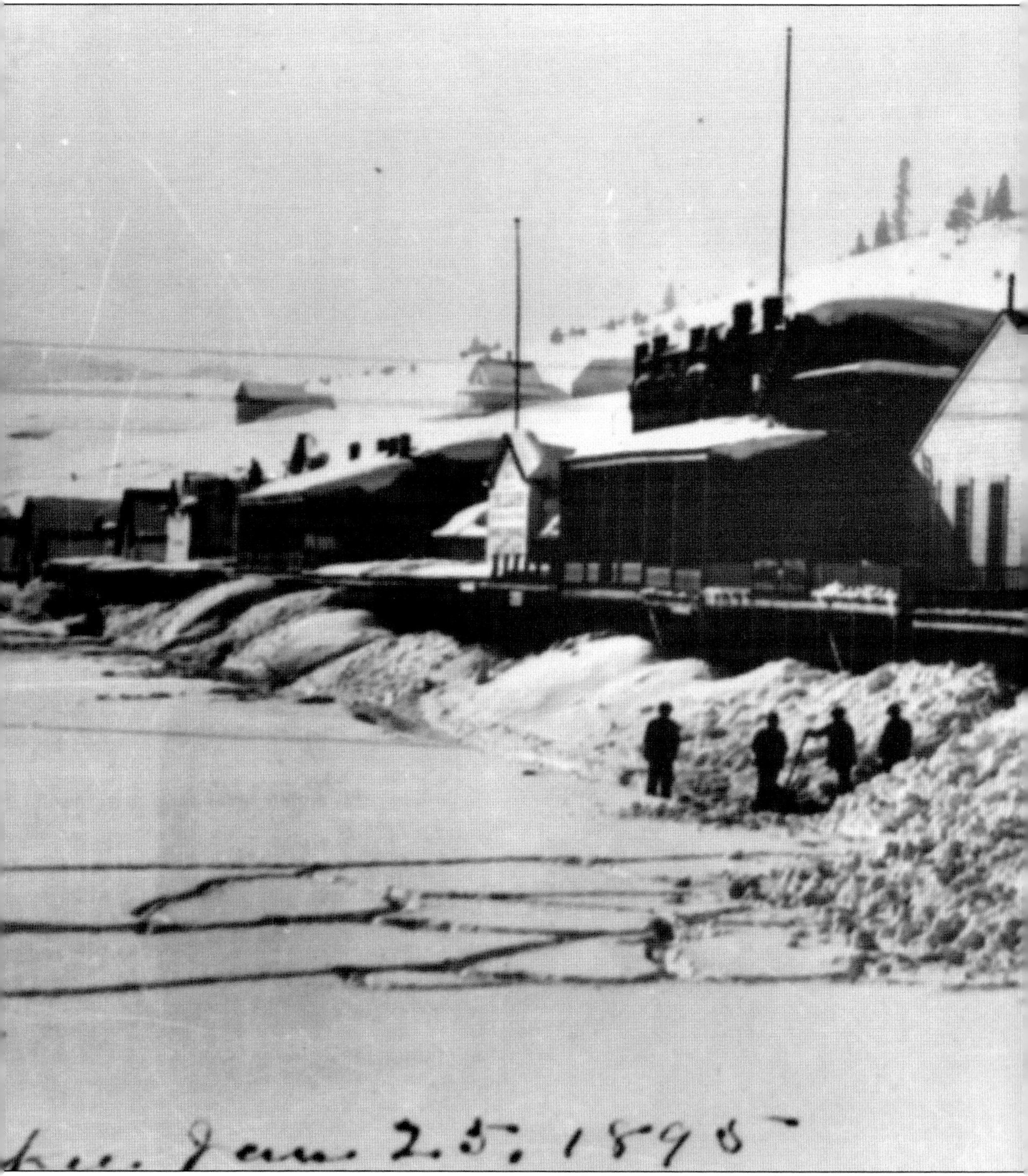


The town of Truckee had all the key components for winter sport: plenty of snowfall; lots of hills for sledding, tobogganing, or skiing; nearby lakes and streams for ice skating; and most important of all, a location adjacent to the transcontinental railroad, which could deliver tourists no matter the weather. In its early decades, the community relied on logging to supply year-round jobs, but as this 1895 photograph shows, most of the nearby trees were gone by the end of the 19th century.

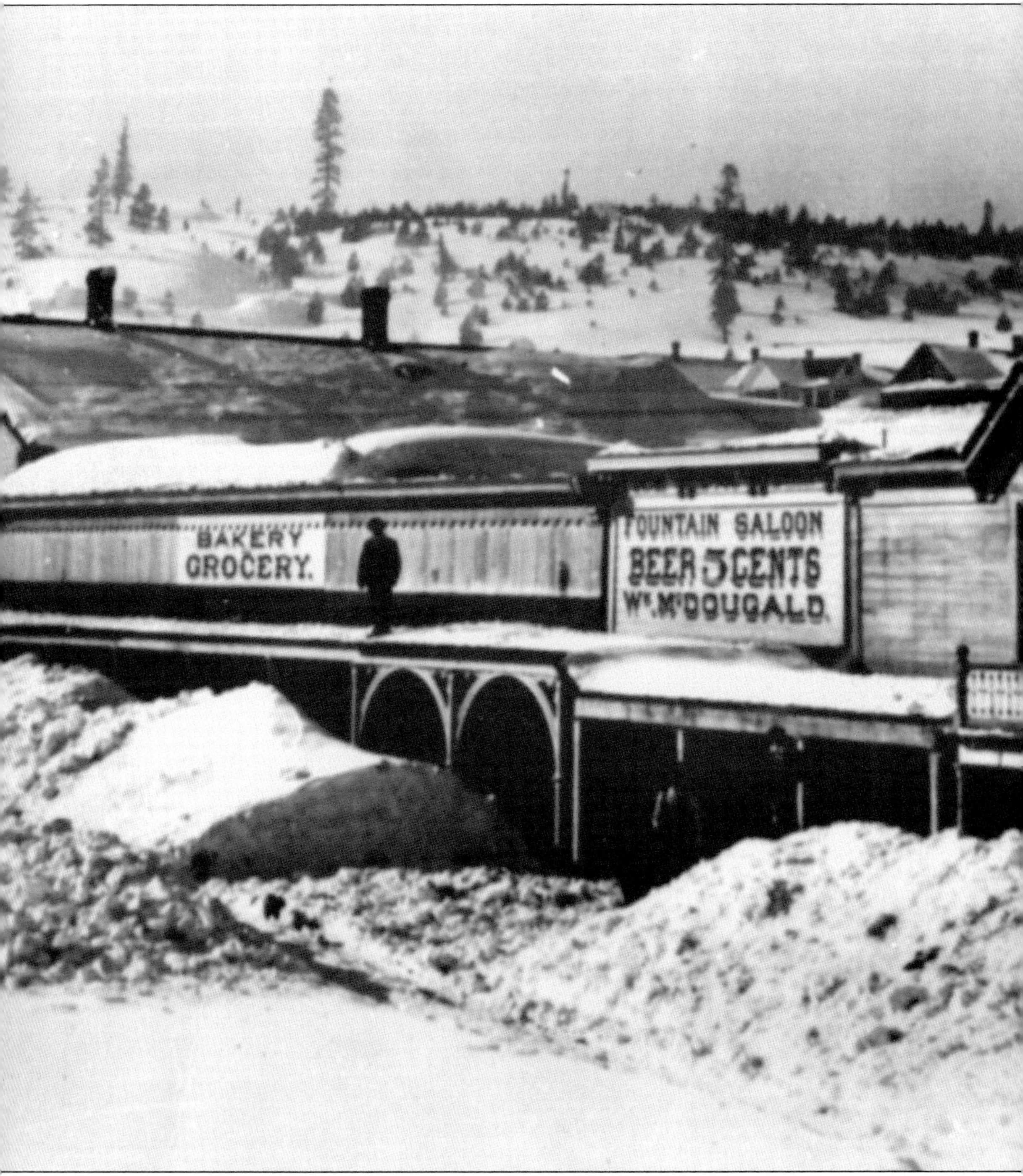


The decline of the Nevada Comstock silver boom was devastating to the whole region; miners, bankers, and business owners abandoned the region in droves. Truckee's commercial ice industry was still producing about 150,000 tons of ice annually and employed more than 600 men for a few months in winter, but this could not make up for the loss of other industries. (Courtesy Truckee Donner Historical Society.)

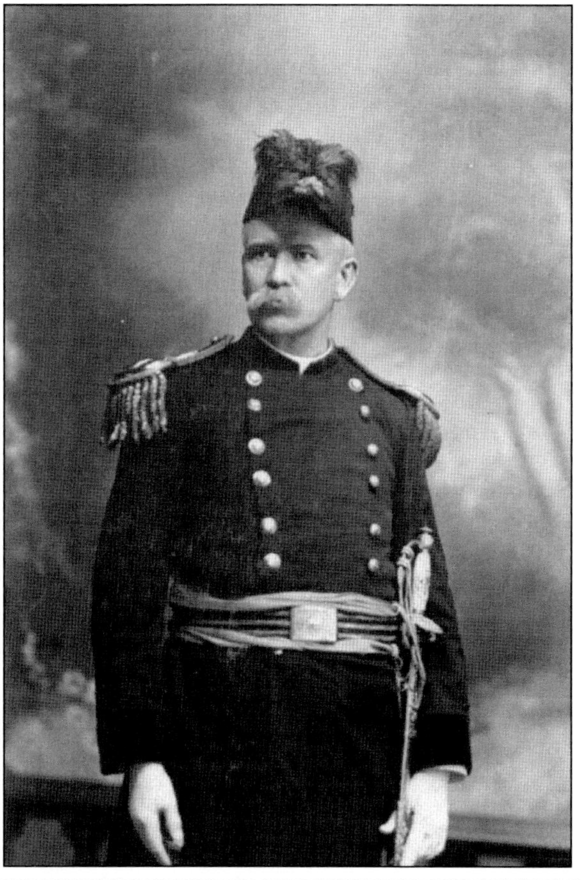

Charles Fayette McGlashan was a driving force behind Truckee's development and expansion of winter tourism. Pictured here in his Fraternal Order of Knights of Pythias brigadier general uniform, McGlashan was a notable figure—a prominent attorney, school principal, and author of the first authentic history of the Donner Party tragedy. He envisioned (correctly) that Truckee, and eventually Lake Tahoe, would become a major attraction for people looking for winter sport excitement. (Courtesy Truckee Donner Historical Society.)

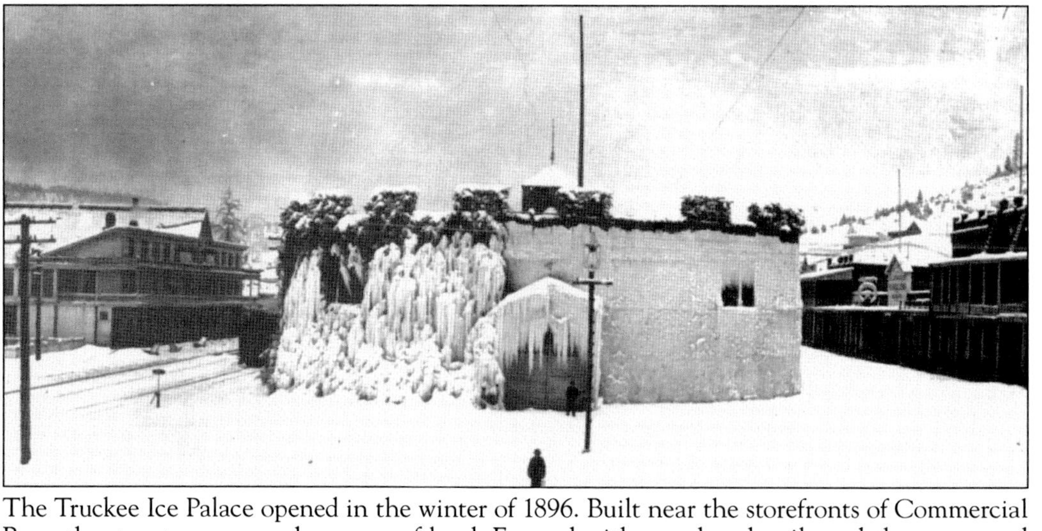

The Truckee Ice Palace opened in the winter of 1896. Built near the storefronts of Commercial Row, the structure covered an acre of land. Framed with wood and nails and then wrapped with wire mesh, it was repeatedly sprayed with water when the temperature fell below freezing, encasing the building in thick ice. The interior was brightly lit and housed a 700-foot oval indoor ice-skating rink where performers serenaded skaters with live music. (Courtesy Truckee Donner Historical Society.)

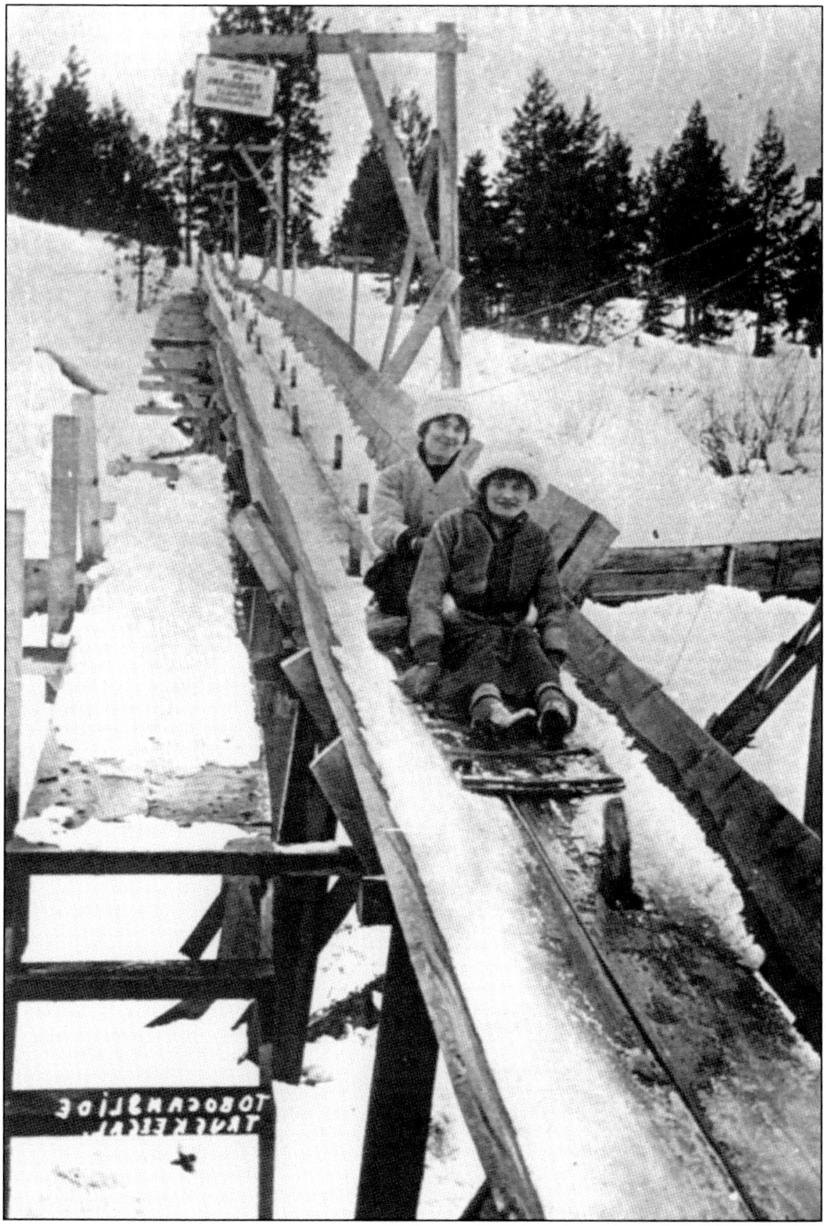

The first ski lift in the United States was this pullback lift installed at Truckee's winter sports area, called Hilltop, in late 1910. Although it was designed and built by Joseph G. Kirchner to transport toboggan riders back up the hill, it was also used by skiers, making it the first mechanical ski lift in America. The carefully groomed toboggan run at Hilltop was fast and nearly 1,000 feet long, so riders were willing to pay for an easy lift back to the top. To power the unit, Kirchner hired ox-drawn wagons to haul in an old steam engine from an abandoned sawmill on the Little Truckee River. This historic uphill lift preceded rope tows by more than two decades. In 1909, Truckee's winter carnival moved activities from downtown to Hilltop. In addition to the standard fare of skating, tobogganing, and sledding, a pair of Norwegian brothers performed ski jumping exhibitions off a snow ramp and offered lessons to anyone daring enough to try. (Courtesy Truckee Donner Historical Society.)

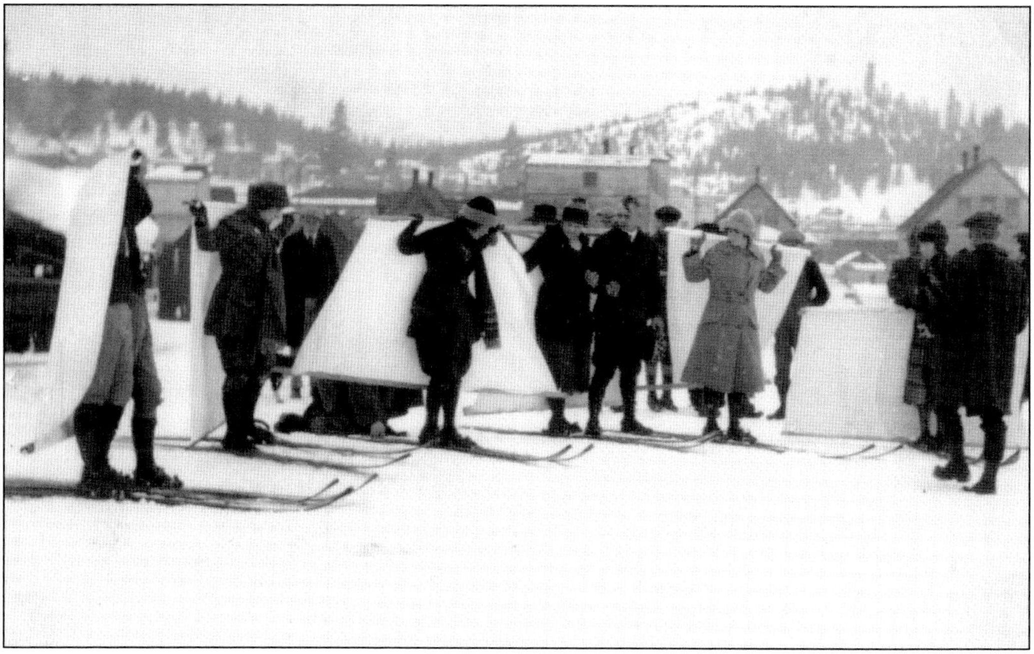

In addition to ski jumping, ice-skating, sleigh rides, cross-country skiing, dogsled races, and tobogganing, the winter carnival also offered wacky amusements like organized snowball fights and snowman-building contests. In this c. 1927 image, female skiers are using cloth sails to tap wind energy for an easy cruise. (Courtesy Truckee Donner Historical Society.)

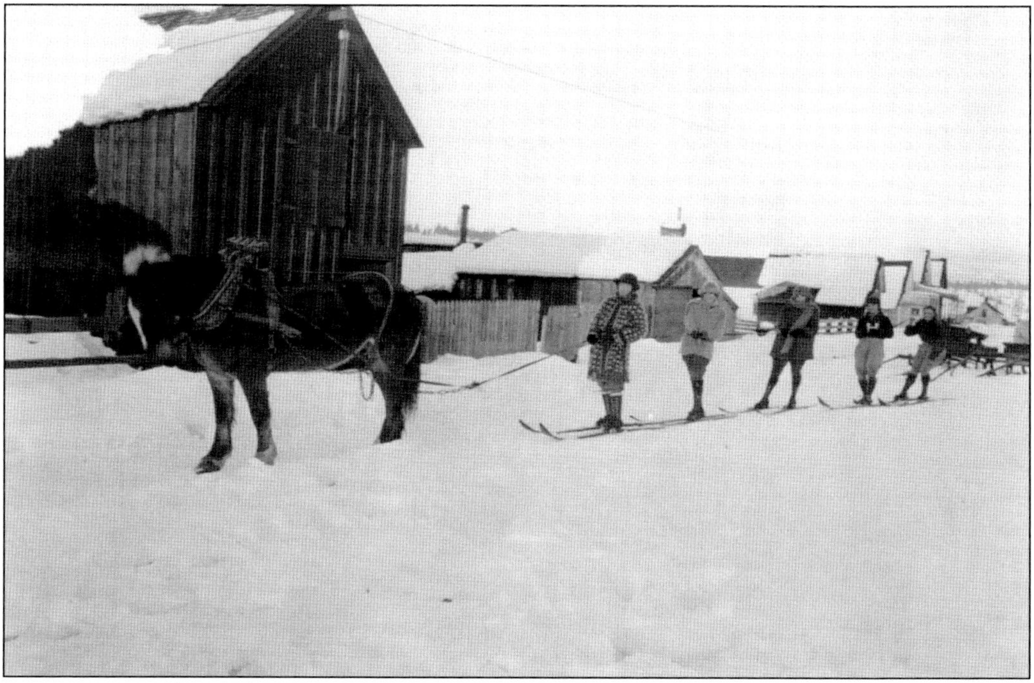

Five young Truckee ladies enjoy skijoring, a winter sport in which a person on skis is pulled by horse, dog, or motor vehicle. Skijoring can be a very fast-paced sport, but it appears that these women have little to worry about. (Courtesy Truckee Donner Historical Society.)

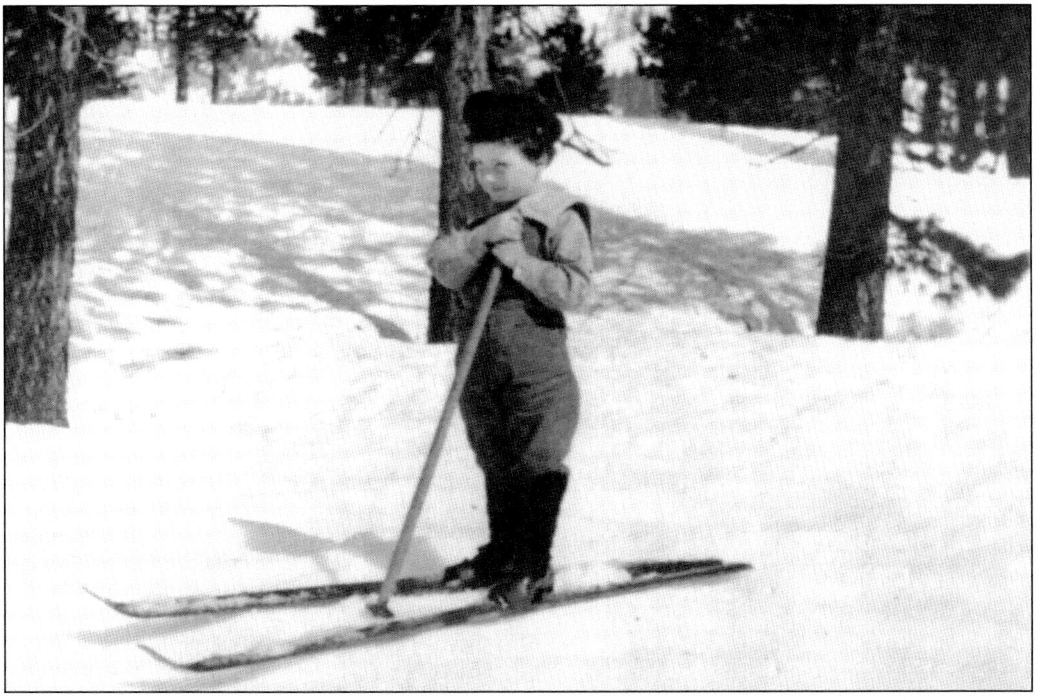

Truckee children learned to ski at a young age, and many of them went on to excel in regional and national competitive ski jumping and downhill events. (Courtesy Truckee Donner Historical Society.)

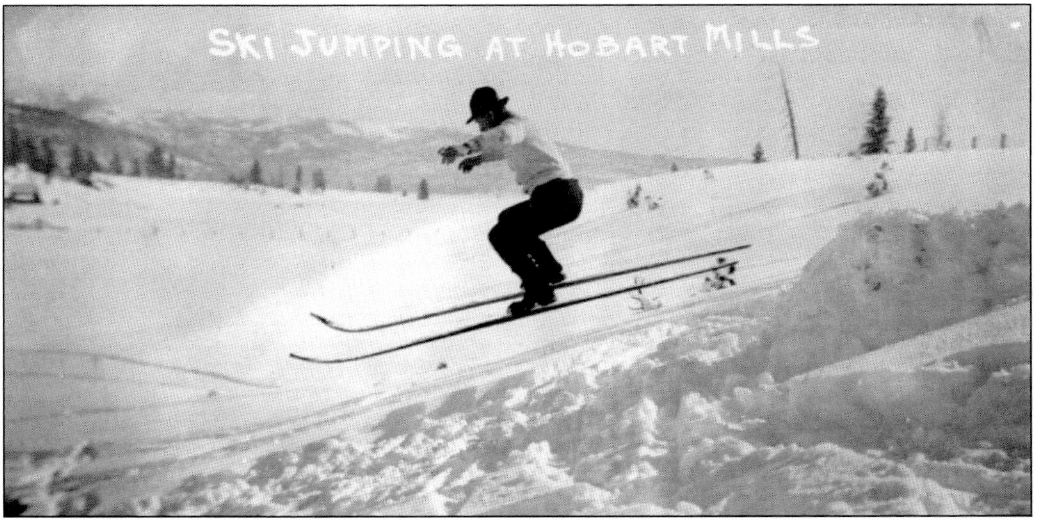


In 1900, ski jumping was popular at the Hobart Mills logging camp near Truckee. Operated by the Sierra Nevada Wood & Lumber Company, saloons were banned at Hobart Mills. For lumberjacks with money, however, Truckee's bars and red-light district were only five miles away. One hundred years later, another nearby logging operation called Schaffer's Mill was transformed into Northstar-at-Tahoe. Today, the old sawmill has found new life as a ski area and one of Tahoe's premier resorts. During the 19th century, logging was a dominant industry that destroyed natural beauty. In the 21st century, the trees near Northstar-at-Tahoe's Schaffer Camp chairlift stand tall while skiers and snowboarders weave through them. (Courtesy Dana Scanlon collection.)

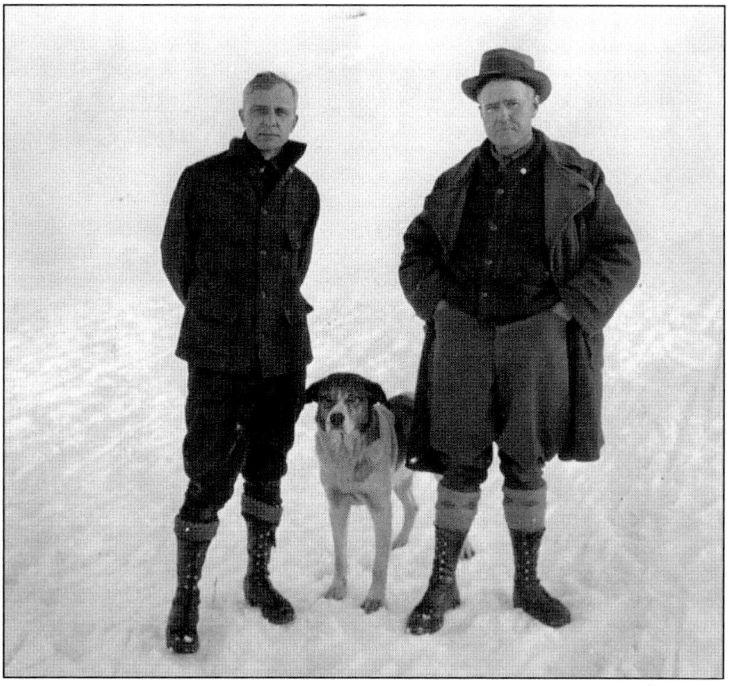

By 1914, Wilbur Maynard (left) and Wally B. Gelatt were very active in promoting Truckee's winter tourism. As manager of the Southern Pacific Hotel in Truckee, Maynard promoted the Truckee region to movie directors and Hollywood film companies as a convenient location for shooting films set in the frozen north. The media exposure expanded awareness of Truckee's winter sports. Carnival events were under the general direction of Gelatt. (Courtesy Truckee Donner Historical Society.)

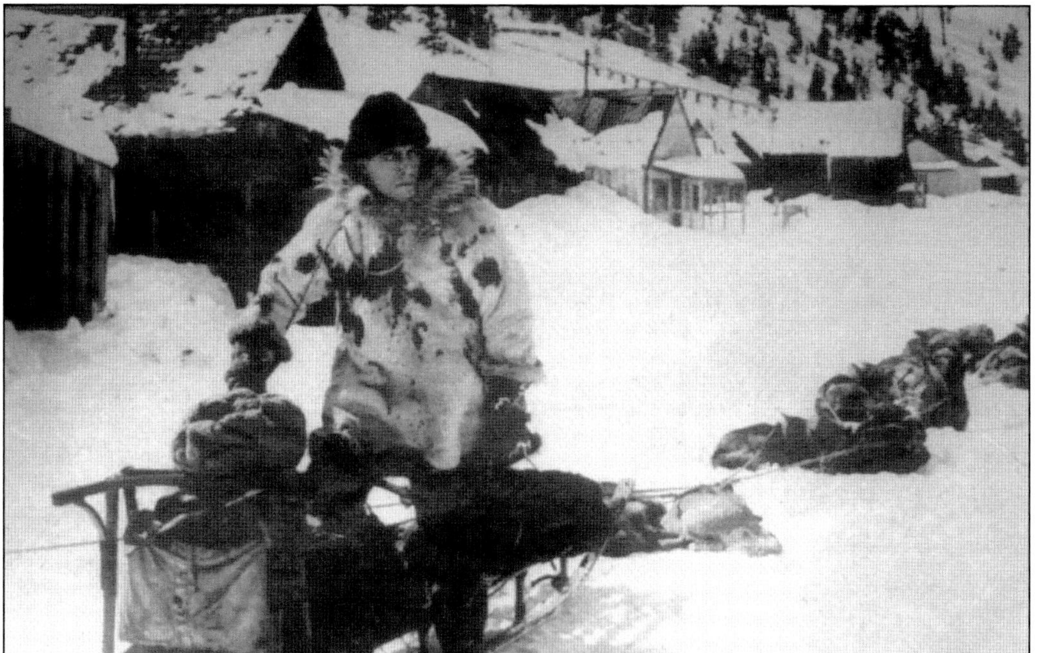

Actor William S. Hart is pictured here on a 1922 movie set for *The Frozen North*, filmed near Truckee. By 1922, Truckee and Lake Tahoe had become principal destinations for motion picture producers and directors. Southern Pacific Railroad had a "location bureau" to assist directors looking for appropriate landscapes and climates. When a movie company arrived by train, Wilbur Maynard was ready to help with any arrangements, providing extras, laborers, carpenters, and even weather forecasts. (Courtesy Truckee Donner Historical Society.)

Hollywood stars such as Buster Keaton and Clark Gable became a common sight in Truckee's restaurants, bars, and hotels. Director and actor Charlie Chaplin filmed scenes for his 1925 silent comedy *The Gold Rush* near Truckee and Donner Pass. Not only did Chaplin and crew patronize local businesses, he hired 600 extras from Truckee and Sacramento for the production. Chaplin grew fond of Truckee and returned often to visit. (Courtesy Truckee Donner Historical Society.)

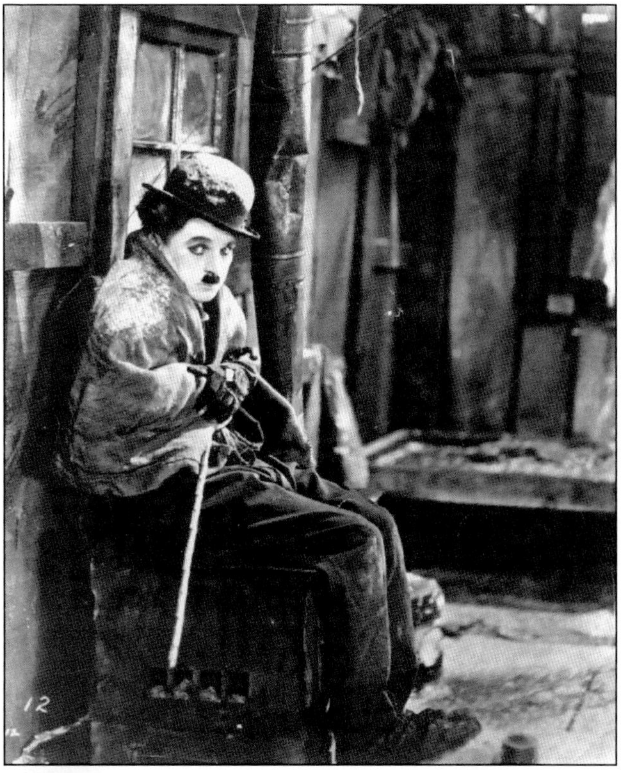

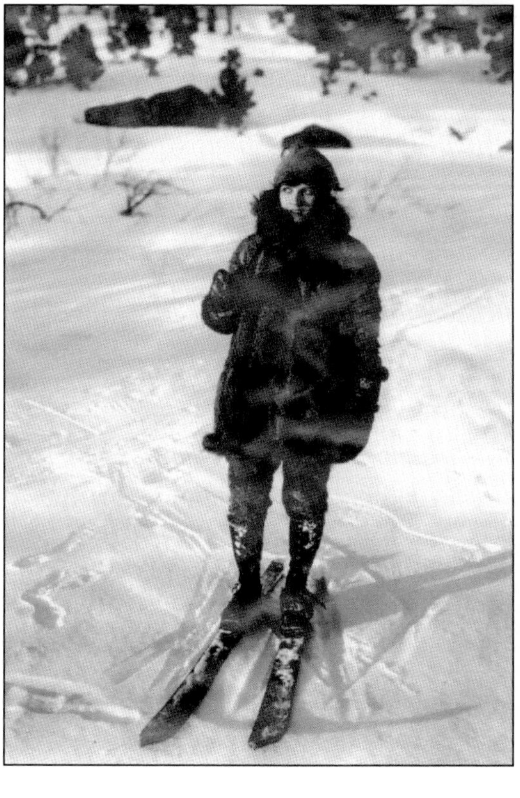

This unidentified actress spent several days learning the basics of skiing for her role in a movie filmed in Truckee. Aggressive advertising efforts by Truckee's chamber of commerce and the Southern Pacific Railroad resulted in the casts and crews of dozens of motion pictures coming to Truckee during the 1920s and 1930s. (Courtesy Truckee Donner Historical Society.)

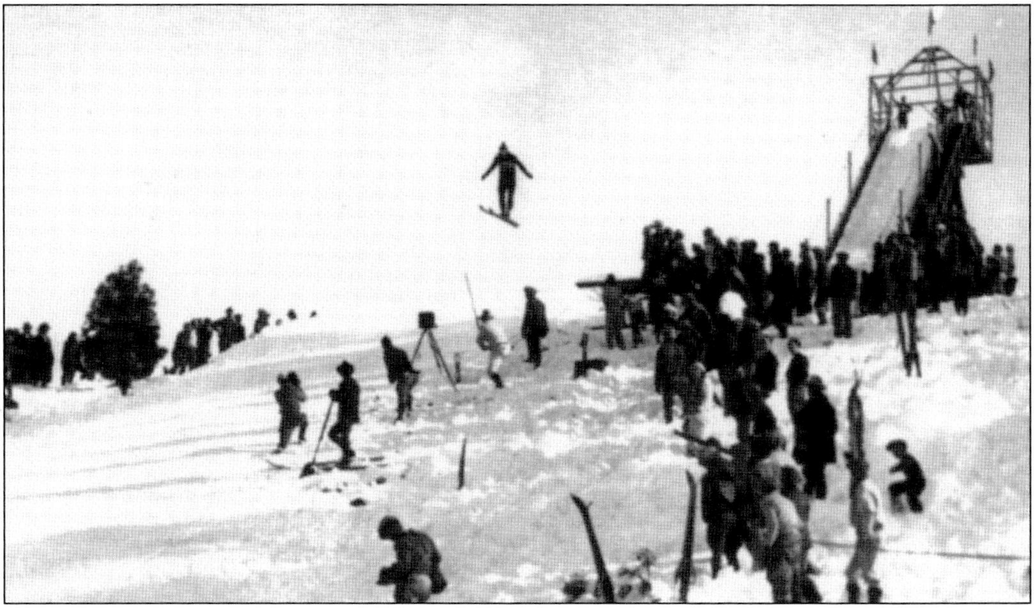

The Truckee Hilltop ski jump attracted skiers from as far away as San Francisco. The wooden scaffold—built across the Truckee River, just south of town—represented the epitome of action-oriented winter sports, with competitors uncorking soaring leaps past crowds of spectators. Jumping contests allowed judges to allocate points for distance and form. Note the large-format camera perched on a tripod underneath the airborne skier. (Courtesy Truckee Donner Historical Society.)

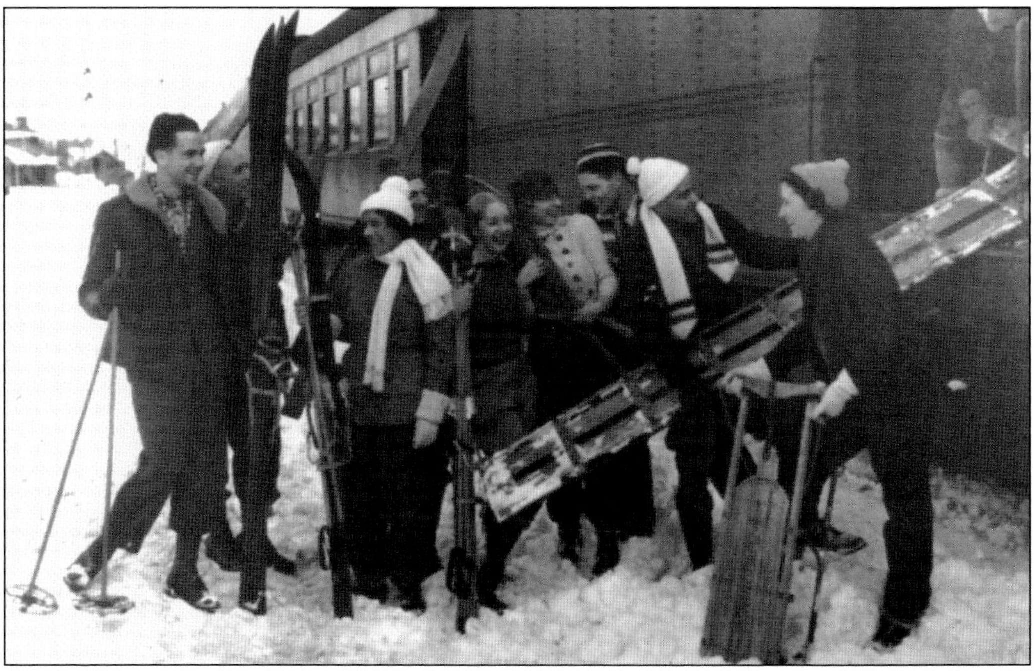

Southern Pacific Railroad capitalized on California winter sports with "Snowball Specials." On weekends, these express party trains conveyed hundreds—sometimes thousands—of tourists from the snowless lowlands to Truckee. Using movies and print media, Southern Pacific promoted Sierra winter sports. (Courtesy William B. Berry collection.)

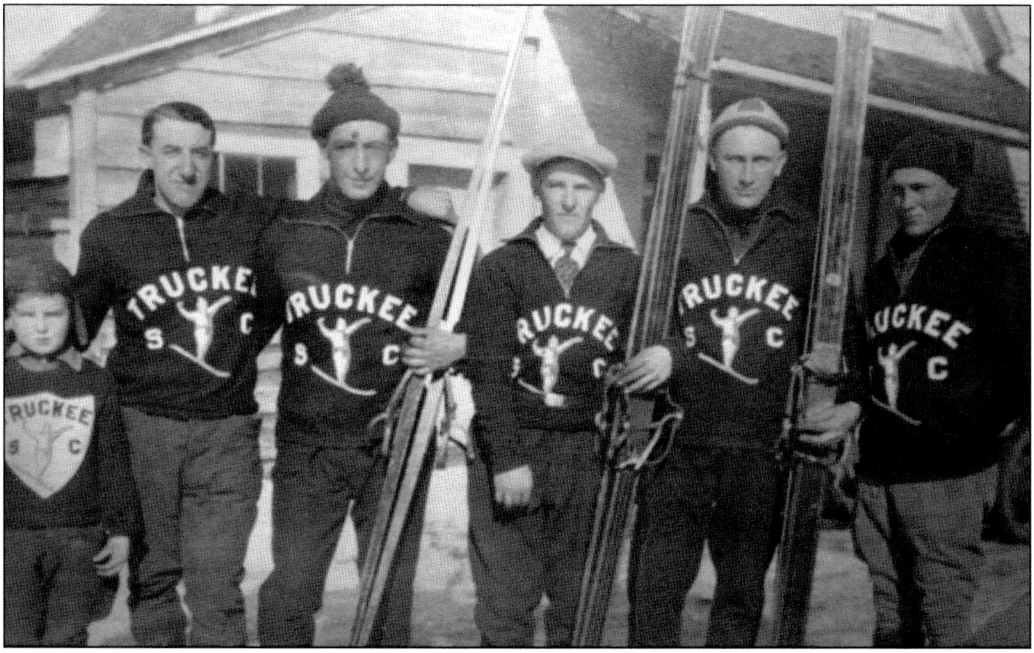

In the late 1920s, ski clubs were formed in Truckee and Tahoe City, and local boys and girls proved their mettle in ski jumping and alpine skiing. The Truckee–Lake Tahoe area became a prime training ground for developing talent, a trend that continues today. The Truckee Ski Club members pictured here in 1930 are, from left to right, "team mascot" Frank Titus, Charles Cozzalio, Pete Passinetti, Earl McKay, Jess Maxom, and Frank Gaiennie. (Courtesy Craig Beck collection.)

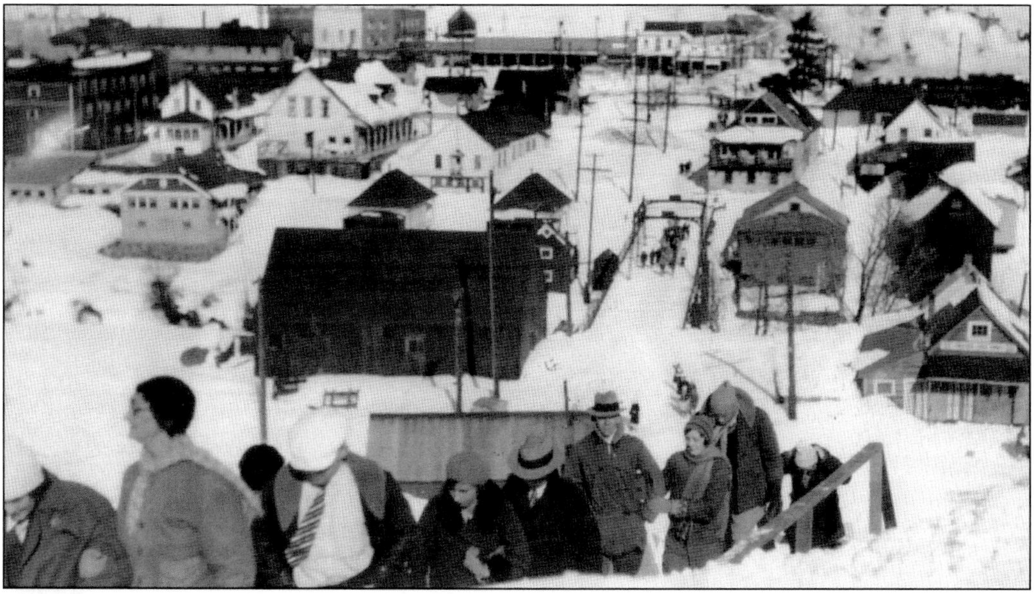

Hilltop's giant wooden scaffold ski jump attracted crowds of spectators willing to climb up the steep hill overlooking Truckee. The town's annual winter carnival led to the increasing popularity of winter sports throughout California and the Sierra Nevada. Ski clubs were formed in the Truckee–Lake Tahoe area, jumps were built, and tournaments and meets were held for skiers of all ages. (Courtesy Truckee Donner Historical Society.)

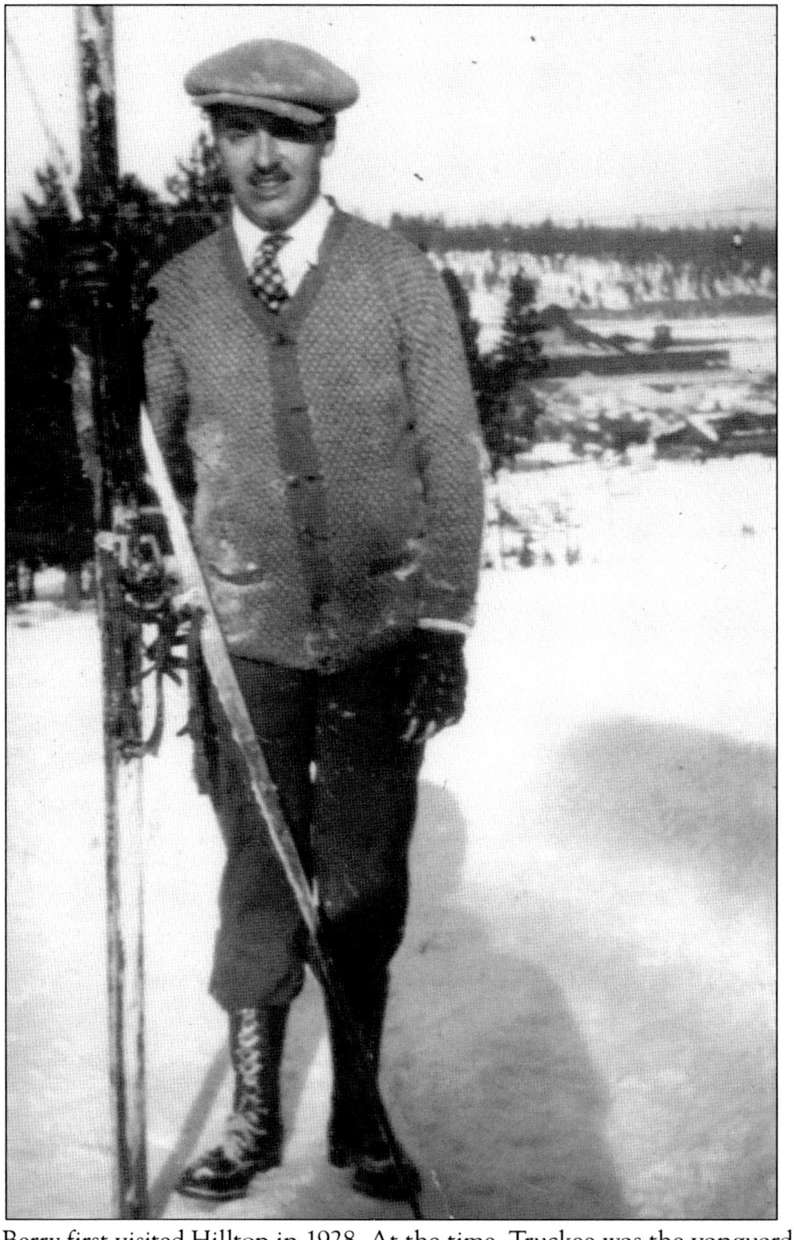

William B. Berry first visited Hilltop in 1928. At the time, Truckee was the vanguard for winter sports, and Hilltop was the pioneer site for American tow-assisted skiing. In 1928, the tow system was a slow-moving cable with steel hooks. Skiers looped their pole baskets over a hook and were pulled up the hill. After his first day skiing at Hilltop, the 25-year-old Berry said, "I realized that this was rather a special occasion. I had never skied down a slope that I had not climbed." A professional journalist who had worked for several major East Coast newspapers, Berry had just moved to Reno, Nevada, where he spent the next 50 years covering regional ski racing. In 1933, Berry began compiling bibliographies and collecting artifacts that became the foundation for the Western SkiSport Museum, located at Boreal Mountain Resort near Donner Pass and founded in 1969. One of Berry's many awards read, "No one has ever, or will ever, see more, write more or do more for skiing." (Courtesy William B. Berry collection.)

# *Three*

# Alpine Skiing Comes of Age (1930s)

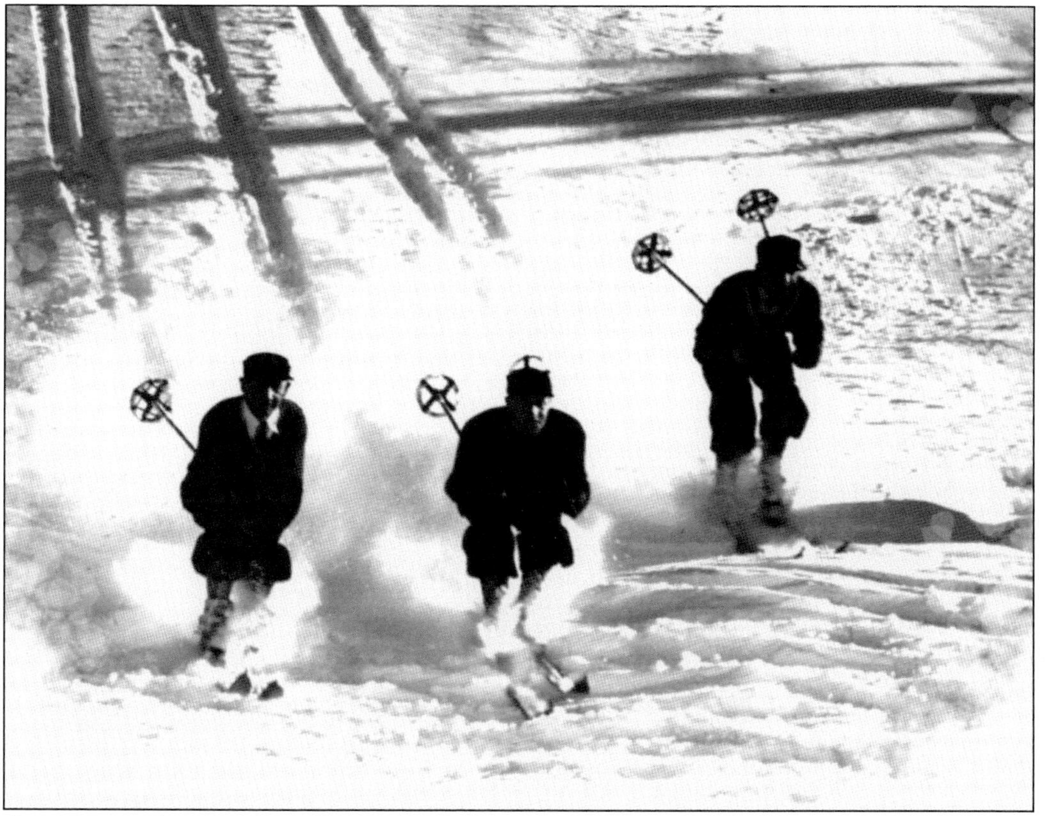

Competitive ski jumping was still popular, but the 1930s was the breakout decade for downhill skiing in the United States. European-trained ski instructors began importing dynamic parallel turning styles from France and Austria. Wooden skis got shorter and easier to turn, while new uphill rope tow systems enabled alpine skiers to make many more runs during the course of a day. (Courtesy Western SkiSport Museum.)

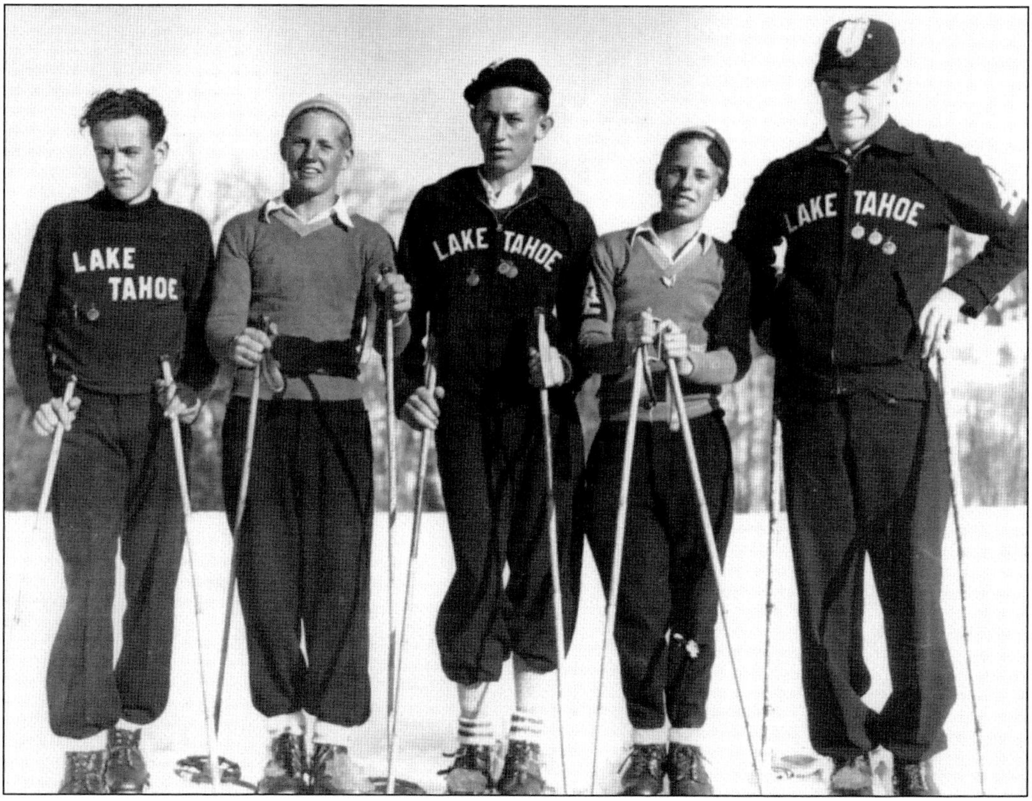


This c. 1936 image shows the Lake Tahoe Ski Club Junior Team. They are, from left to right, James Worden, Charles Henrikson, Carl Bechdolt Jr., Oliver Henrikson, and Al Henry Jr. The Lake Tahoe Ski Club formed in 1928 to give young residents a chance to compete at the new Winter Sports Grounds, located at the present-day site of Granlibakken resort. The Lake Tahoe Ski Club has produced more national champions and Olympians than any ski club in the United States. (Courtesy North Lake Tahoe Historical Society.)

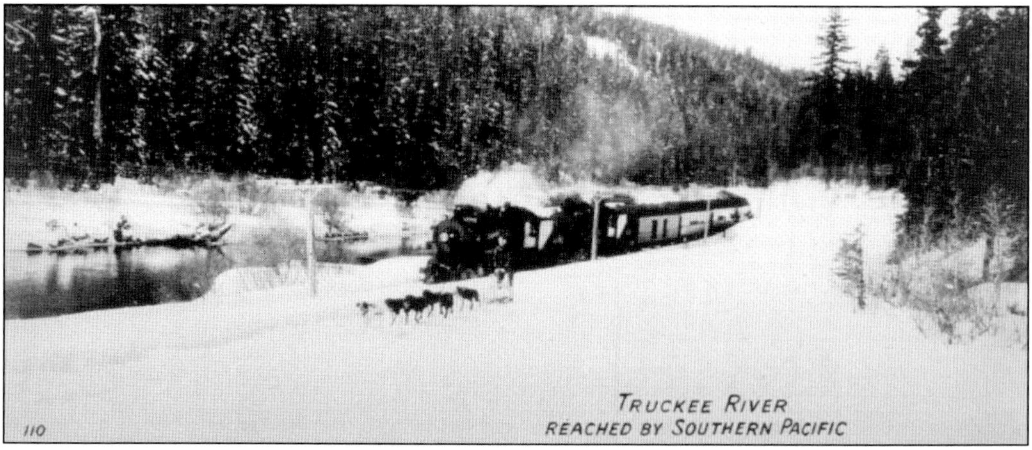


During winter months, Southern Pacific Railroad provided transportation from the transcontinental line in Truckee to Tahoe City. In 1926, Southern Pacific purchased the Tahoe Tavern, a 223-room, European-style luxury hotel near Tahoe City. To accommodate winter tourists, the new management opened the facility from December to March. (Courtesy Nevada Historical Society.)

Truckee had a head start with the town's wooden scaffold, but ski jumping competitions at the Winter Sports Grounds near Tahoe City quickly grew in popularity. Unlike the tower built on Truckee's Hilltop, the jump near Tahoe City was graded into the side of a hill at a cost of $10,000. Views of spectacular Lake Tahoe attracted top-name competitors and crowds of spectators. (Courtesy William B. Berry collection.)

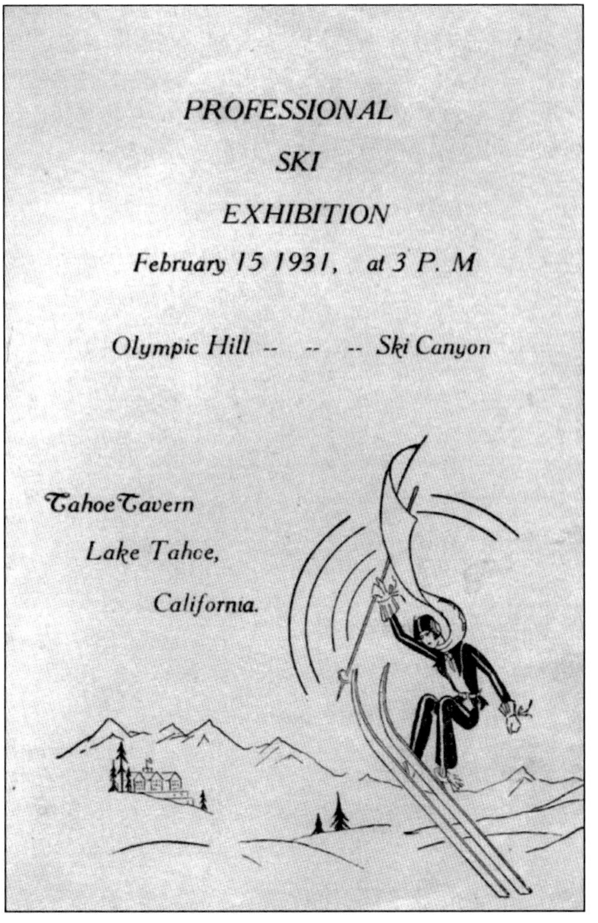


Caught in action, this ski jumper is launching off Tahoe City's "Olympic Hill" during a 1932 national competition. Note Lake Tahoe in the background. In 1929, the United States was chosen to host the 1932 Winter Olympics. Tahoe City made a bid for the games, but California delegates chose Yosemite to represent the state. During the bidding process, the Tahoe Tavern's Winter Sports Grounds area was optimistically renamed Olympic Hill. (Courtesy North Lake Tahoe Historical Society.)

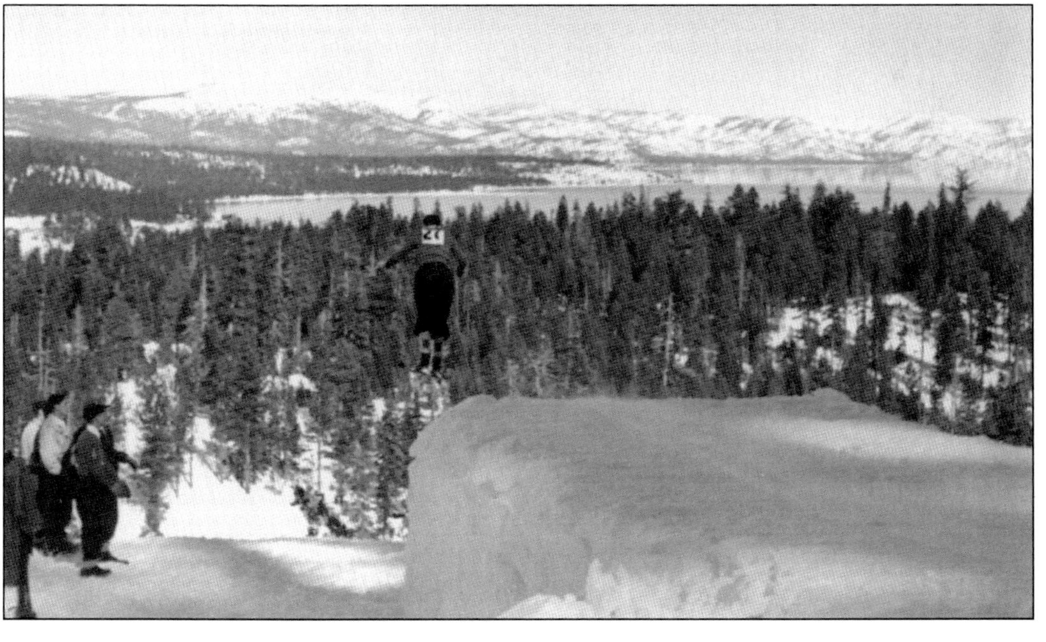

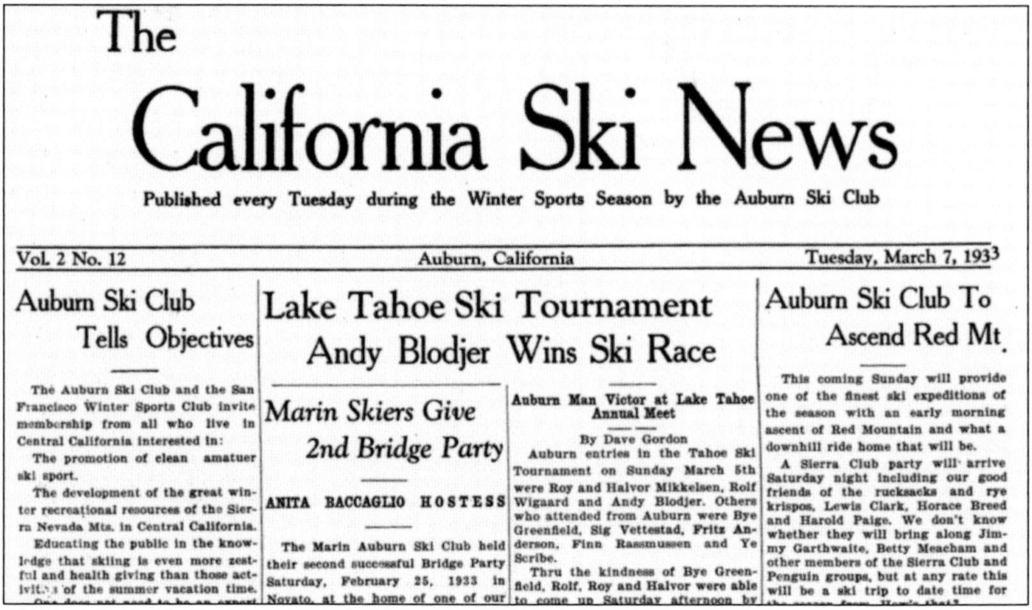

The

# California Ski News

Published every Tuesday during the Winter Sports Season by the Auburn Ski Club

Vol. 2 No. 12 | Auburn, California | Tuesday, March 7, 1933

## Auburn Ski Club Tells Objectives

The Auburn Ski Club and the San Francisco Winter Sports Club invite membership from all who live in Central California interested in:

The promotion of clean amatuer ski sport.

The development of the great winter recreational resources of the Sierra Nevada Mts. in Central California.

Educating the public in the knowledge that skiing is even more zestful and health giving than those activities of the summer vacation time.

## Lake Tahoe Ski Tournament Andy Blodjer Wins Ski Race

### *Marin Skiers Give 2nd Bridge Party*

ANITA BACCAGLIO HOSTESS

The Marin Auburn Ski Club held their second successful Bridge Party Saturday, February 25, 1933 in Novato, at the home of one of our

### Auburn Man Victor at Lake Tahoe Annual Meet

By Dave Gordon

Auburn entries in the Tahoe Ski Tournament on Sunday March 5th were Roy and Halvor Mikkelsen, Rolf Wigaard and Andy Blodjer. Others who attended from Auburn were Bye Greenfield, Sig Vettestad, Fritz Anderson, Finn Rassmussen and Ye Scribe.

Thru the kindness of Bye Greenfield, Rolf, Roy and Halvor were able

## Auburn Ski Club To Ascend Red Mt.

This coming Sunday will provide one of the finest ski expeditions of the season with an early morning ascent of Red Mountain and what a downhill ride home that will be.

A Sierra Club party will arrive Saturday night including our good friends of the rucksacks and rye krispos, Lewis Clark, Horace Breed and Harold Paige. We don't know whether they will bring along Jimmy Garthwaite, Betty Meacham and other members of the Sierra Club and Penguin groups, but at any rate this will be a ski trip to date time for

The National Ski Association held its annual championship tournament at Tahoe City's Olympic Hill in February 1932. It was the first one held west of the Rocky Mountains, and it drew 120 professional and amateur skiers from around the country. Word soon spread that California had great skiing, and Lake Tahoe went on to host competitions like this 1933 event won by California's champion cross-country ski racer Andrew Blodjer. (Courtesy William B. Berry collection.)

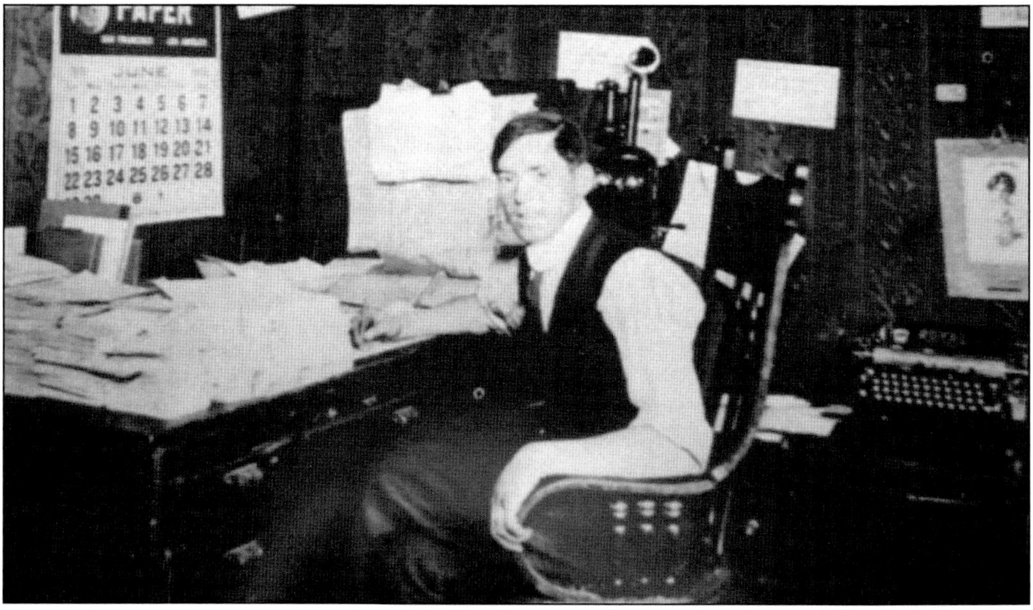

Winter sports promoter Bert A. Cassidy is pictured here in his office in 1914. An avid outdoorsmen and successful businessman, Cassidy used his ownership of the *Truckee Republican* newspaper to popularize Truckee's winter carnival. He later moved to Auburn, California, and purchased the *Auburn Journal* and *Placer Country Republican* newspapers. Elected to the state senate in 1929, Cassidy was a strong political force for the expansion of winter sports throughout the northern Sierra. (Courtesy Craig Beck collection.)

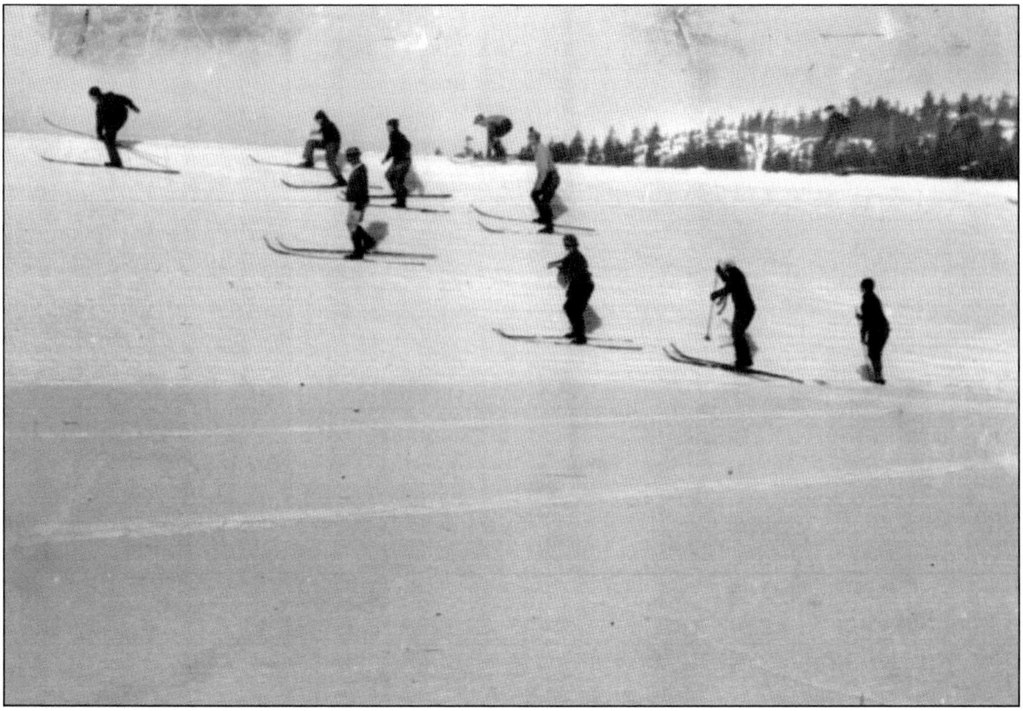

The 1932 Tahoe City tournament focused on jumping and cross-country skiing because alpine skiing was still in its infancy. Before the advent of rope tows and chairlifts, skiers looking for turns had to climb for them. It was a challenging sport for even the most physically fit and determined warrior. Skiers hoping for convenient uphill tow systems had a few years to wait. (Courtesy Truckee Donner Historical Society.)

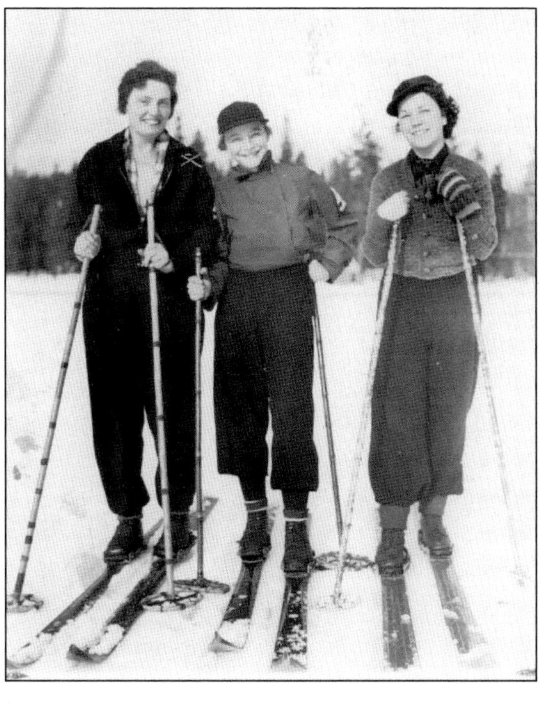

This 1930s photograph includes Lake Tahoe Ski Club members Marie Henry (left), Kathleen Anderson (center), and Lillian Vernon. As ski equipment and instruction improved, recreational skiers began looking for more thrills. A few ski instructors started to teach students how to make European-style alpine turns, a skill that required practice to master. In the mid-1930s, Tahoe City residents Bill and Carl Bechdolt set up a rope tow near town. (Courtesy North Lake Tahoe Historical Society.)

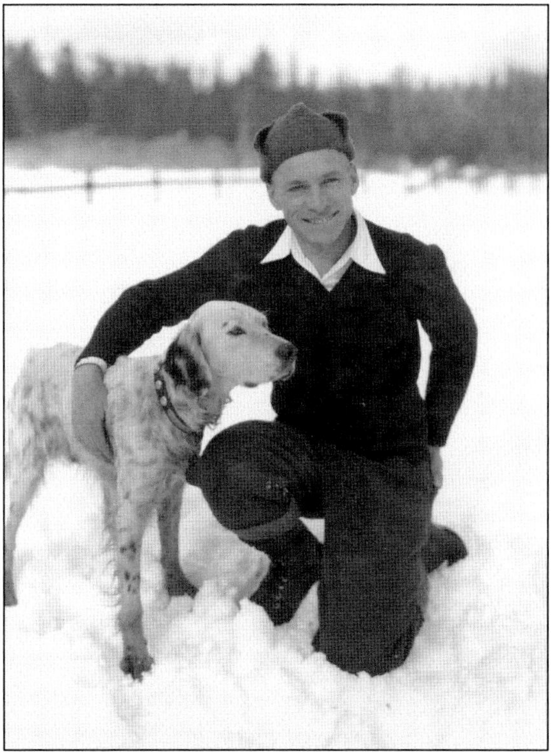

Wendell T. Robie was an Auburn, California, businessman with a passion for the outdoors. Recognizing the health benefits of winter sports, he helped organize the Auburn Ski Club in late 1928. When the National Ski Association approved the formation of the California Ski Association in 1931, Robie was elected its first president. (Courtesy Western SkiSport Museum.)

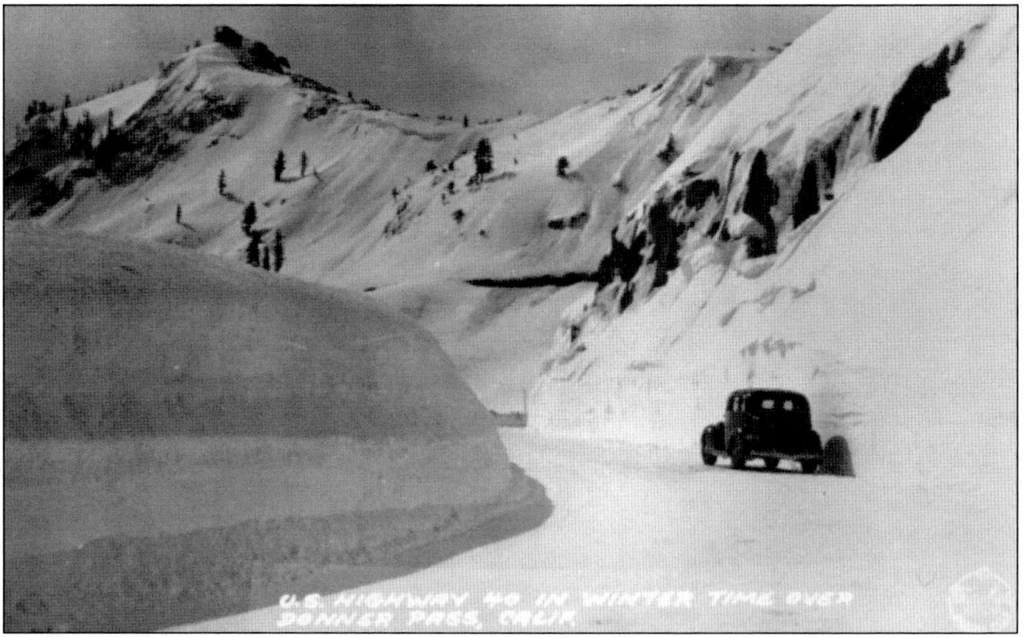


Before 1931, the California Highway Department did not plow US Highway 40 over Donner Pass in the winter; the Auburn Ski Club convinced the state legislature to clear the road in order to create access to the snowbound High Sierra. To supply their growing ranks, Wendell T. Robie used his Auburn Lumber Company to make bulk mail-order purchases of skis and poles to sell to club members. (Courtesy Frank Titus collection.)

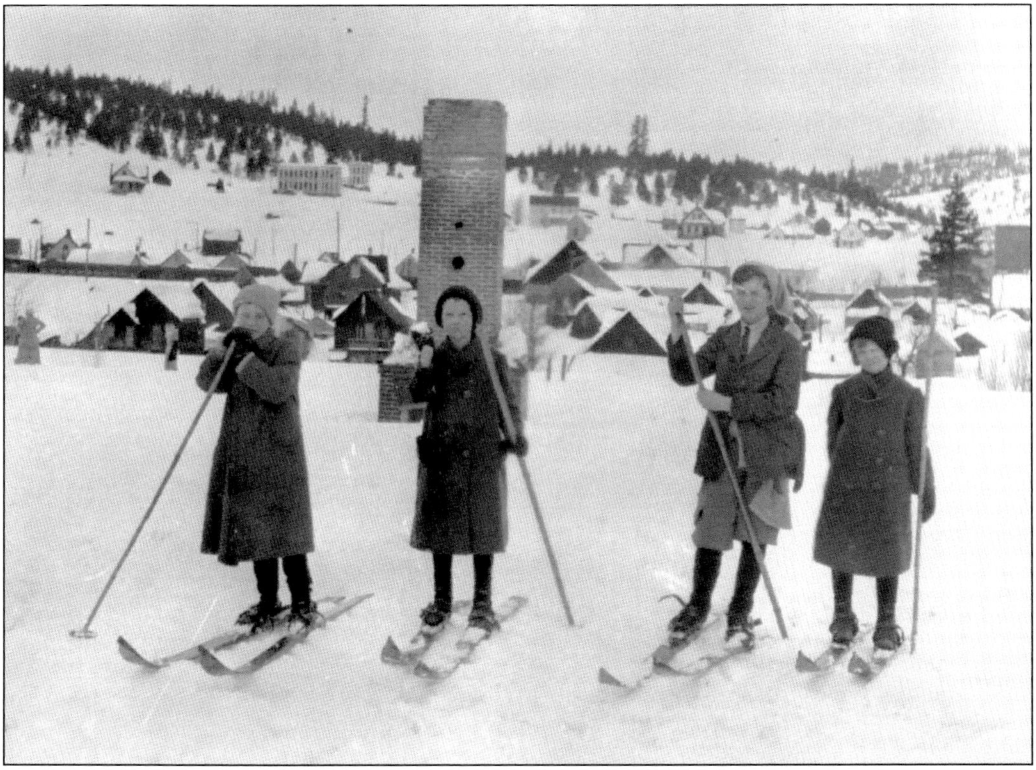

Pictured around 1916, these young skiers in Truckee represent a vanishing style of skiing that relied on the use of one pole. Within a few years, European-trained instructors began utilizing two poles to turn. The children are, from left to right, Ted McDonald, Maud Koepke, Elmer McDonald, and Roberta Koepke. Ted and Elmer McDonald were descendants of James McDonald, co-owner and superintendent of the Sierra Lakes Ice Company at nearby Prosser Creek and Boca. (Courtesy McDonald-Lundblade family collection.)

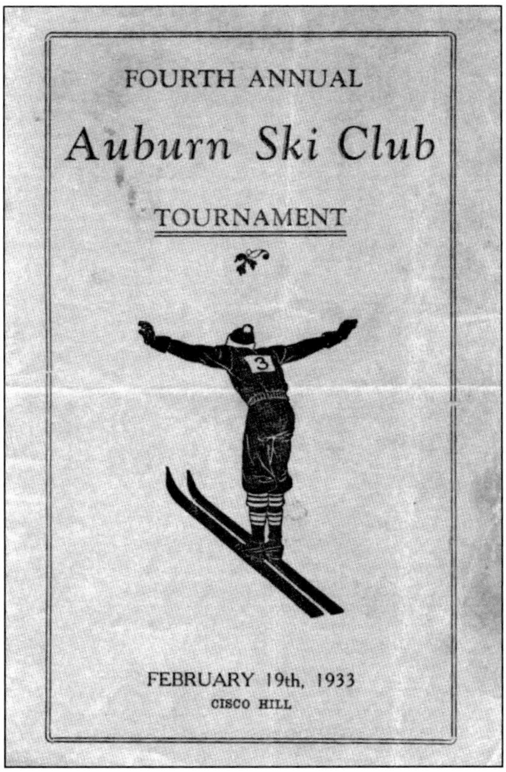


Once the state began plowing US 40 for winter traffic in 1932, the Auburn Ski Club built a new Winter Park facility at 6,000 feet elevation on the Sierra west slope, near Cisco. The club, which boasted several of the country's best skiers, constructed a warming hut and California's first modern-designed ski jump. Club president Wendell T. Robie wasted no time in scheduling widely advertised winter competitions. (Courtesy William B. Berry collection.)

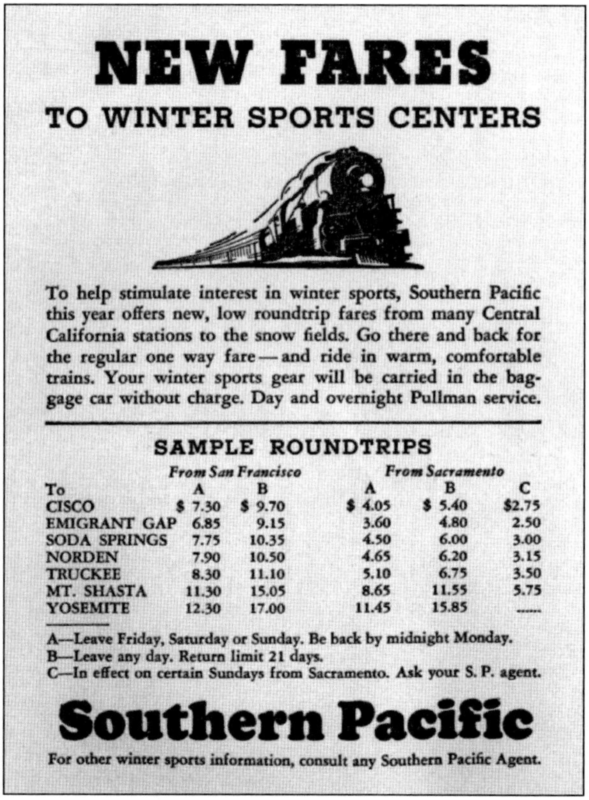

# NEW FARES

## TO WINTER SPORTS CENTERS

To help stimulate interest in winter sports, Southern Pacific this year offers new, low roundtrip fares from many Central California stations to the snow fields. Go there and back for the regular one way fare—and ride in warm, comfortable trains. Your winter sports gear will be carried in the baggage car without charge. Day and overnight Pullman service.

### SAMPLE ROUNDTRIPS

| | *From San Francisco* | | *From Sacramento* | | |
|---|---|---|---|---|---|
| To | A | B | A | B | C |
| CISCO | $ 7.30 | $ 9.70 | $ 4.05 | $ 5.40 | $2.75 |
| EMIGRANT GAP | 6.85 | 9.15 | 3.60 | 4.80 | 2.50 |
| SODA SPRINGS | 7.75 | 10.35 | 4.50 | 6.00 | 3.00 |
| NORDEN | 7.90 | 10.50 | 4.65 | 6.20 | 3.15 |
| TRUCKEE | 8.30 | 11.10 | 5.10 | 6.75 | 3.50 |
| MT. SHASTA | 11.30 | 15.05 | 8.65 | 11.55 | 5.75 |
| YOSEMITE | 12.30 | 17.00 | 11.45 | 15.85 | ...... |

A—Leave Friday, Saturday or Sunday. Be back by midnight Monday.
B—Leave any day. Return limit 21 days.
C—In effect on certain Sundays from Sacramento. Ask your S. P. agent.

**Southern Pacific**

For other winter sports information, consult any Southern Pacific Agent.

This c. 1933 flyer documents Southern Pacific Railroad Company travel fares. The California Highway Department was plowing snow on Highway 40 by the early 1930s, but Southern Pacific knew there were plenty of skiers who would rather pay to travel in the comfort and convenience of a passenger coach than make the long, stressful drive on icy roads. Eastbound trains left San Francisco on weekend nights and arrived at the winter sports areas by the following morning. (Courtesy Mark McLaughlin.)

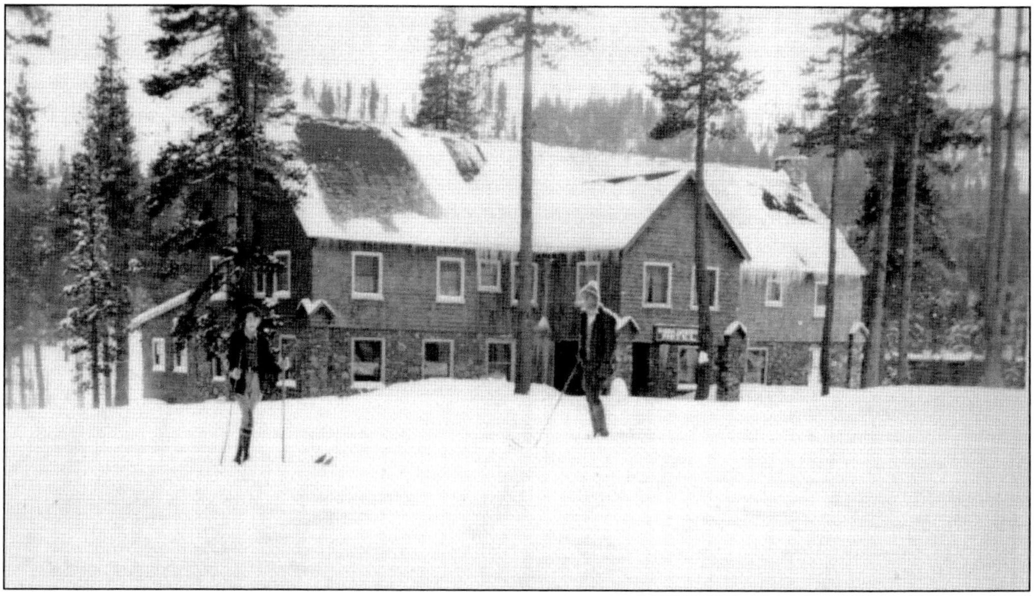

Brothers Oscar and Herstle Jones built the 20-room Soda Springs Hotel in 1927. At the time, it was the only commercial business that offered meals and accommodations in the snow country near Donner Pass and could be easily accessed by skiers taking the train from San Francisco. Visitors could ski down to Donner Lake and then ride a horse-drawn sleigh back to the hotel. (Courtesy Donner Summit Historical Society/Norm Sayler collection.)

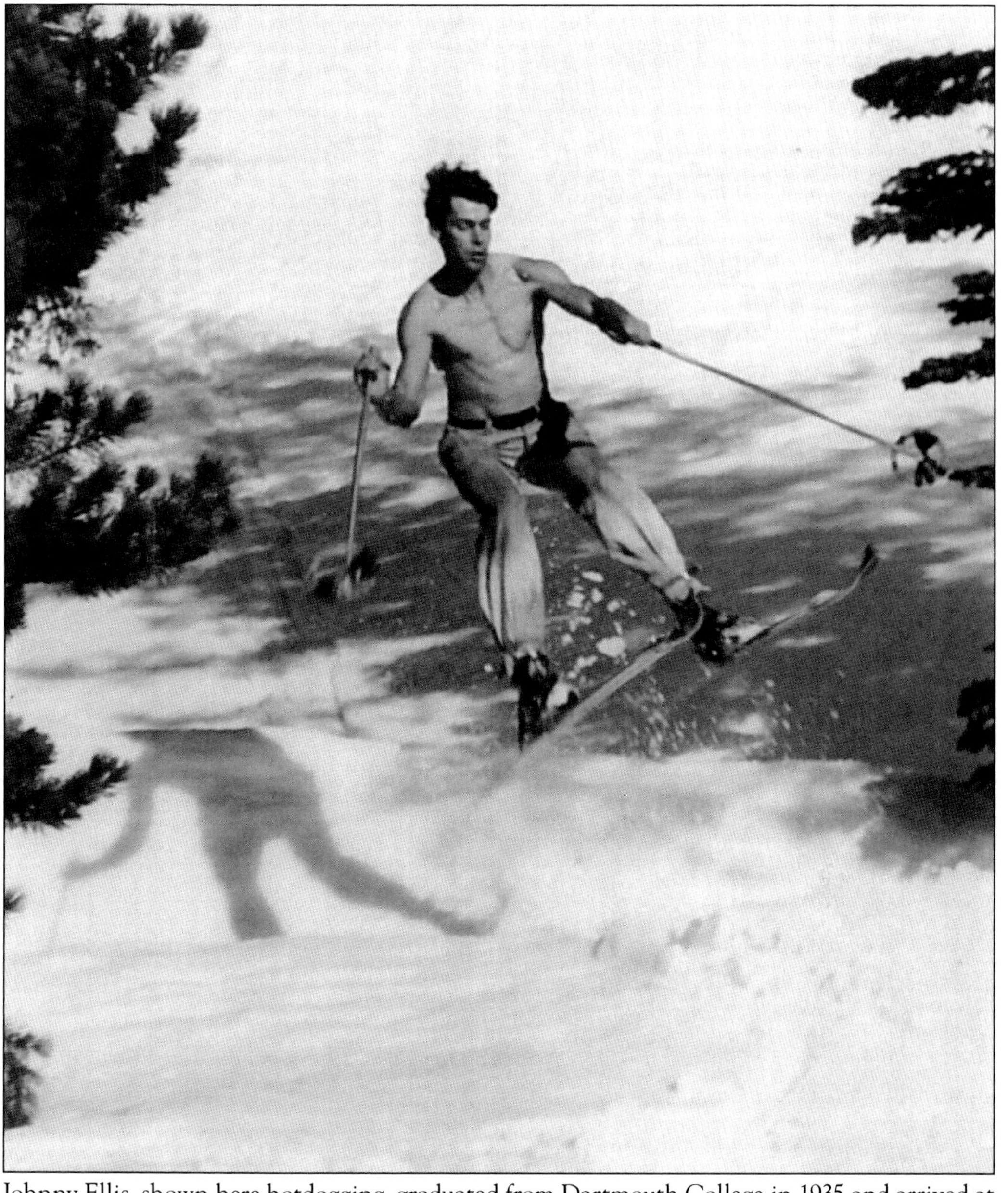

Johnny Ellis, shown here hotdogging, graduated from Dartmouth College in 1935 and arrived at Donner Summit that summer, just in time to help complete the Sierra Club's new Clair Tappaan Lodge. In 1937, Ellis installed a rope tow above Lake Mary, near the site of the future Sugar Bowl ski area. His electrically driven system was later extended to reach 1,200 feet up the lower slope of Mount Judah. Ellis claimed that his was the first rope tow in the West, but the Sierra Club had a rope tow running at about the same time. There was also a J-bar operation at Sonora Pass that winter. A J-bar uses a cross bar for skiers to sit on, which makes it less fatiguing than trying to grip an icy manila rope while being pulled uphill. Ellis, one of the true pioneers in alpine ski development in the region, recognized the economic opportunities and installed more rope tows across the highway at Signal Hill, future site of Donner Ski Ranch. (Courtesy Donner Summit Historical Society/Norm Sayler collection.)

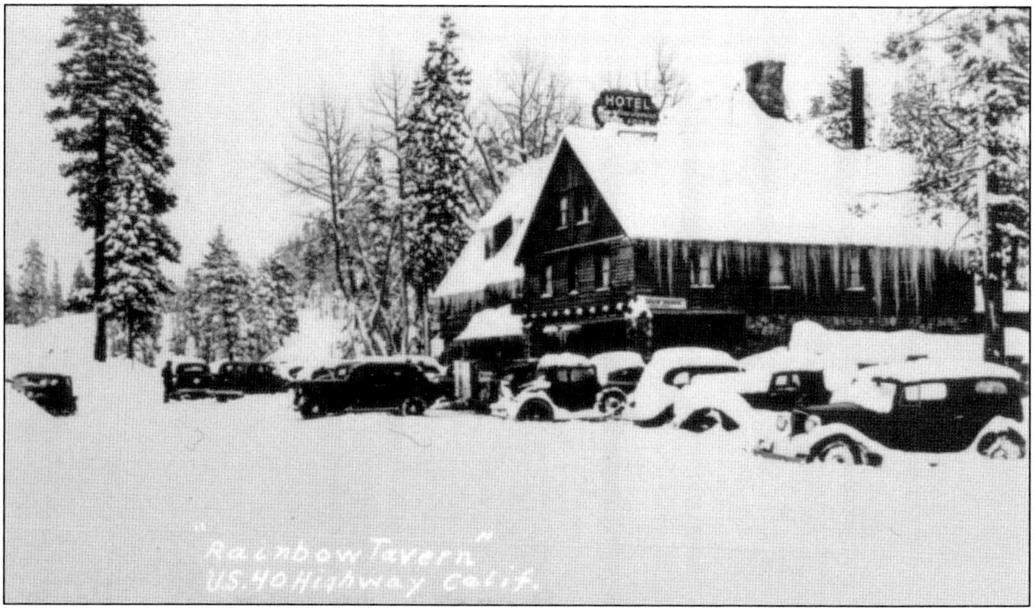


By 1930, the Rainbow Lodge had become a popular destination for skiers traveling Highway 40. Built along the south fork of the Yuba River, the structure was originally used as a stage stop in the late 1800s. Businessman Herstle Jones took it over in 1927 and upgraded and enlarged the building. He and his brother Oscar anticipated the 1930s surge in winter traffic along Highway 40 and established some of the first destination resorts in the Donner Summit area. (Courtesy Frank Titus collection.)

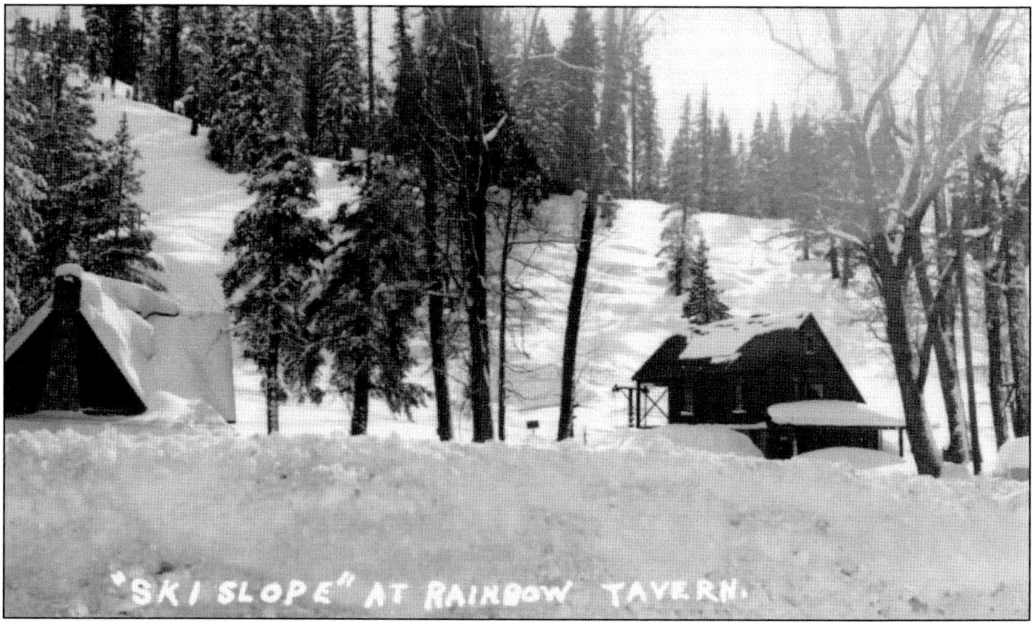


After Herstle Jones acquired the Rainbow Lodge, he renamed it Herstle Jones' Rainbow Tavern and Trout Farm. Jones marketed it as a year-round resort, with access to both summer and winter sports. By 1939, Jones' had a J-bar rope tow that pulled his skiing guests 500 feet up the hill near the lodge for 25¢ a ride. (Courtesy Donner Summit Historical Society/Norm Sayler collection.)

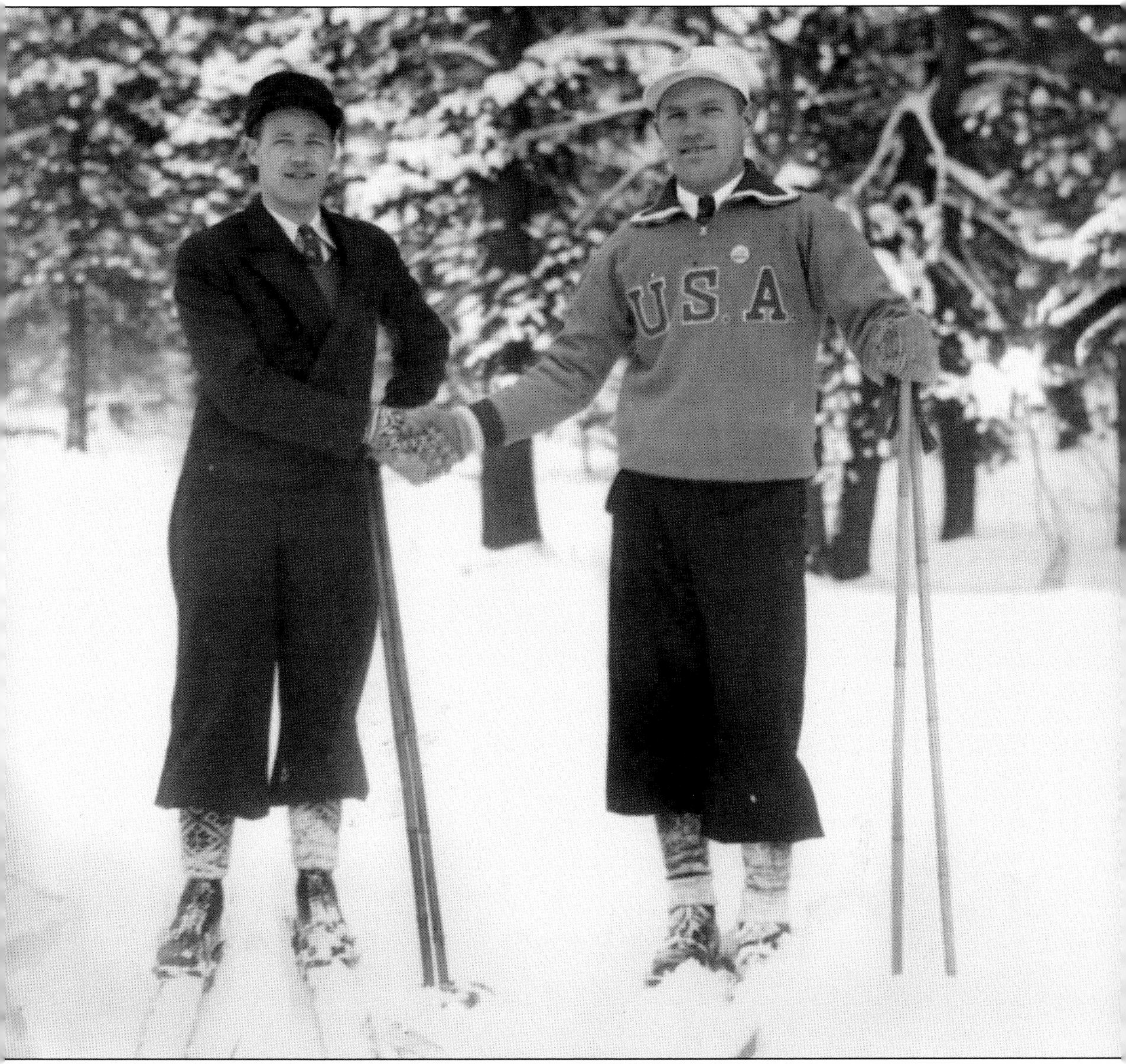


For many years, Sig Vettestad (left) and Roy Mikkelsen were champion jumpers with the Auburn Ski Club. The California Ski Championships were held at the club's new facilities at Cisco in January 1932. Events included a slalom race—skiing around staggered gates—which was becoming popular in Europe. This sanctioned competition was the first slalom race in California (and possibly the United States). Mikkelsen was a national champion twice and reigned as California's top jumper for nearly 15 years. (Courtesy Mark McLaughlin.)

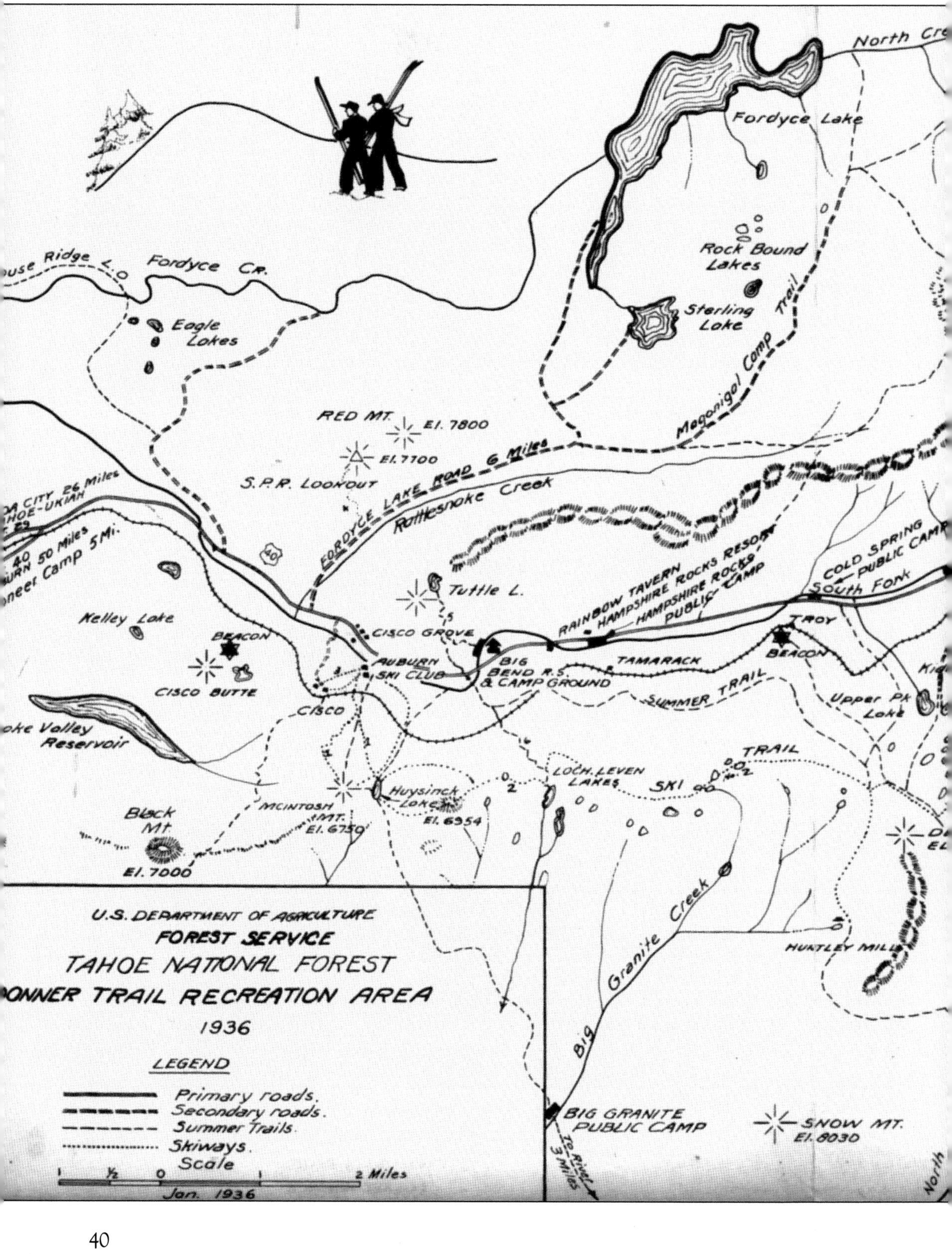

North Cr
Fordyce Lake
Rock Bound Lakes
Sterling Lake
Magonigol Camp Trail
Fordyce Cr.
Eagle Lakes
RED MT. El. 7800
El. 7700
S.P.R. LOOKOUT
FORDYCE LAKE ROAD 6 Miles
Rattlesnake Creek
Tuttle L.
Kelley Lake
BEACON
CISCO BUTTE
CISCO GROVE
AUBURN SKI CLUB
CISCO
BIG BEND R.S. & CAMP GROUND
RAINBOW TAVERN
HAMPSHIRE ROCKS RESORT
HAMPSHIRE ROCKS PUBLIC CAMP
COLD SPRING PUBLIC CAMP
South Fork
TROY
BEACON
TAMARACK
SUMMER TRAIL
Upper Pk Lake
LOCH LEVEN LAKES
SKI TRAIL No. 2
Huysinck Lake El. 6954
McINTOSH MT. El. 6750
Black Mt. El. 7000
Valley Reservoir
HUNTLEY MILL
Big Granite Creek
BIG GRANITE PUBLIC CAMP
To River 3 Miles
SNOW MT. El. 8030
U.S. DEPARTMENT OF AGRICULTURE
FOREST SERVICE
TAHOE NATIONAL FOREST
DONNER TRAIL RECREATION AREA
1936
LEGEND
Primary roads.
Secondary roads.
Summer Trails.
Skiways.
Scale
1 ½ 0 1 2 Miles
Jan. 1936

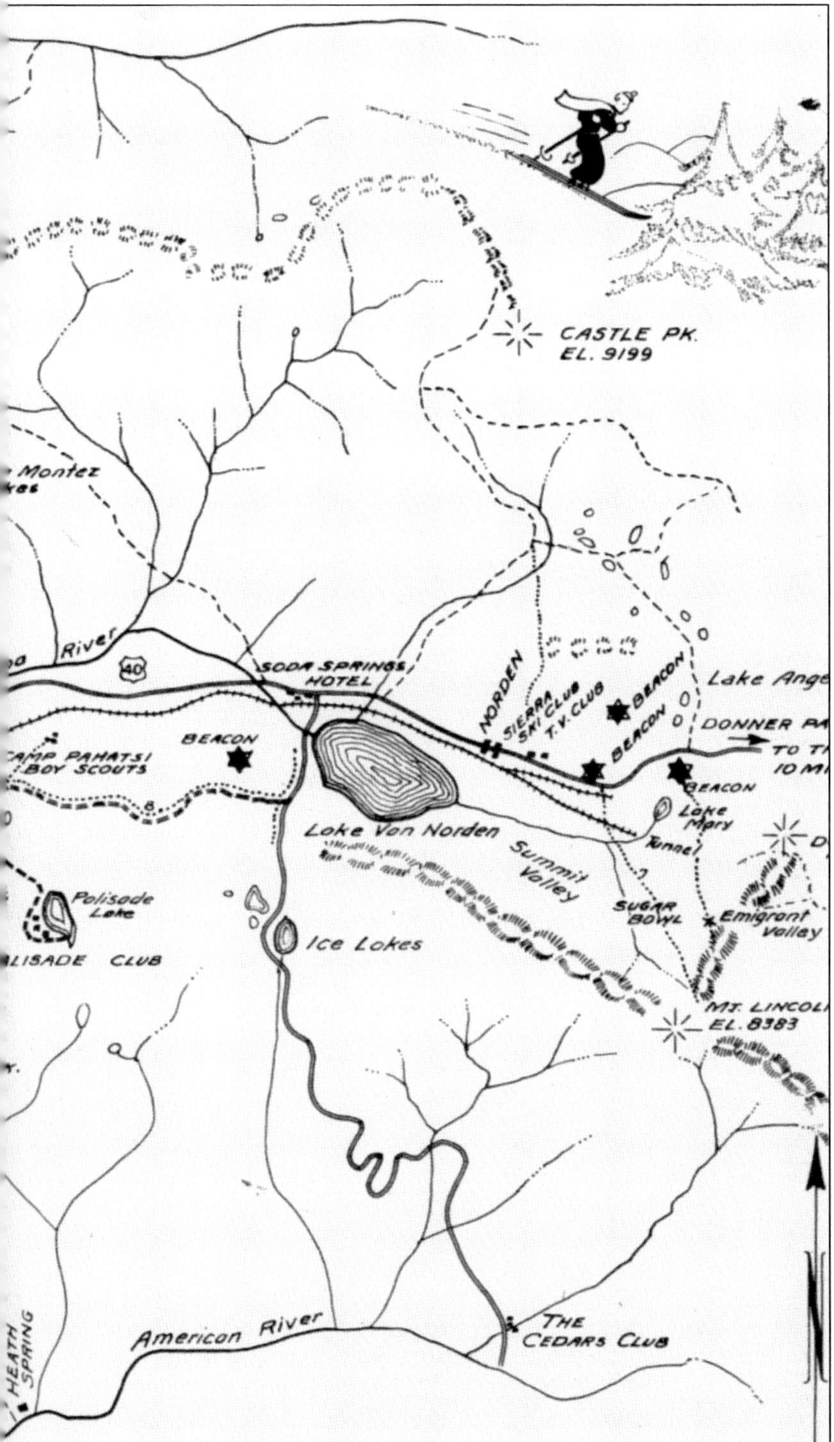


By 1936, there were already a handful of ski-oriented facilities between the Auburn Ski Club's winter park at Cisco (west) and Donner Lake (east). In the years leading up to World War II, many more were established, with rope tow operations dotting the Highway 40 corridor. Note how Highway 40 and the transcontinental railroad parallel each other most of the way. Skiers and winter sports enthusiasts could take the train to snow country if they did not want to drive. Also note the Skiways icon in the map legend for cross-country skiing along marked trails. (Courtesy William B. Berry collection.)

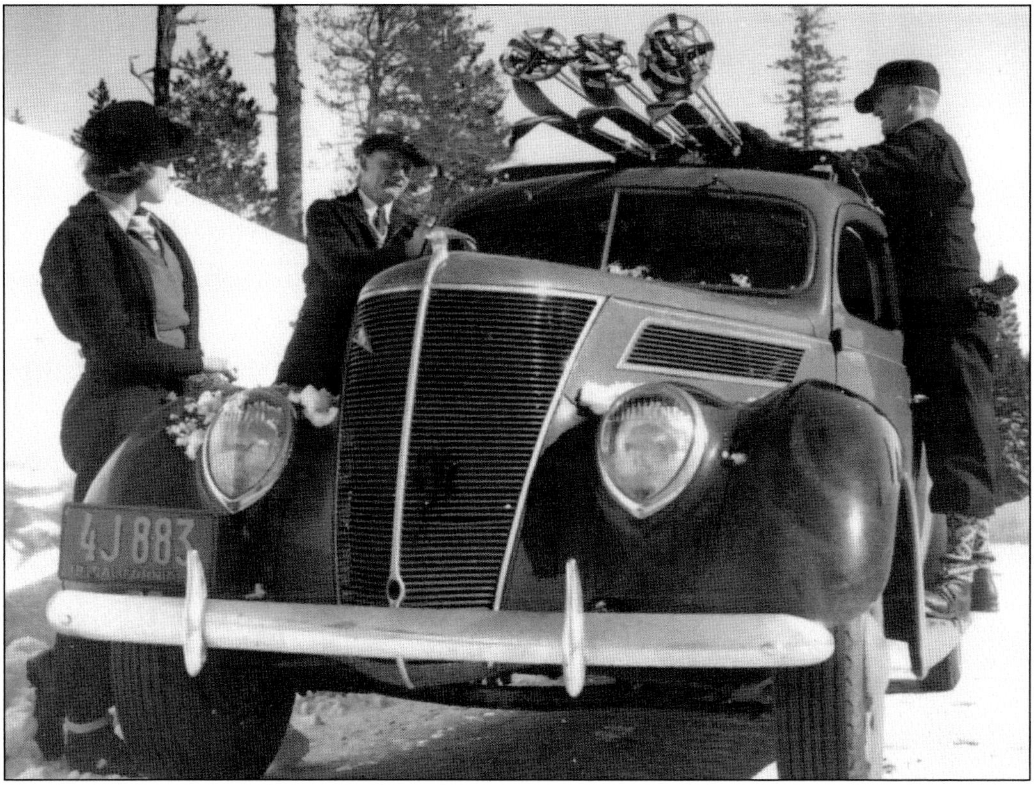


By 1940, ski business was booming along the Highway 40 corridor in the Donner Pass region. Rope tows had made the sport more fun, but it was lessons taught by trained instructors that made the difference. Dr. Joel H. Hildebrand, a University of California, Berkeley, chemistry professor and future president of the Sierra Club, played an influential role in the promotion of alpine skiing. Dr. Hildebrand encouraged the Sierra Club to construct the Clair Tappaan Lodge in the snowbelt near Donner Pass. For professional ski instruction, Dr. Hildebrand imported two Austrian brothers, Wilhelm "Bill" and Ferdinand "Fred" Klein. They joined American Dennis Jones, son of entrepreneur Oscar Jones, who had learned to ski while attending school in Switzerland. In the early 1930s, Jones cleared ski runs, built an up-ski contraption, and started a ski school that offered equipment rental. (Both, courtesy Donner Summit Historical Society/Norm Sayler collection.)

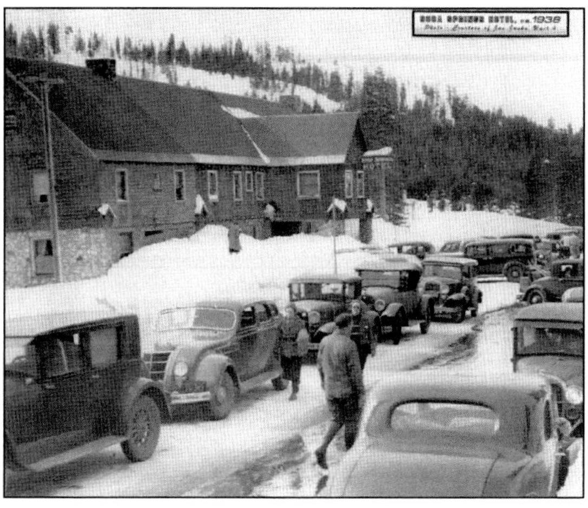

# *Four*

# Skiing Ramps Up before World War II

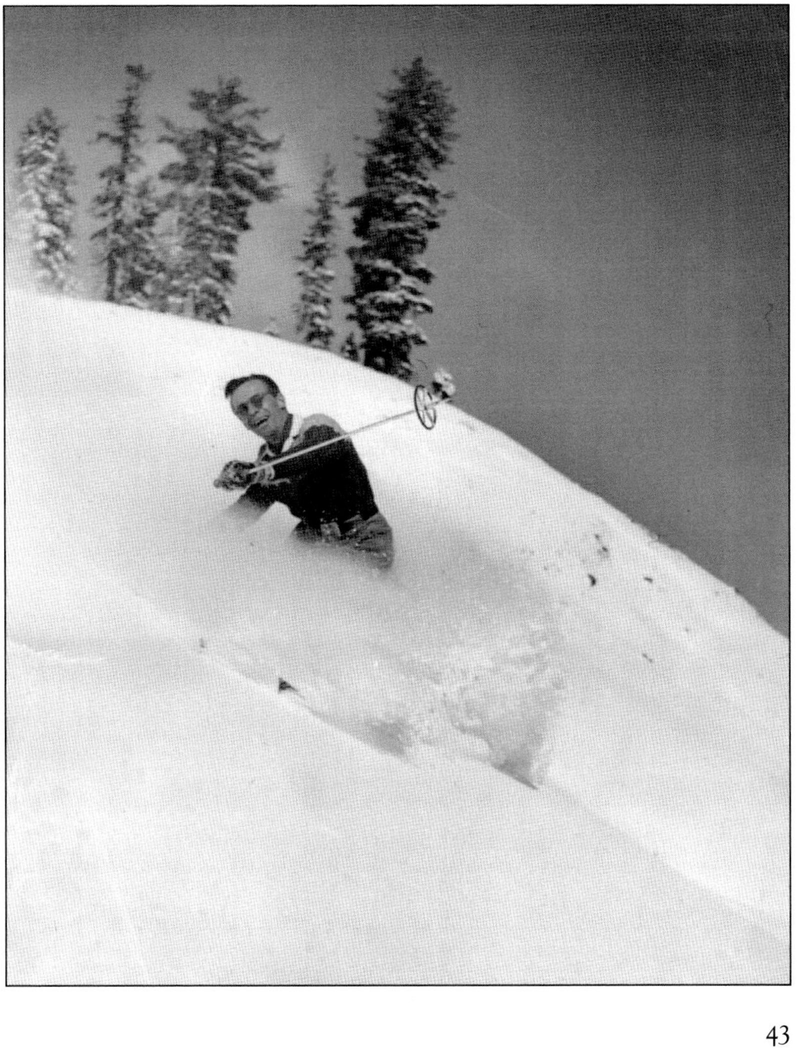

In this photograph, Larry Gratz Powers, director of the ski school at Donner Ski Ranch, makes a dynamic powder turn. Around 1930, ski instructors in the Alps ditched the old methods of simply schussing straight without turns or using the telemark turn with one knee bent forward. Students were taught to aggressively link parallel turns for a fast but controlled descent. Over time, the best qualities from several European techniques merged to become the basis of modern downhill skiing. (Courtesy Donner Summit Historical Society/Norm Sayler collection.)

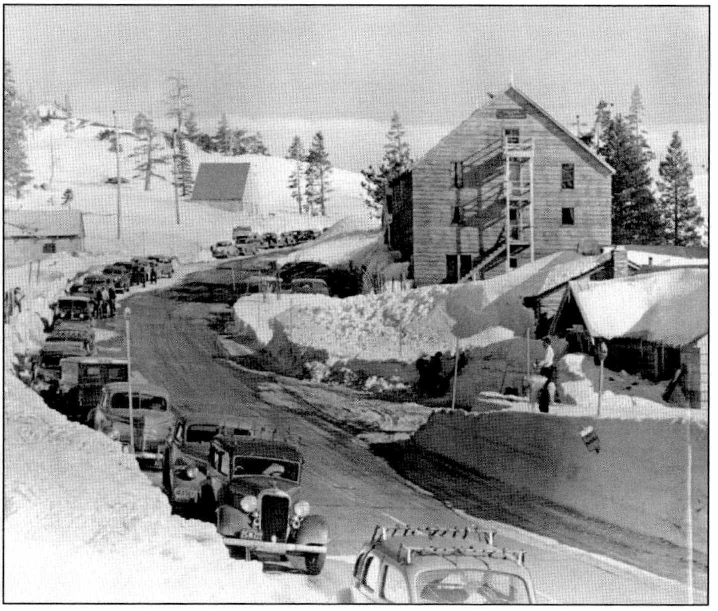

The House of Vanderford ski lodge (shown here) was constructed before World War II near the Sierra crest just west of Donner Pass. Mrs. Jessie A. Vanderford operated the ski lodge, while William Strickland, a popular and well-known skier, provided ski school instruction. After more resorts popped up between Reno and Sacramento, the Highway 40 corridor was promoted as "America's Finest Ski Area." (Courtesy Donner Summit Historical Society/Norm Sayler collection.)

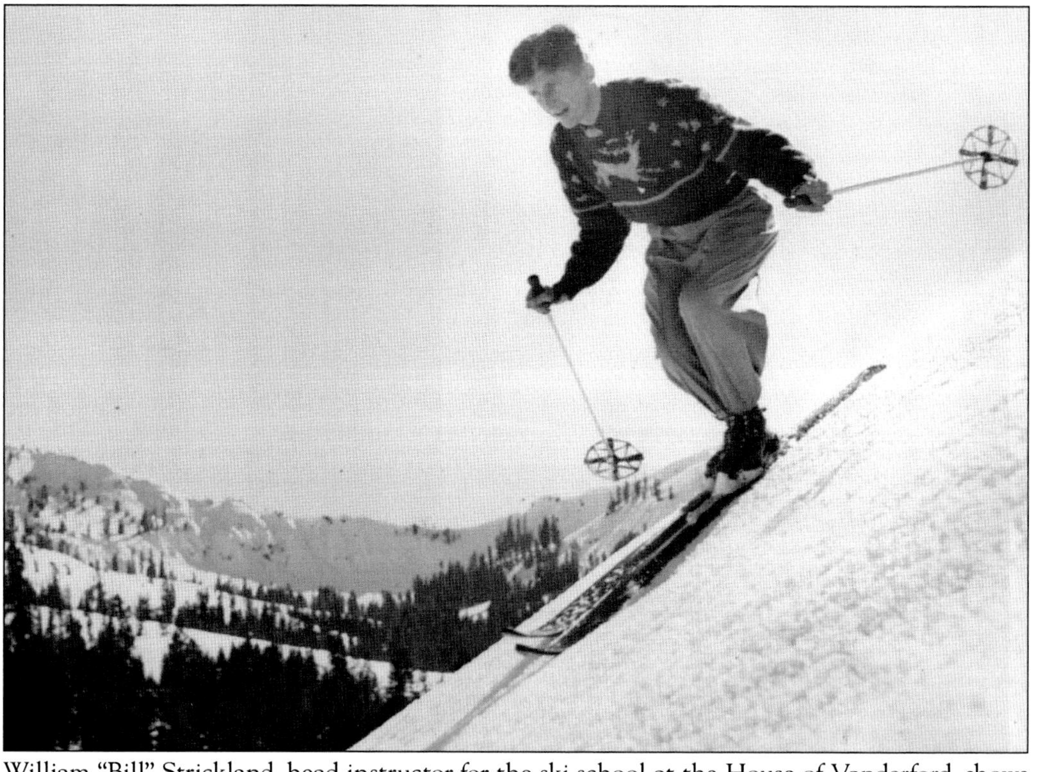

William "Bill" Strickland, head instructor for the ski school at the House of Vanderford, shows his style near the Sugar Bowl ski area. The Donner Pass/Norden area was a skier's paradise, with reliable snow and a variety of rope tows operated by entrepreneurs like Johnny Ellis or organizations like the Sierra Club. Ski clubs from Sacramento, Stockton, Oakland, and others provided inexpensive overnight accommodations. (Courtesy Donner Summit Historical Society/Norm Sayler collection.)

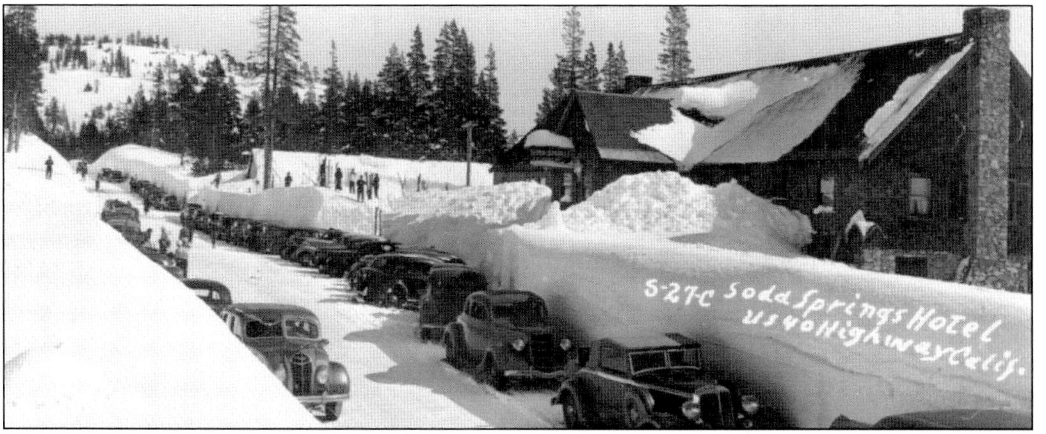


By 1941, the Soda Springs Hotel was under the new management of Herb and Ollie Bruck. Avid skiers, the couple revamped the lodge, installed a Swiss beer cellar in the basement, and built observation porches off the bar. The hotel could accommodate 75 guests in steam-heated rooms that contained a bath. Hotel rates in the Donner Summit area ranged from $1 to $4 per day, and meals cost 25¢ to a dollar per day. (Courtesy Donner Summit Historical Society/Norm Sayler collection.)

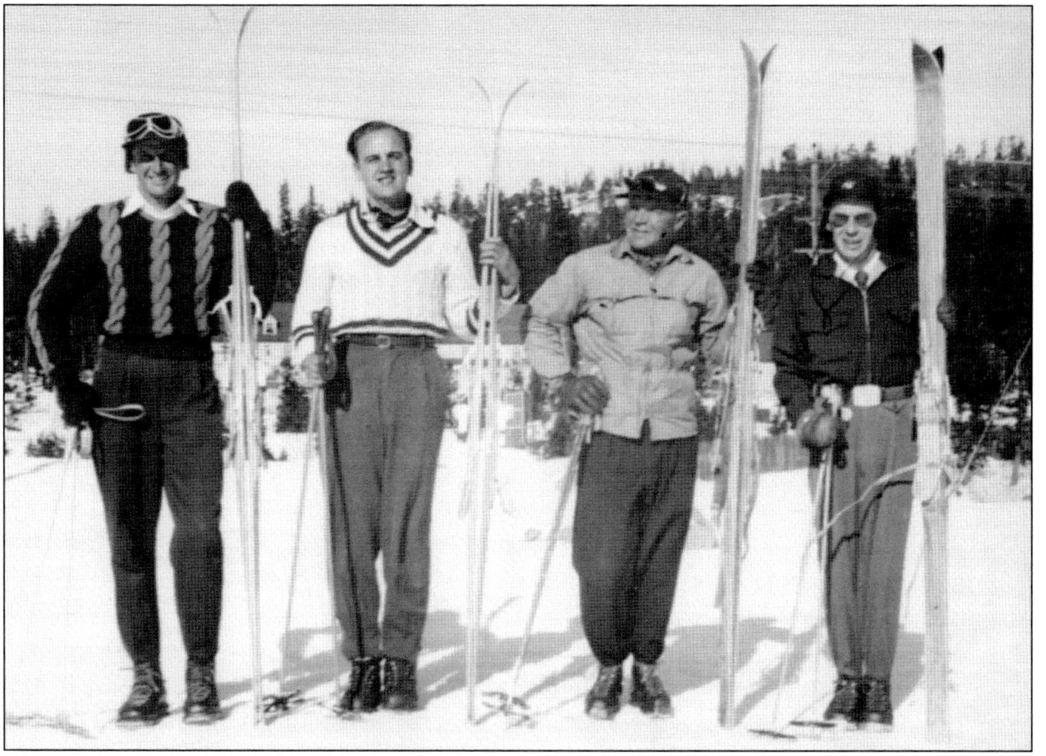

Early ski instructors at Soda Springs included, from left to right, William Strickland, Bud Zorich, John Johanson, and Larry Gratz Powers. By 1941, there were ski areas with rope tows all along Highway 40 from Yuba Gap to Donner Pass. As a testament to Dr. Joel Hildebrand's advocacy for professionalism in ski instruction, most of the ski hills were staffed with certified instructors who taught students the latest techniques. (Courtesy Donner Summit Historical Society/Norm Sayler collection.)

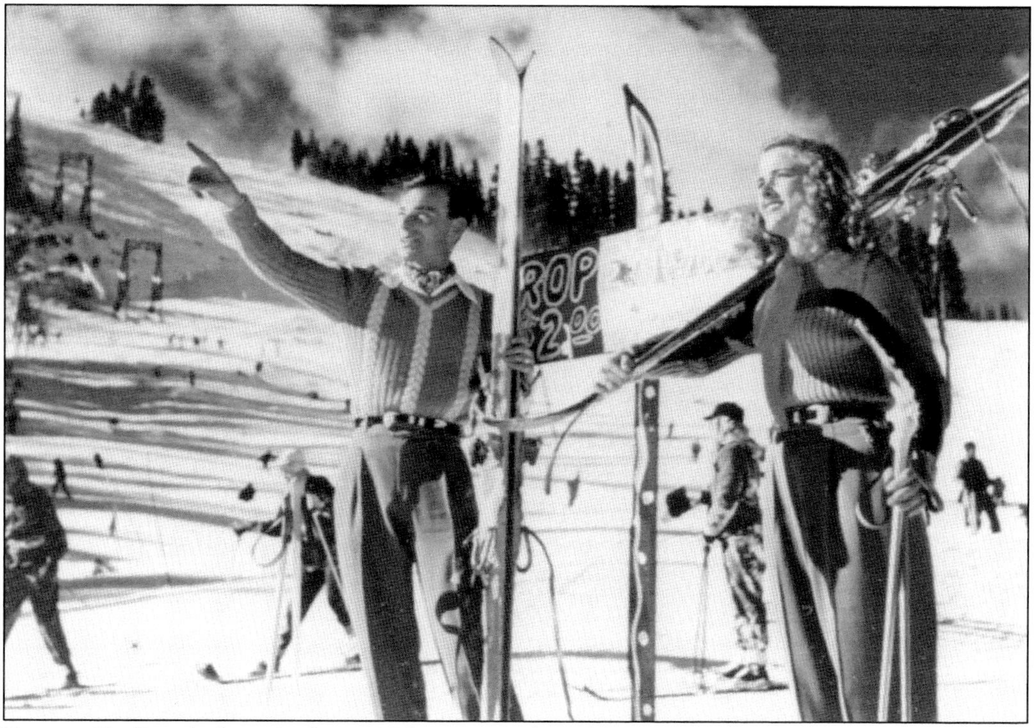

Donner Ski Ranch, launched in 1937 by Stan and Madelyn Walton, was located on Signal Hill, across Highway 40 from the House of Vanderford. Over the years, they added rope tows and built up a steady and loyal clientele. Madelyn was the daughter of pioneer Donner Summit ski entrepreneur Oscar Jones and a sister to Dennis Jones, one of the first ski instructors in the region. Ski instructor Phillip Sullivan is pictured here in 1948 with an unidentified student. (Courtesy Donner Summit Historical Society/Norm Sayler collection.)

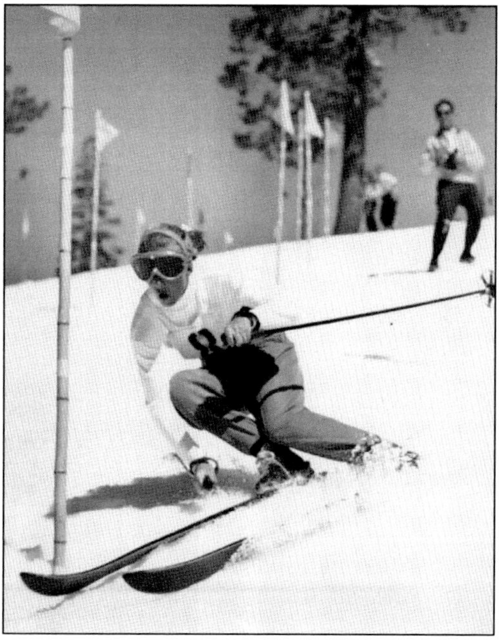

Donner Summit native Starr Walton shows her dynamic racing technique while skiing gates in 1962. The daughter of Stan and Madelyn Walton, Starr learned to ski at age three. A broken foot kept her off the 1960 US Olympic squad, but she carried the Olympic torch into Squaw Valley that year on old-fashioned barrel stave skis. Walton was the top American finisher in the downhill during the 1964 Olympic Winter Games in Innsbruck, Austria. (Courtesy Donner Summit Historical Society/Norm Sayler collection.)

This 1947 image captures three Donner Ski Ranch instructors—Larry "Gratz" Powers (left), Lee Peroni (center), and Al McIntyer. As the head buyer for the Emporium Ski Shop in San Francisco, Powers was heavily involved in the ski industry. Not only was he one of the first to import skis from Japan, Powers also designed the popular Thunderbird ski. (Courtesy Donner Summit Historical Society/Norm Sayler collection.)

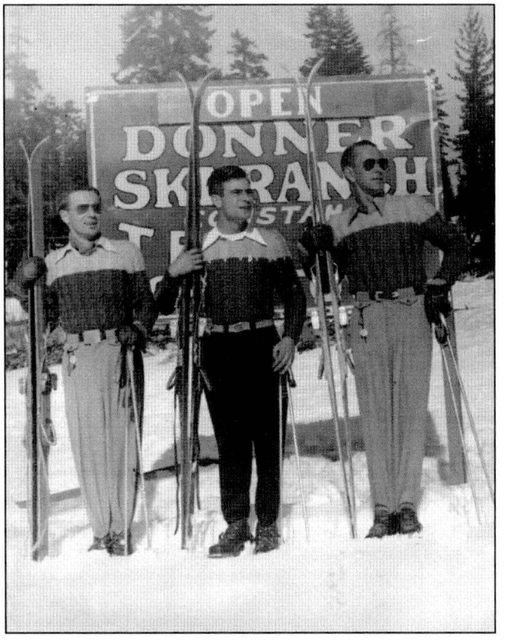


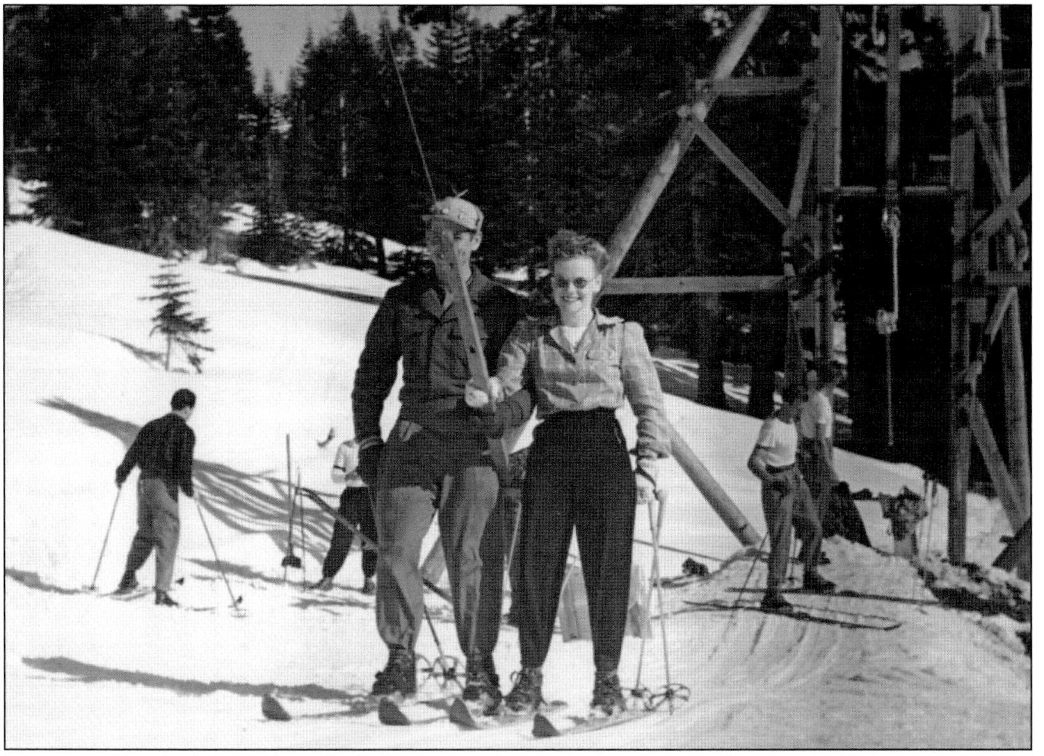

The Donner Ski Ranch installed this new T-bar in 1946. For nearly 50 years, Norm Sayler ran the "Ranch" with a business philosophy that focused on fun, not restrictions. Sayler set many modern industry precedents at his resort, including allowing snowboarders, providing programs for the disabled, and becoming the first California resort to provide lift-served telemark skiing and racing. (Courtesy Donner Summit Historical Society/Norm Sayler collection.)

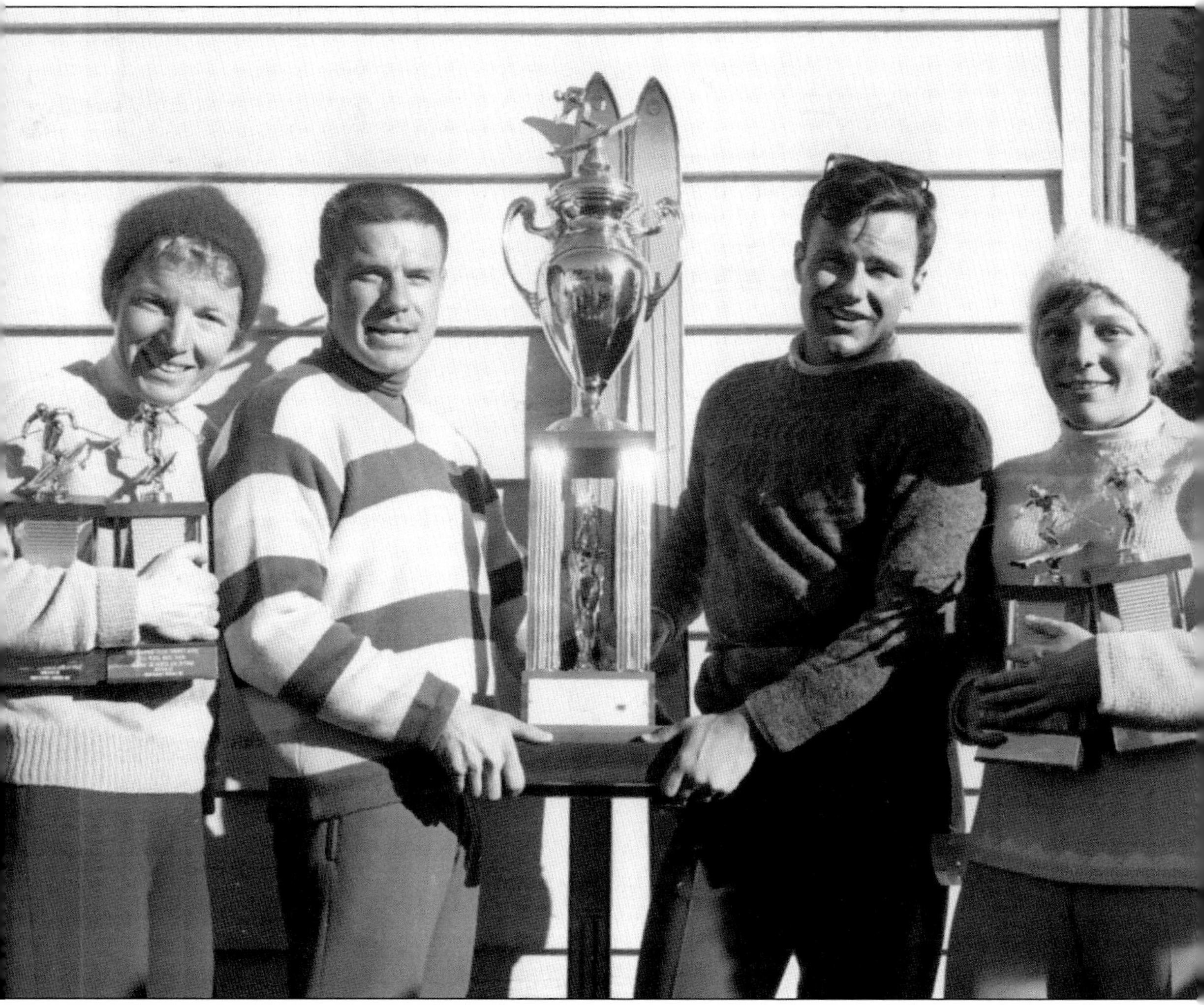

The Donner Ski Ranch Thunderbird Trophy Race attracted the best skiers from the Lake Tahoe region. The winners of this early 1960s race are, from left to right, Babette Haueisen, Norm Sayler, Dick Dorworth, and Patti Formichelli. Popular ski instructor Haueisen and her student Formichelli hold the individual "take-home" trophies, while Sayler and Dorworth hoist the impressive Thunderbird trophy. The race was sponsored by Larry Gratz Powers and the Thunderbird ski company. Haueisen did not start skiing until age 19, but she won the prestigious Sugar Bowl Silver Belt race just six years later. After just missing the cut at the 1956 Olympic Trials, she began a lifelong career in Tahoe as one of the nation's top ski instructors. After his stint with the 10th Mountain Division, Sayler got a job at Donner Ski Ranch in the 1950s digging postholes for a new ski lift. He eventually took over the ownership and operation of the resort where he worked for 46 years. Dorworth set world records in speed skiing and became an acclaimed ski writer. (Courtesy Donner Summit Historical Society/Norm Sayler collection.)

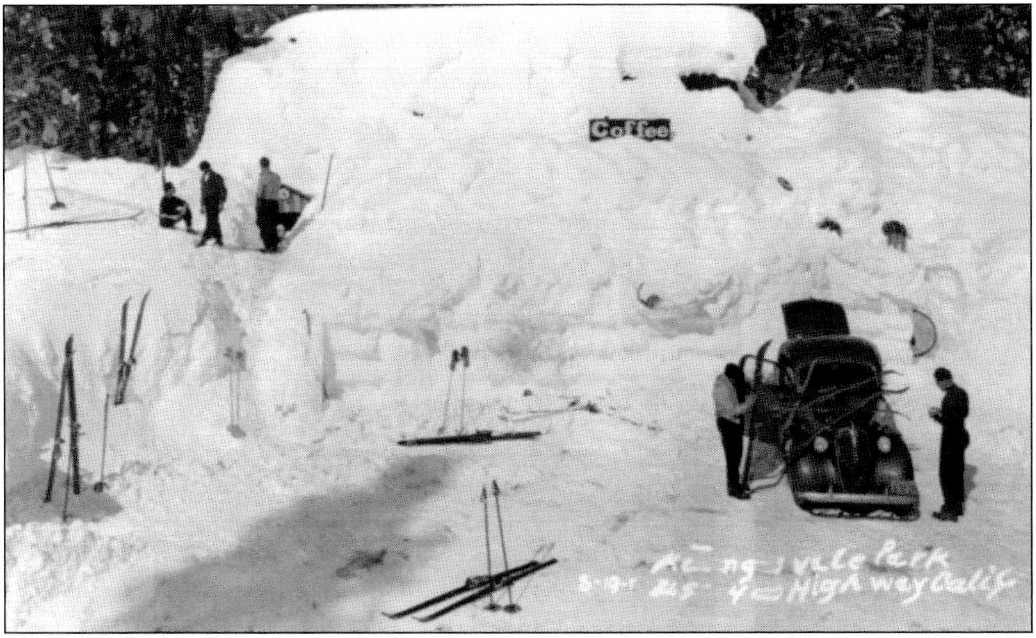


Before the construction of modern Interstate 80, Highway 40 was the hub for winter sports in the northern Sierra. There were tourist accommodations, inns, restaurants, and gas stations all along the route to Truckee. Most of these businesses are now gone, as motorists today use the interstate. By 1940, hot coffee and ski rentals were already available at the Kingvale Snow Park (now Kingvale). (Courtesy Donner Summit Historical Society/Norm Sayler collection.)

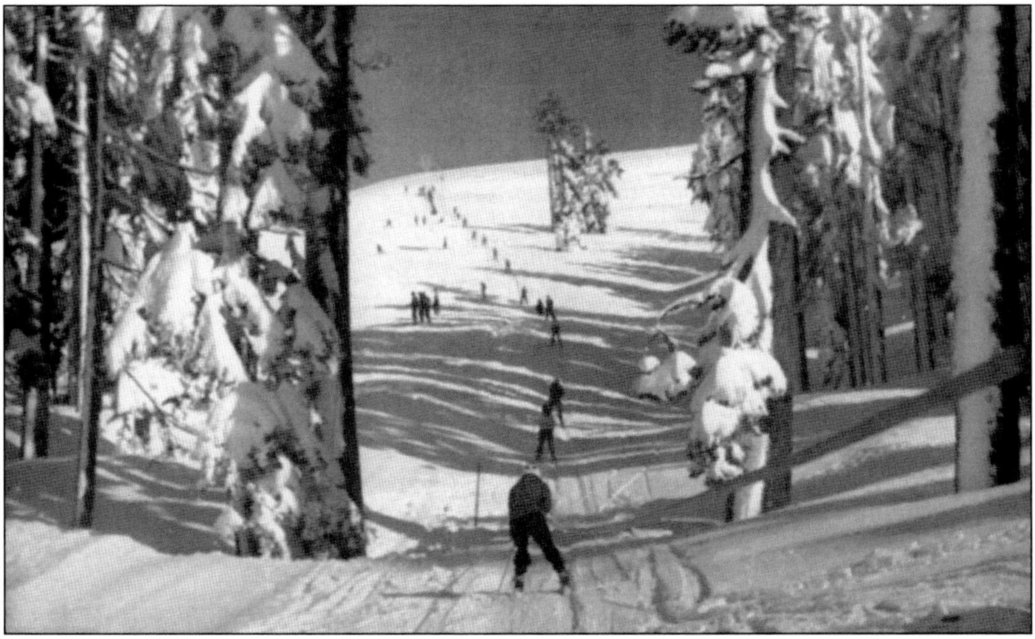

The Sierra Club rope tow gave skiers one heck of a ride. Dr. Joel Hildebrand had learned to parallel ski in Europe and became an advocate for the sport. He encouraged the Sierra Club to install one of the first rope tows in the region, where members received professional ski instruction from Bill and Fred Klein. (Courtesy Sierra Club Bulletin, March 1948.)

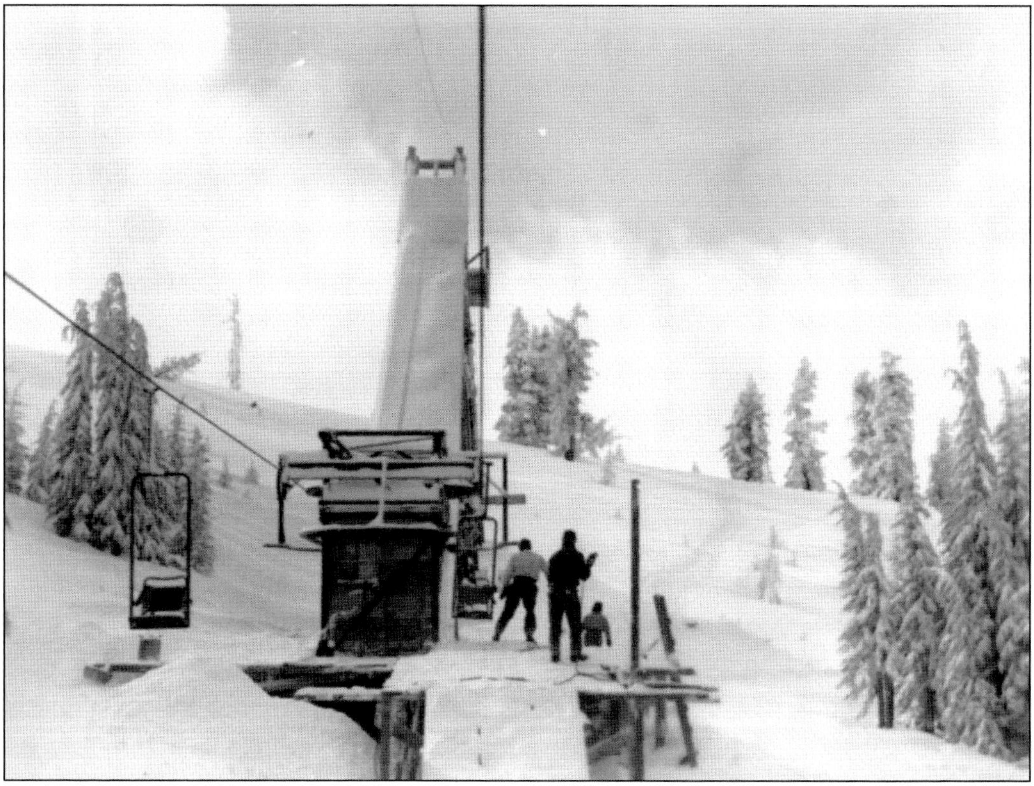

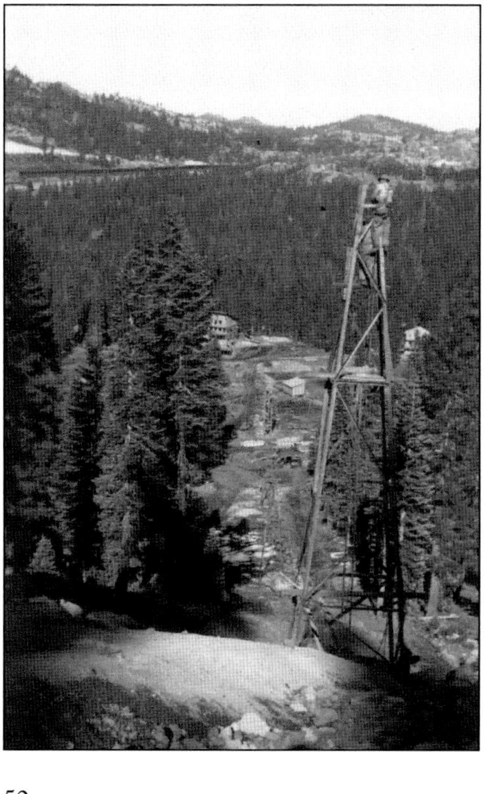

By the summer of 1939, construction was well underway on the Sugar Bowl ski resort and California's first chairlift. A two-man power saw was used to cut down large trees, and dynamite helped blast out the tower footings. The lift cost $39,000 to build, and when completed, it whisked skiers 1,000 vertical feet up to the Sierra ridge in just six and a half minutes. Ski lift rates were 25¢ per ride, $2 per day, or $10 per week. Due to the lodge's distance from the Southern Pacific Railroad, during the first winter, a horse-drawn sleigh was used to transport skiers from the train to the lodge. Note the long stretch of the Southern Pacific wooden snowshed in the upper distance. The sheds protected the trains and track from avalanches and snow buildup. (Both, courtesy Donner Summit Historical Society/Norm Sayler collection.)

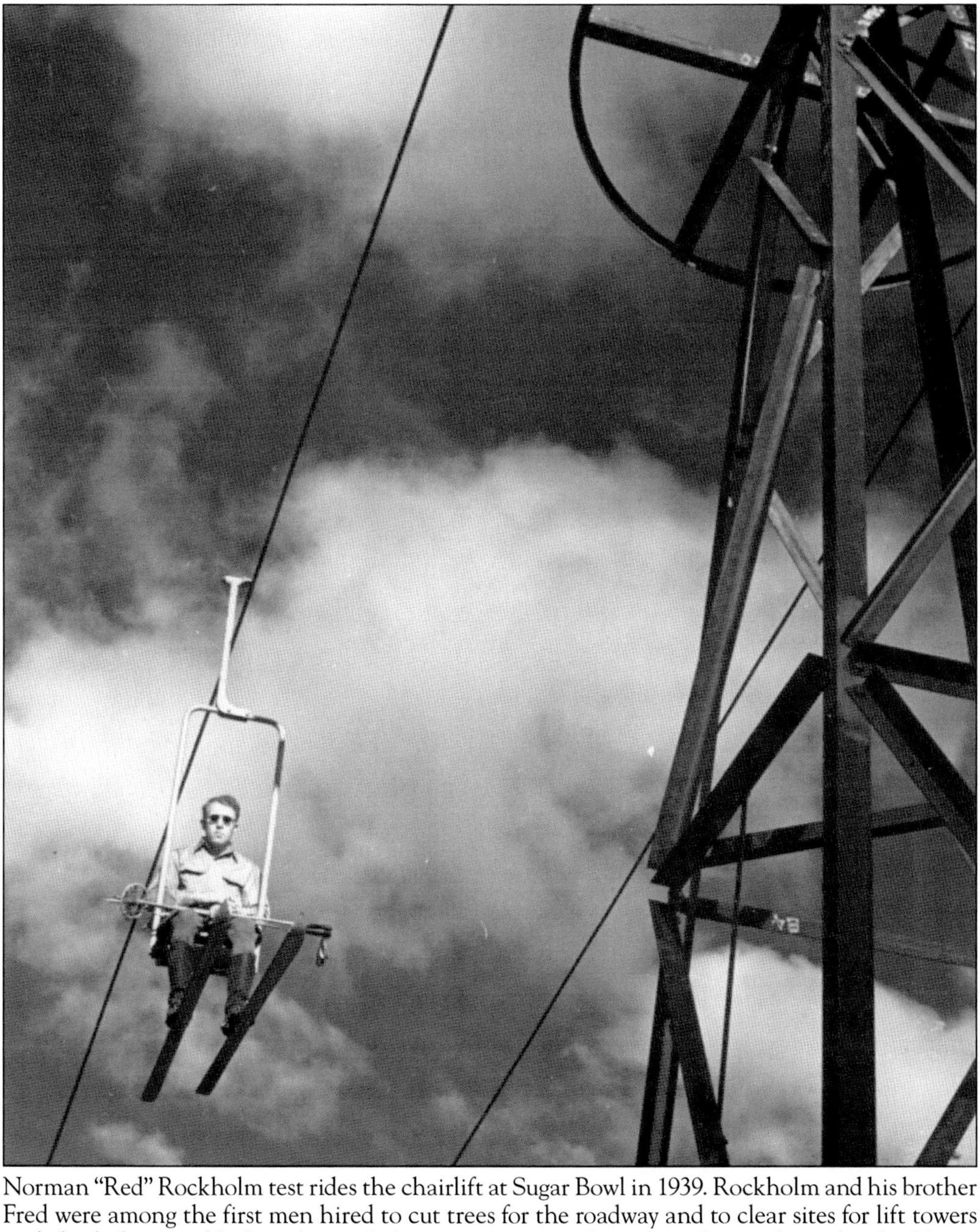

Norman "Red" Rockholm test rides the chairlift at Sugar Bowl in 1939. Rockholm and his brother Fred were among the first men hired to cut trees for the roadway and to clear sites for lift towers and the lodge. Rockholm admitted that it was scary riding the solitary chair that had been attached to the cable just the night before, "but the thought of being the first man to ride the first chairlift in California relieved the tension a little." Southern Pacific Railroad organized the promotional pictures, but the female model, Norma Brooks, became nauseated as the chair swung during the shoot. As soon as Sugar Bowl opened, on December 15, 1939, skiers fell in love with its perfect blend of European charm coupled with the exuberance of California. The legendary animator Walt Disney was an avid skier and an early investor in the resort. Sugar Bowl quickly became popular with movie stars and the rich and famous. (Courtesy Donner Summit Historical Society/Norm Sayler collection.)

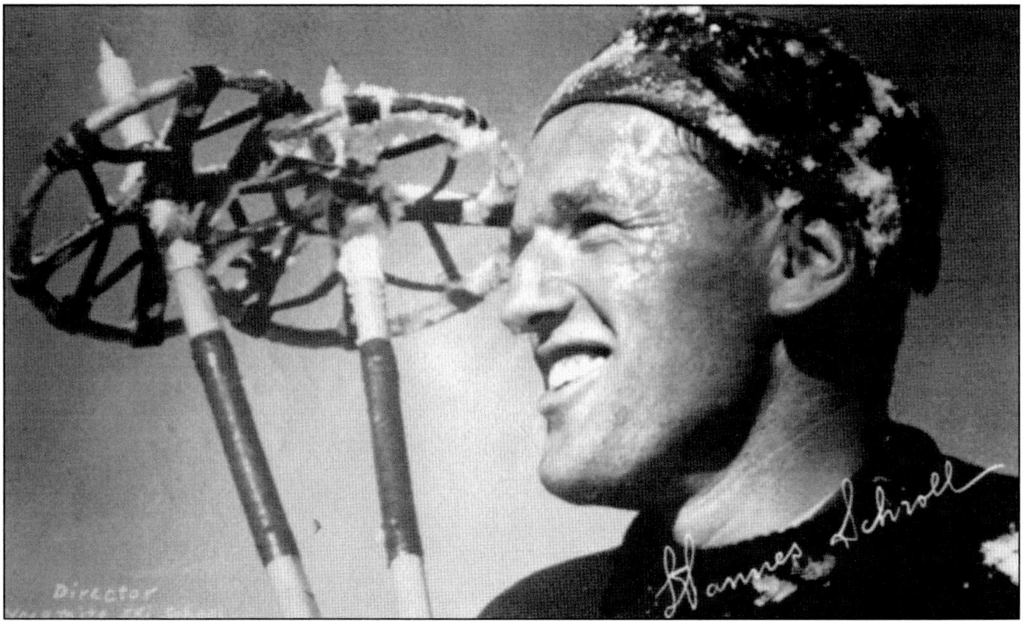


Hannes Schroll, a world-class ski racer from Austria, took America by storm. Formerly the director of the Yosemite Ski School, Schroll and San Francisco–based investors purchased the land needed for the Sugar Bowl resort in 1938 for less than $7,000. Schroll was a flamboyant character known for yodeling and skiing fast. A natural at drawing publicity, Schroll inaugurated the first annual Silver Belt race in 1940, a legendary giant slalom that plummeted 1,300 vertical feet down steep terrain. (Courtesy Bill Klein collection.)

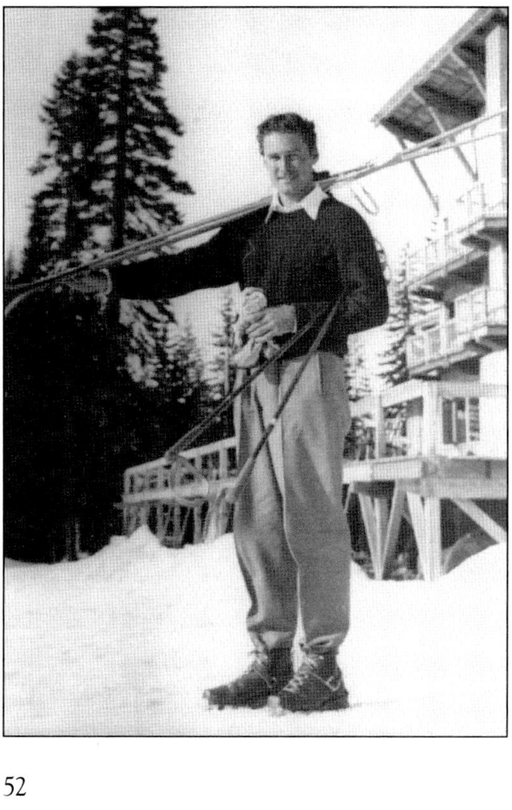

Movie legend Errol Flynn enjoys a day of skiing Sugar Bowl in 1942. The resort drew celebrities from across the country, including glitterati like Howard Hughes, Claudette Colbert, Lowell Thomas, Norma Shearer, and others. The Sugar Bowl Lodge (background) was designed by noted architect William Wilson Wurster and constructed in a Tyrolean style within walking distance of the lifts. (Courtesy Truckee Donner Historical Society.)

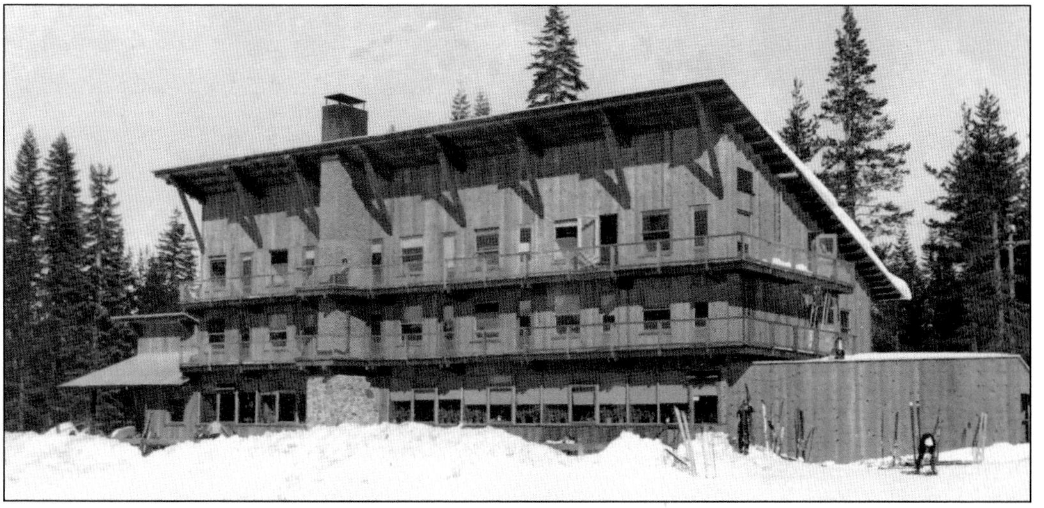

The Sugar Bowl Lodge could accommodate up to 20 people in private rooms, with two dormitories (one for men and one for women) that each slept 10. Below the lodge were a ski shop, ski rental department, lockers, and restrooms—all open to the public. Business was so good that Southern Pacific began running "Snowball Special" trains every day of the week during ski season. (Courtesy Truckee Donner Historical Society.)

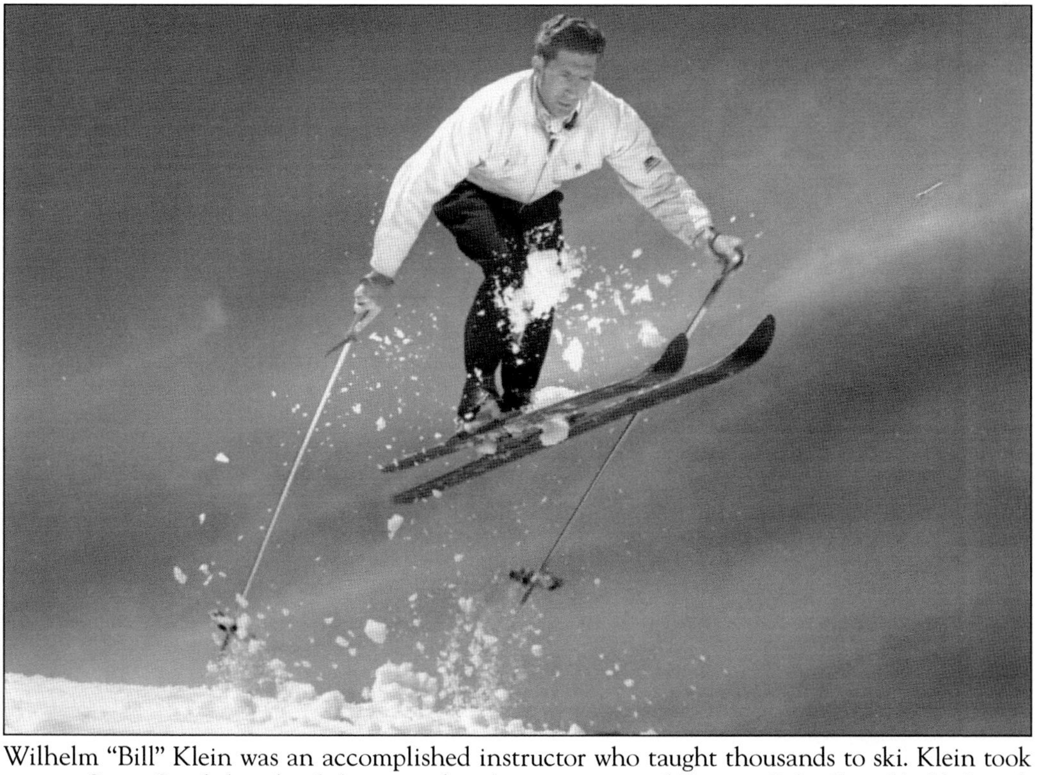

Wilhelm "Bill" Klein was an accomplished instructor who taught thousands to ski. Klein took over as Sugar Bowl ski school director after the retirement of Hannes Schroll and held the job until 1957, when he decided to change careers and offered the position to Yosemite's Badger Pass director Luggi Foeger. For more than 20 years, Klein taught skiing with a confident style that inspired students to succeed. (Courtesy William B. Berry collection.)

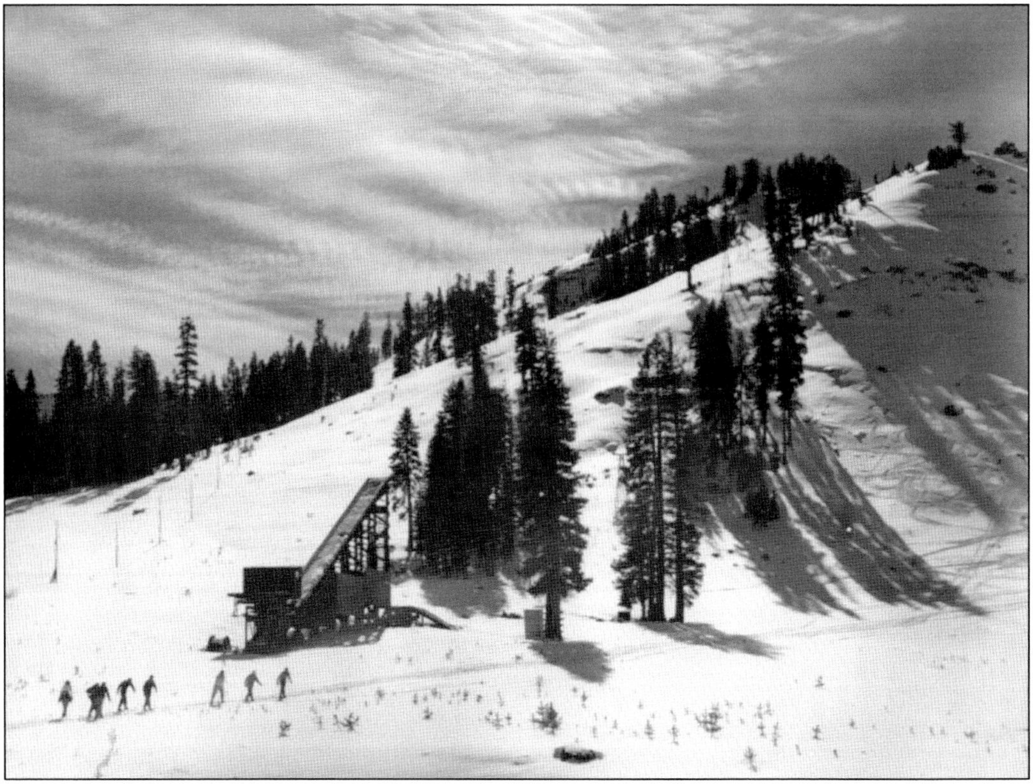

The highest elevations of Sugar Bowl, named for its prodigious snowfall, boasted big mountain cliffs, chutes, and expert terrain. The new chairlift effortlessly transported skiers to the challenges on the upper slopes. After a locomotive killed some horses pulling the sleigh from the train station, mechanical tractors were used until the "Magic Carpet" gondola was built in 1953 to carry skiers from the train to the lodge. (Courtesy Donner Summit Historical Society/Norm Sayler collection.)

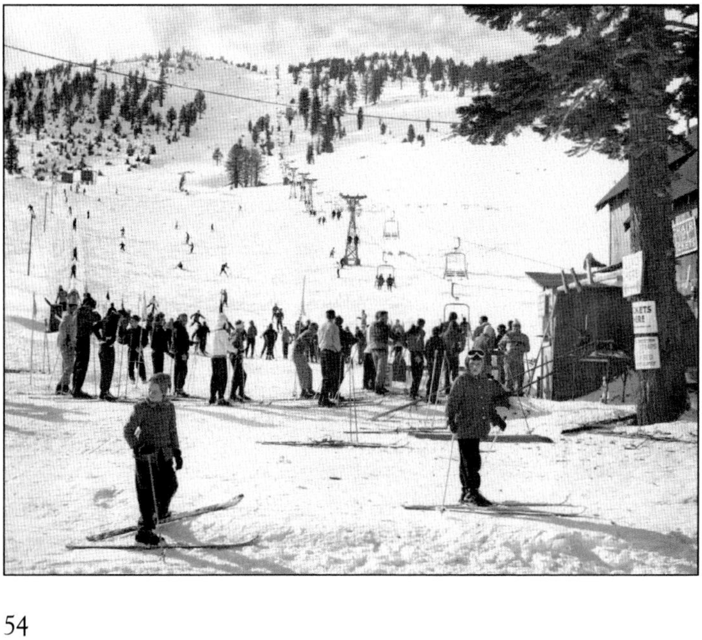

Because of its proximity to the transcontinental railroad, access to Sugar Bowl was closed for national security reasons during and shortly after World War II. In the postwar era, the resort upgraded to a modern double chairlift to replace its first single-seat model, a primitive version that tended to sway in the wind and made some skiers seasick. (Courtesy Donner Summit Historical Society/Norm Sayler collection.)

# *Five*

# Downhill Sprouts at Lake Tahoe

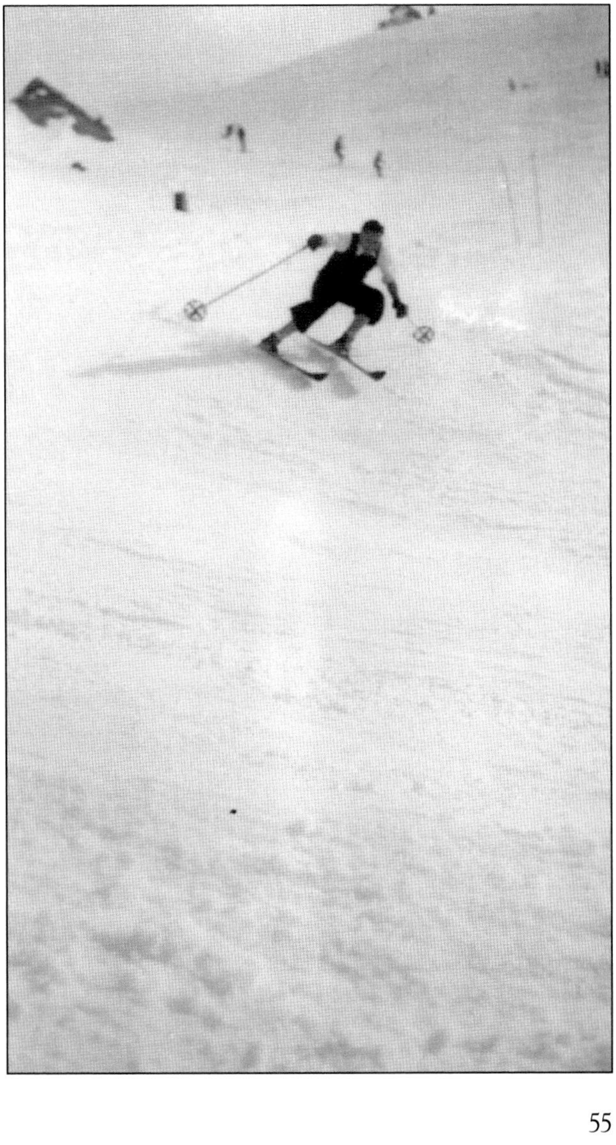

Raymond I. "Pappy" Smith makes turns on Poulsen's Hill, near Mount Rose, Nevada. In the late 1930s, Wayne Poulsen, former captain and later coach of the University of Nevada ski team, set up a rope tow on the hill. Poulsen established a ski school and gave lessons—the first in the Silver State. Inspired by the prospect, Smith, owner of Harold's Club casino, donated $6,000 to start ski-area development in the Mount Rose area southwest of Reno. (Courtesy William B. Berry collection.)

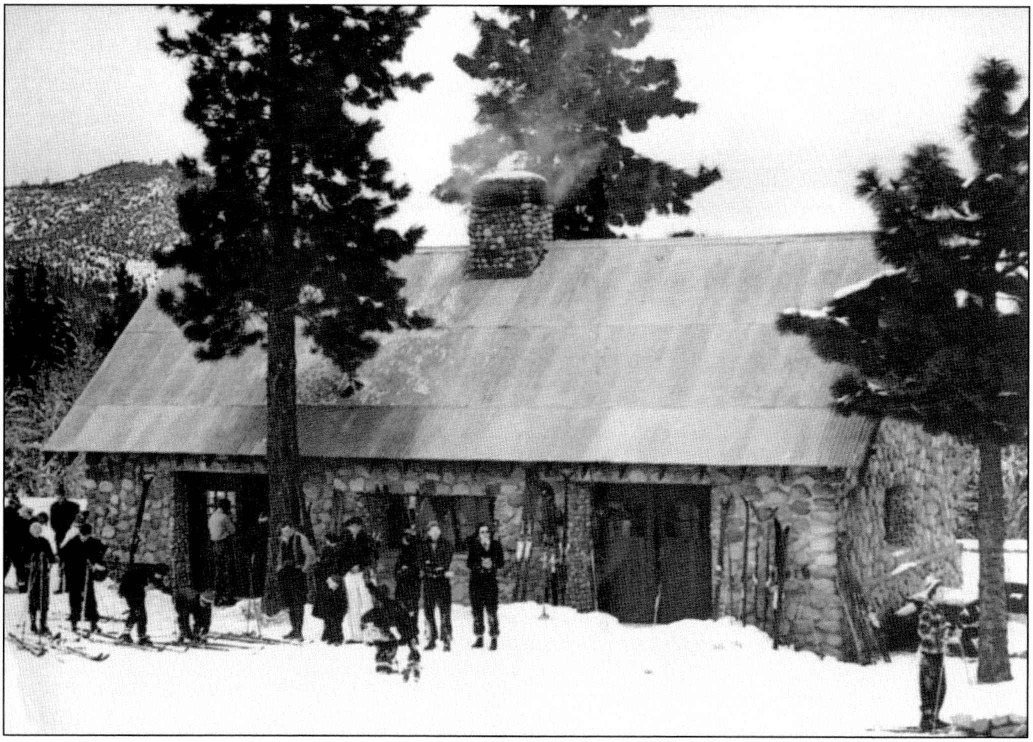

The Galena Creek Ski Hut was built in 1937 by the Works Progress Administration, a Depression-era federal program designed to put unemployed Americans to work. This stone warming hut, near Mount Rose, Nevada, provided shelter for enthusiasts enjoying the nearby ski jump and large ice-skating rink. Galena Creek was a popular winter sport center for University of Nevada ski competitions. (Courtesy Nevada Historical Society.)

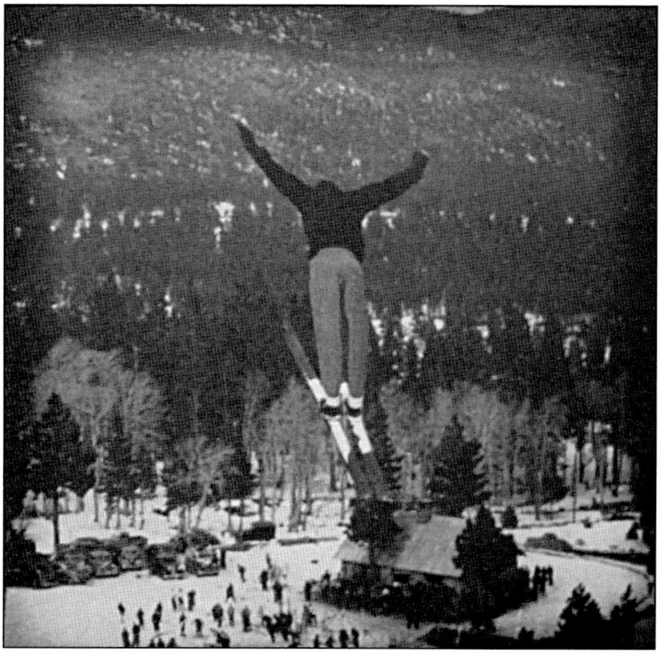

Galena Creek was the spot for Reno-area skiers in the late 1930s. Before World War II, local residents and University of Nevada ski team members flocked to the Galena Creek winter sports center. The university held its very popular annual Intercollegiate Winter Sports Carnival there, attracting college ski teams from throughout the west. (Courtesy Nevada Historical Society.)

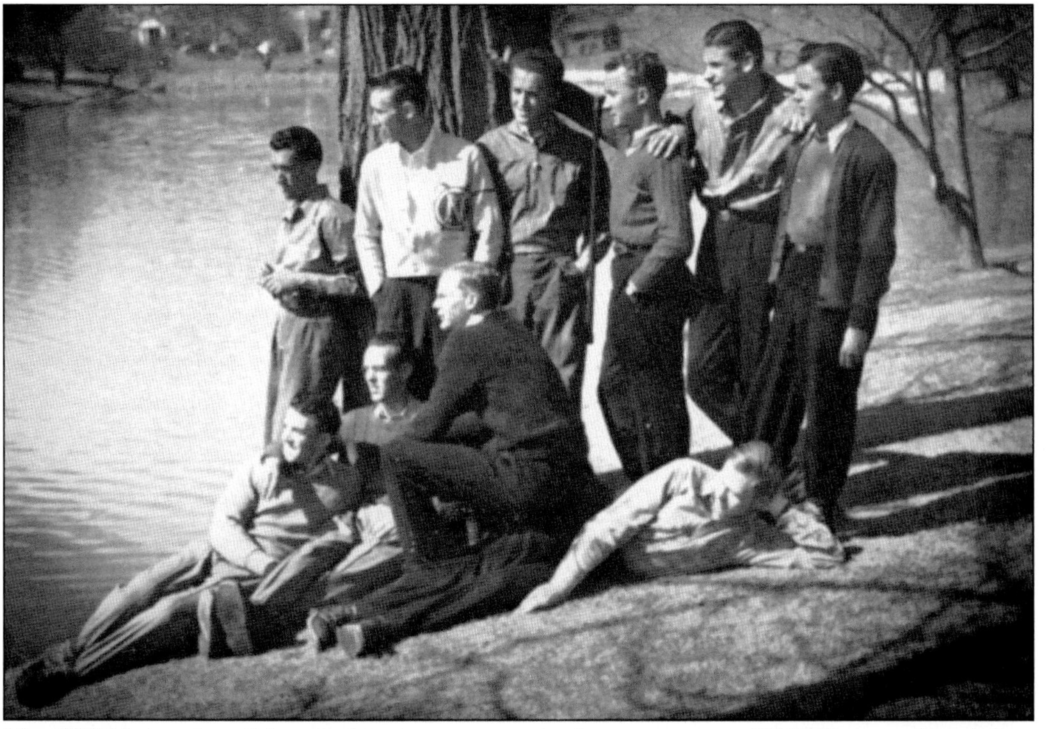

The 1939 University of Nevada ski team poses on the Reno campus in 1939. They are, from left to right, (first row, on the ground) ? Johnson, James Worden, Jack Starratt, and Fraser West; (second row, standing) Martin "Marti" Arrougé, Carl Bechdolt Jr., Earl Edmunds, Wayne Poulsen, Don McMeekin, and Frank Titus. In 1939, the talented team outscored every college it competed with and became champion of the Western region. There was not a national sanctioning authority for intercollegiate skiing until 1954. (Courtesy Nevada Historical Society.)

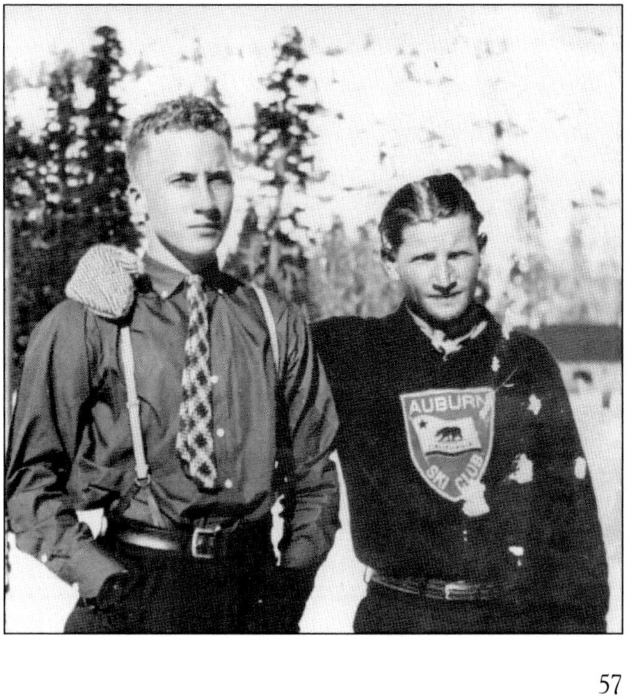


Wayne Poulsen (left) and his friend Joe Caffney are pictured in 1938. Poulsen was captain of the University of Nevada ski team; he excelled in jumping and alpine skiing. After graduation, he stayed on to encourage the fledgling ski program he had started at the university and coached the 1939 squad to an undefeated season. Wayne Poulsen, future founder of Squaw Valley, was a true pioneer in the development of Lake Tahoe skiing. (Courtesy Donner Summit Historical Society/Norm Sayler collection.)

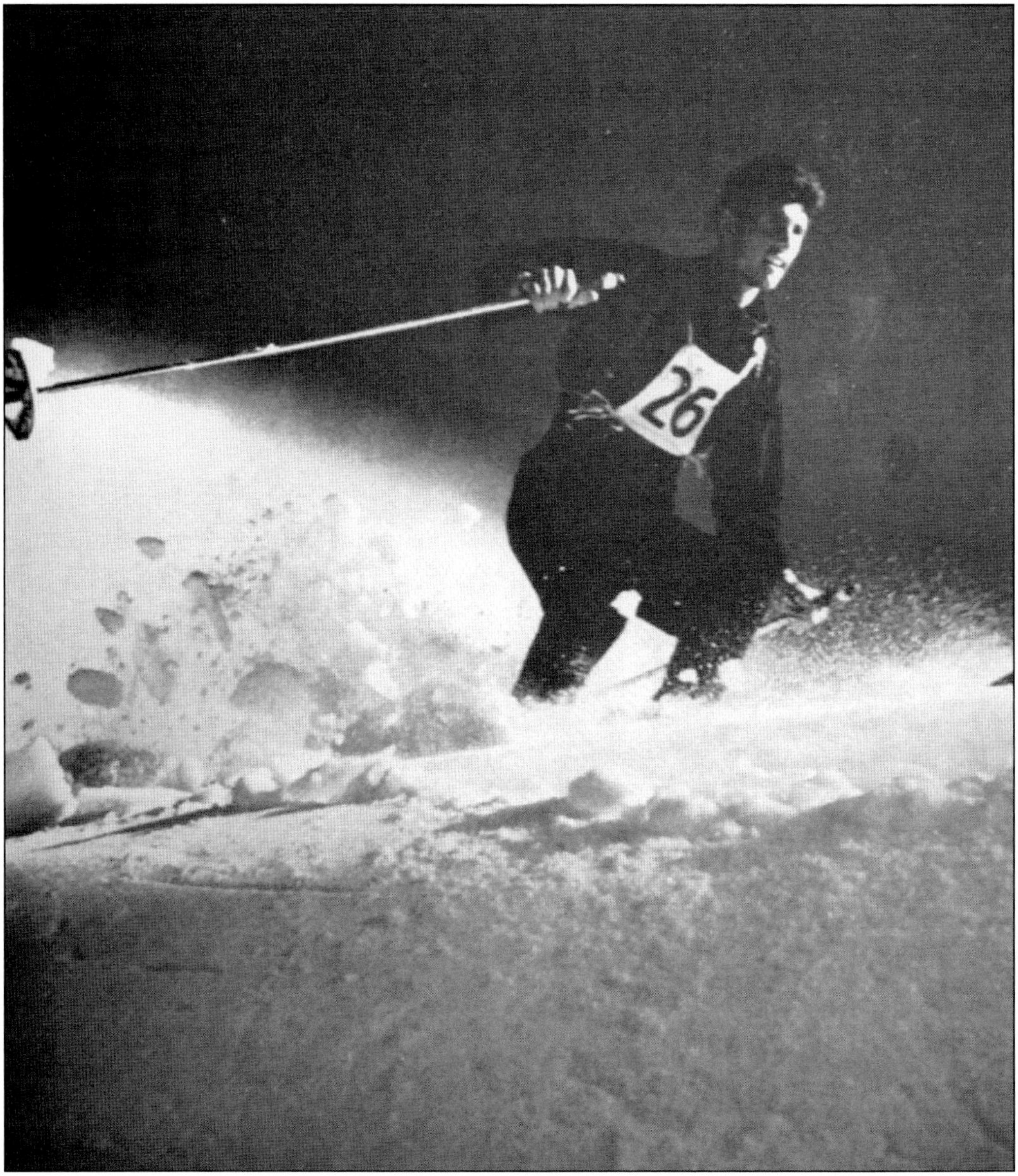


This is University of Nevada, Reno (UNR) ski team member Robert Cameron in a 1939 competition. The 1939 Nevada ski team was an exceptional group of young men who proved their mettle on the ski hill before graduating to prove their courage in World War II. The skill and determination that they showed in competition were the same characteristics that made them heroes in both war and peacetime. Among the squad were a future Marine lieutenant colonel, an Air Force colonel, three naval aviators (counting coach Wayne Poulsen), and a brigadier general. William Moran, who did not make the first team, became an admiral. Tragically, Lt. Col. Robert Cameron was killed in a helicopter explosion, and Don McMeekin, a Navy lieutenant, died while serving in the Aleutian Islands. The ongoing high performance of Nevada ski teams inspired Wayne Poulsen to say, "The UNR ski team has produced more national champions, more Olympic team members and more national and international recognition than any other group of athletes from UNR." It is a legacy that Poulsen was proud of. (Courtesy Nevada Historical Society.)

Challenged by disease, Tahoe City's Carl Bechdolt Jr. was still racing gates in 1941. Before Bechdolt was stricken with polio in 1939, his University of Nevada teammates figured Bechdolt was a shoo-in for the 1940 Winter Olympics, which were cancelled due to war. An outstanding competitor in all four ski disciplines, Bechdolt continued to be a top performer in national meets for the next few years despite his disability. (Courtesy North Lake Tahoe Historical Society.)

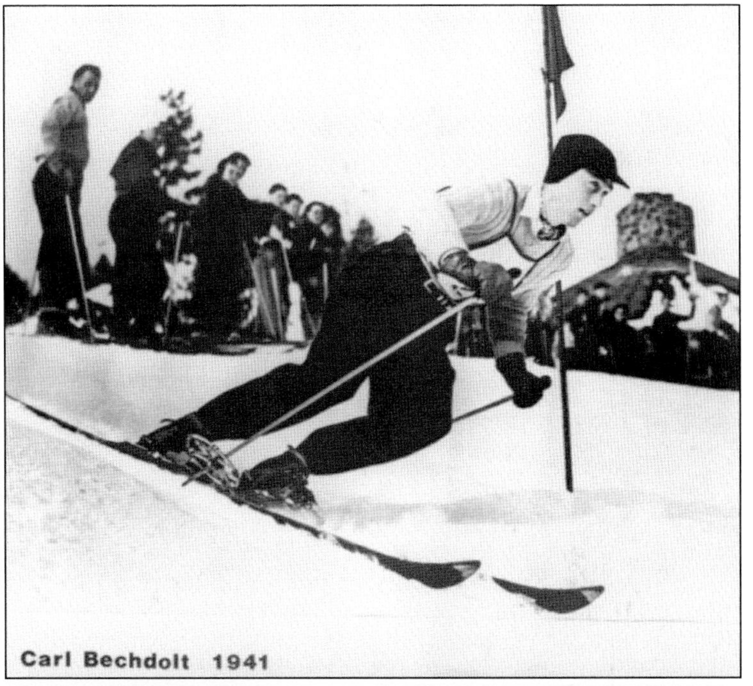


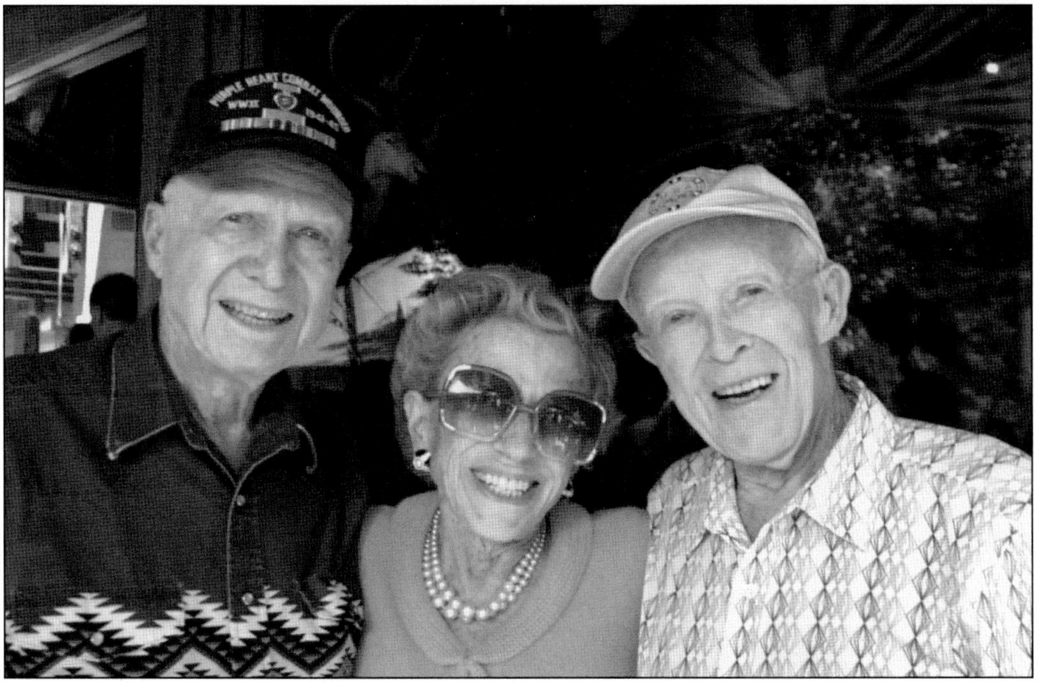

Lake Tahoe skiing pioneers Fraser West (left), Gladys "Sandy" Poulsen (center), and Frank Titus were photographed together in 2007. West and Titus were on the 1939 University of Nevada championship team, and both were officers in World War II. In 1949, West headed up the first ski patrols at Squaw Valley. After the war, Truckee resident Titus became a pharmacist but continued to teach others how to ski. Until her death in 2007, Sandy Poulsen—the wife of Wayne Poulsen—was known as the "Grand Dame of Squaw Valley." (Courtesy Mark McLaughlin.)

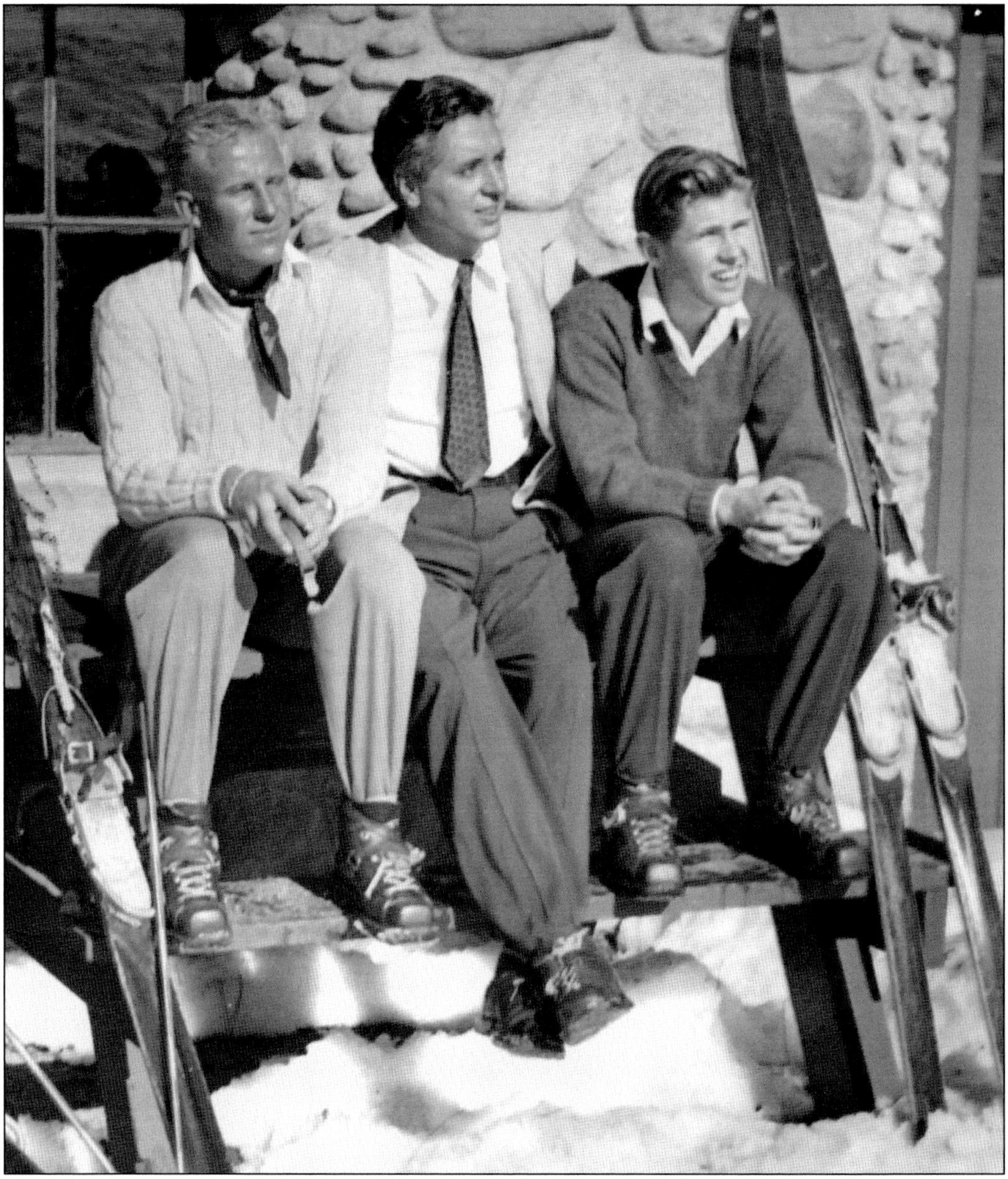

Noted ski journalist William B. Berry (center) relaxes with his two sons, Joseph "Barnes" (left) and Hal, at Nevada's Galena Creek winter sports center in 1942. After a stint doing stunt skiing as a double in an Abbott & Costello musical comedy on Donner Summit in 1942, Barnes Berry joined what became the 10th Mountain Division, in which soldiers at Camp Hale, Colorado, were trained to fight in cold weather and ski rugged alpine terrain. The story of the 10th Mountain Division's contribution to the Allied victory in Europe during World War II is legendary. About 15 skiers from the Lake Tahoe region became ski troopers or Army instructors in the 10th Mountain Division, including Chelton Leonard (Reno), William Bechdolt (Tahoe City), Karl Kielhofer and Peter Vanni (Truckee), Roy Mikkelsen (Auburn), and William "Bill" Klein and Larry Gratz Powers (Soda Springs). (Courtesy Mark McLaughlin.)

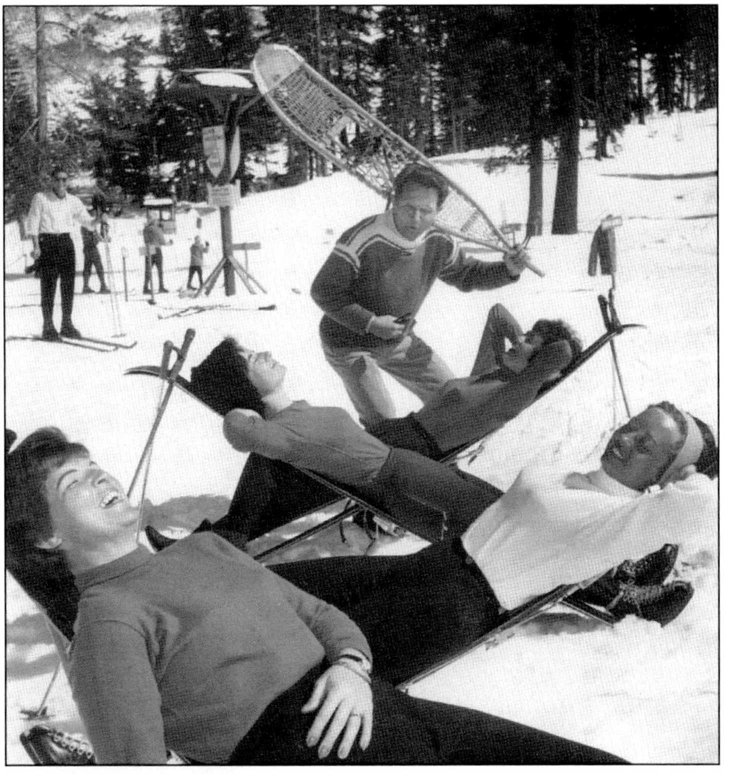

During World War II, Austrian-born Luggi Foeger fled to the United States. An expert skier, he taught survival skills to members of the 10th Mountain Division in Colorado. At Lake Tahoe, he worked as a ski instructor at Alpine Meadows. Known for his sense of humor, Foeger is seen here hamming it up at Alpine Meadows around 1963. He later helped develop Ski Incline (now Diamond Peak). (Courtesy North Lake Tahoe Historical Society.)

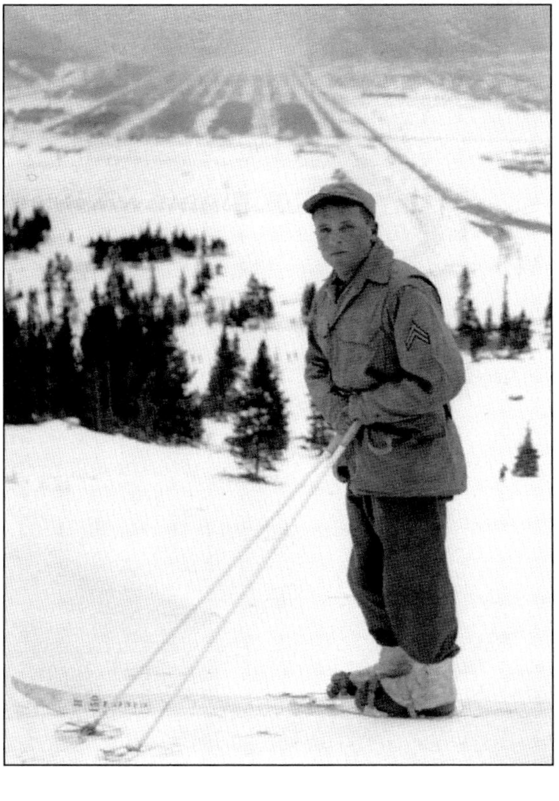

This 1943 image shows Reno resident Chelton Leonard training as a ski trooper at Camp Hale, Colorado. Returning soldiers fired up America's modern ski industry by publishing magazines, opening ski schools, designing equipment, managing ski shops, and establishing new areas like Vail, Aspen, Diamond Peak, Sugarbush, Whiteface Mountain, and others. At least 62 resorts were founded by, managed by, or employed head ski instructors who were 10th Mountain Division veterans. (Courtesy Chelton Leonard collection.)

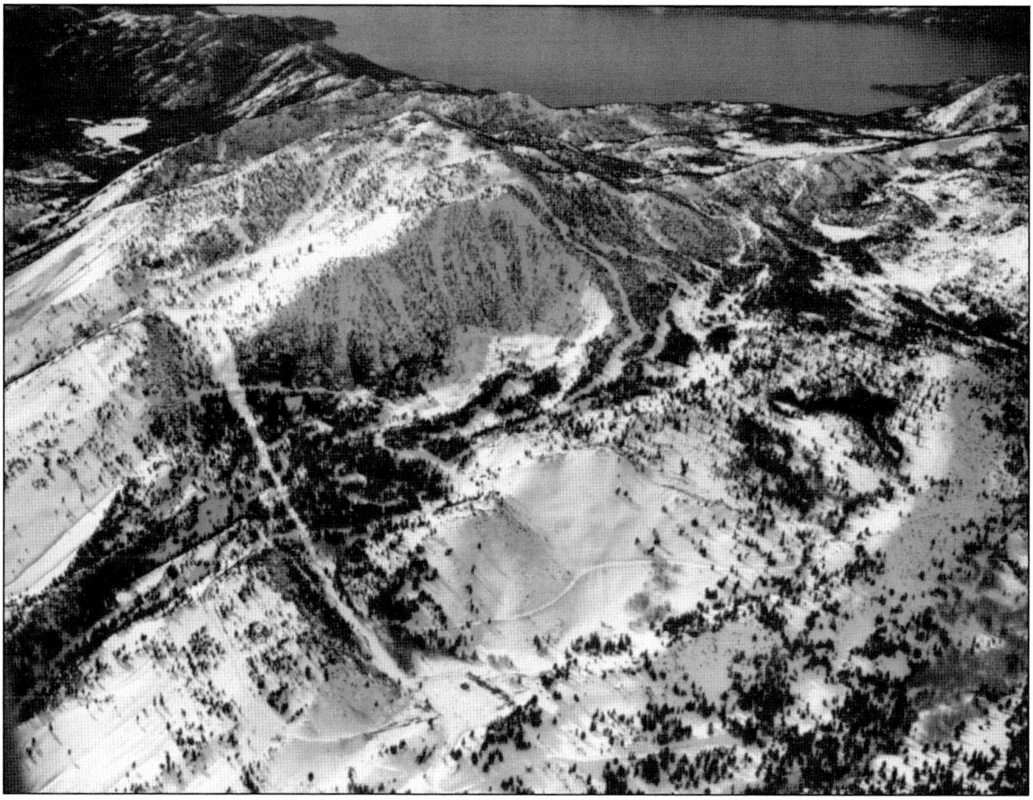

A 1940 photograph shows an aerial view of Mount Rose and Slide Mountain, southwest of Reno, Nevada. In late 1938, Wayne Poulsen and his partner, Edward Heath, opened Nevada's first ski area with a rope tow and ski school at 8,000 feet elevation in the Mount Rose bowl. Because of his snow surveying with University of Nevada professor Dr. James Church, Poulsen knew that the northeastern quadrant of the Lake Tahoe Basin combined radical terrain with dry powder snow. (Courtesy Donner Summit Historical Society/Norm Sayler collection.)

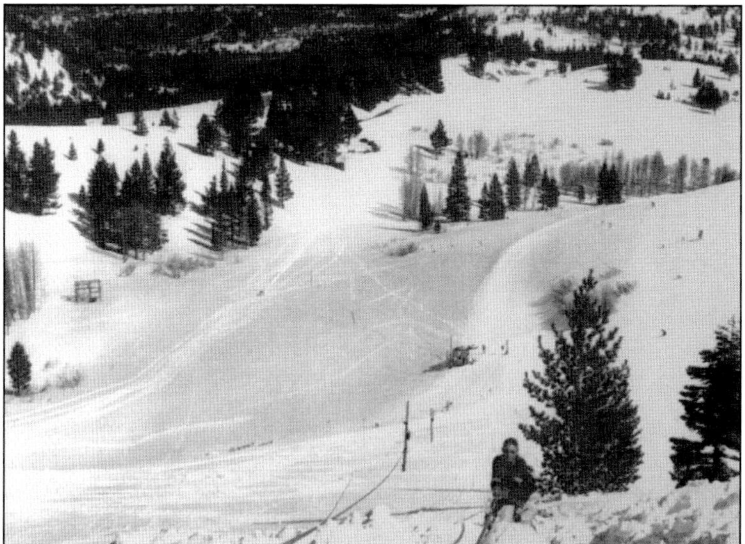

By 1940, Poulsen and Heath's rope tow was transporting skiers 560 vertical feet. Poulsen's "Mt. Rose Upski and Ski School Tyrol" was Nevada's first ski school. Members of the University of Nevada ski team helped Poulsen clear the slope, build a warming hut, and mount wheels on wooden posts to support the automobile-powered rope tow. (Courtesy Keston Ramsey collection.)

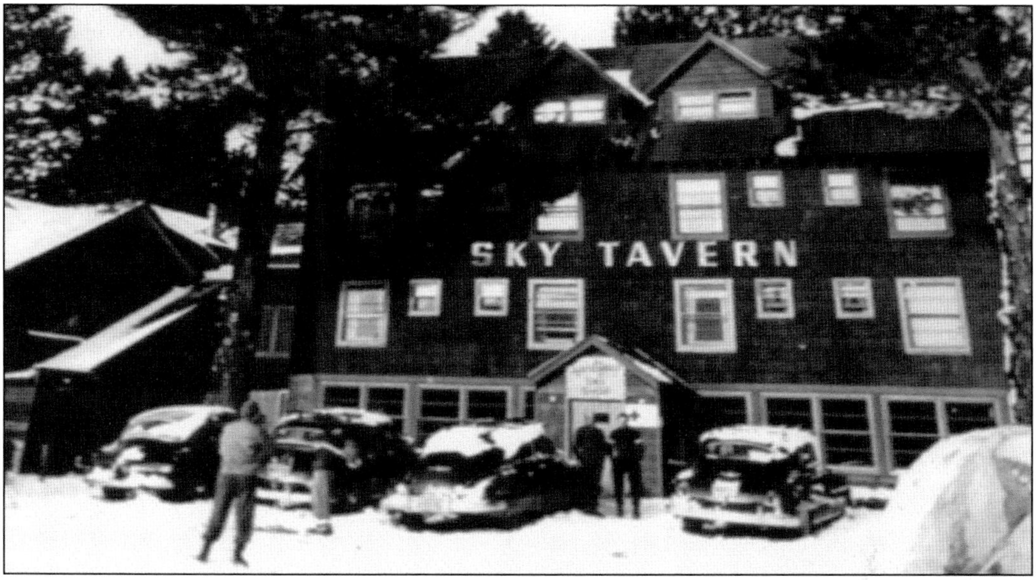


The Sky Tavern Lodge, located near Mount Rose, was completed in 1945. In 1941, Wayne Poulsen's lease to operate a rope tow in the Mount Rose bowl was cancelled by the landowner, Robinson Neeman, who promptly purchased a T-bar rope tow and built a small ski resort. In 1945, Reno contractor Keston Ramsey acquired the acreage and ski operation when Neeman was forced to sell after running into trouble with the Las Vegas mob over gambling debts. (Courtesy Keston Ramsey collection.)

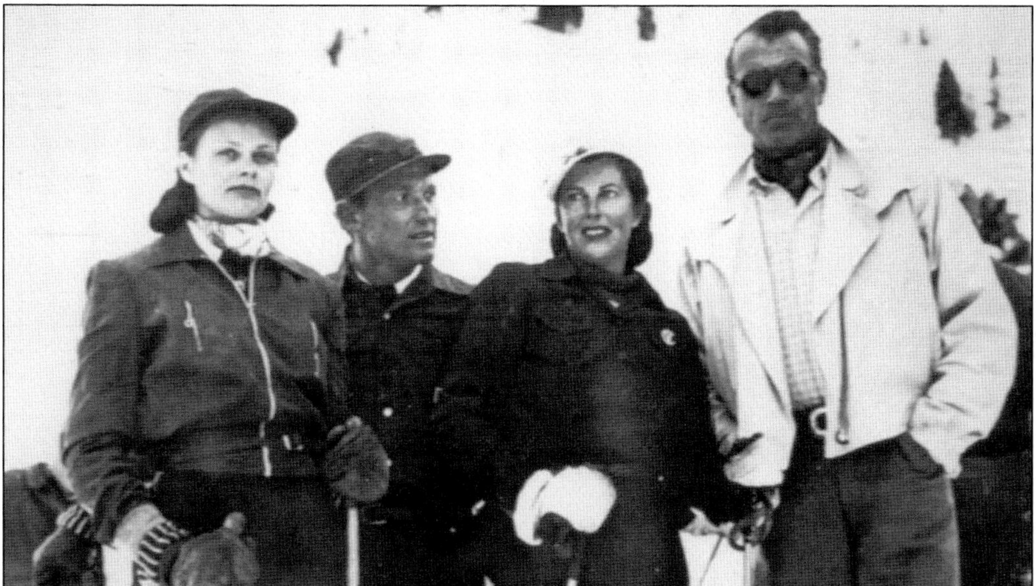

From left to right, Peggy Engle and her husband, renowned Sun Valley skiing icon Sigi Engle, and actress Veronica "Rocky" Cooper and her husband, film star Gary Cooper, mingle at Sky Tavern in 1948. The resort opened just as World War II ended, when America's rich and famous were taking up skiing as a sport. The Sky Tavern was less than 20 miles from Reno's Hubbard Field airport and had a small gaming operation run by William "Bill" Harrah. (Courtesy Keston Ramsey collection.)

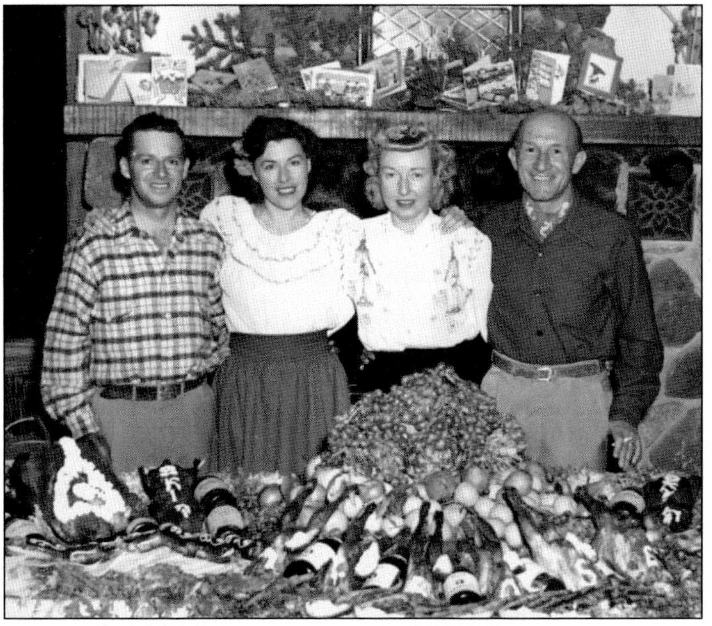

This 1949 photograph depicts Christmas dinner at Sky Tavern with the original partners (from left to right) Keston Ramsey; his wife, Carlisle; and Ruth and George Tett. To develop the property into a destination resort, Ramsey used his construction company to build a modern four-story, 21-room hotel with a coffee shop, graded the parking lot, and installed a new sewage system and water supply. From start to finish, Ramsey did the work in less than four months. (Courtesy Keston Ramsey collection.)

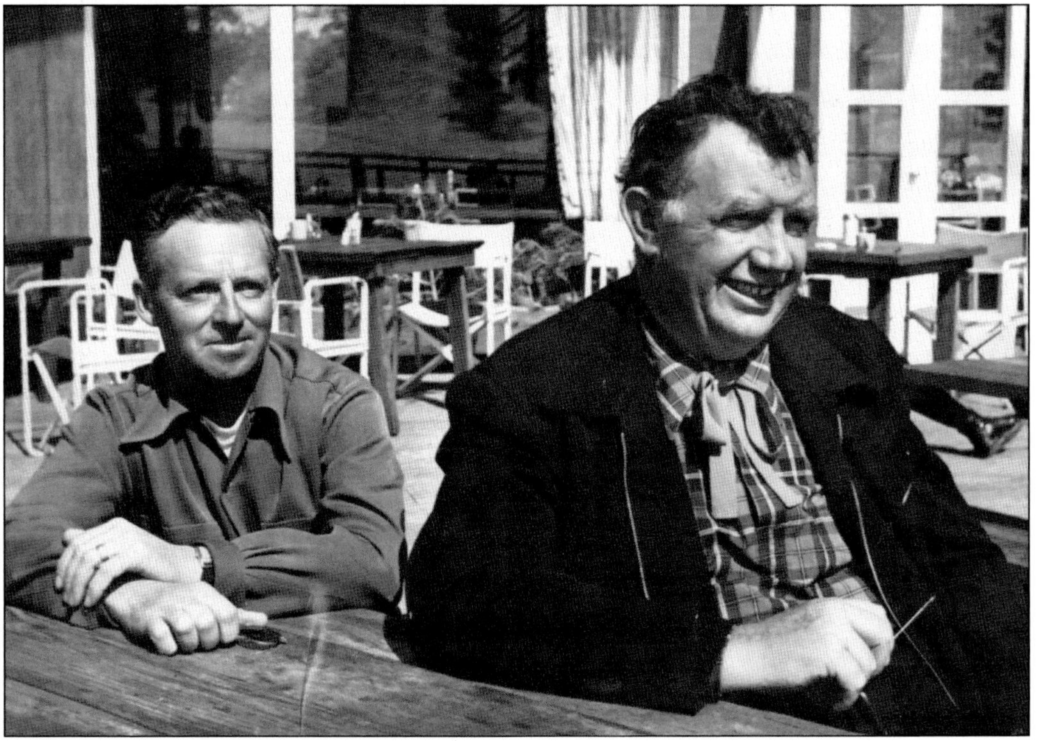

Keston Ramsey (left) relaxes with famed comic actor Andy Devine on the deck at Sky Tavern in 1948. Before the development of major Tahoe resorts in the 1950s, movie stars, prominent San Francisco socialites, and famous personalities flocked to the slopes of Mount Rose. Celebrities like Rita Hayworth and Ingrid Bergman were frequent guests. Lowell Thomas, an avid skier and well-known radio newsman, once gave a national broadcast live from Sky Tavern. (Courtesy Keston Ramsey collection.)

In 1948, Sky Tavern owner Keston Ramsey convinced Sun Valley's top ski-racing coach, Hal Codding, to take over as ski school director and to train the Sky Tavern's new junior ski team. Codding had mastered the most advanced techniques in Europe and had great coaching ability. He had been selected as a member of the 1940 US Olympic team competing in downhill and slalom until those Winter Games were cancelled. (Courtesy Nevada Historical Society.)

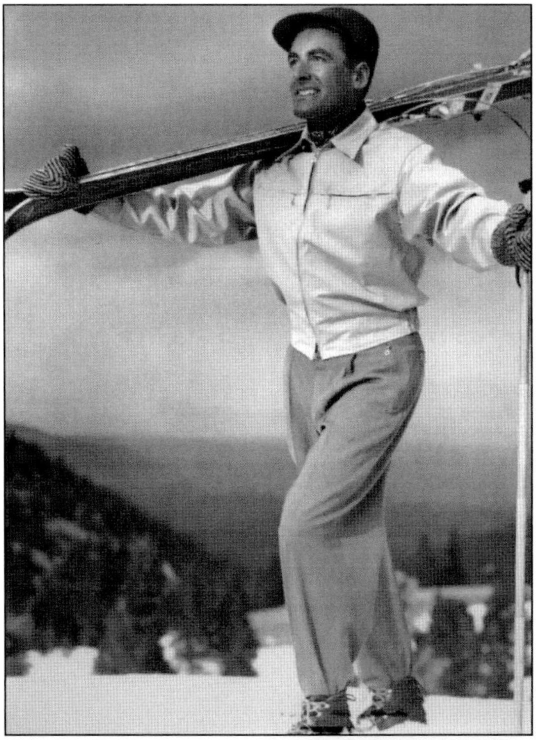

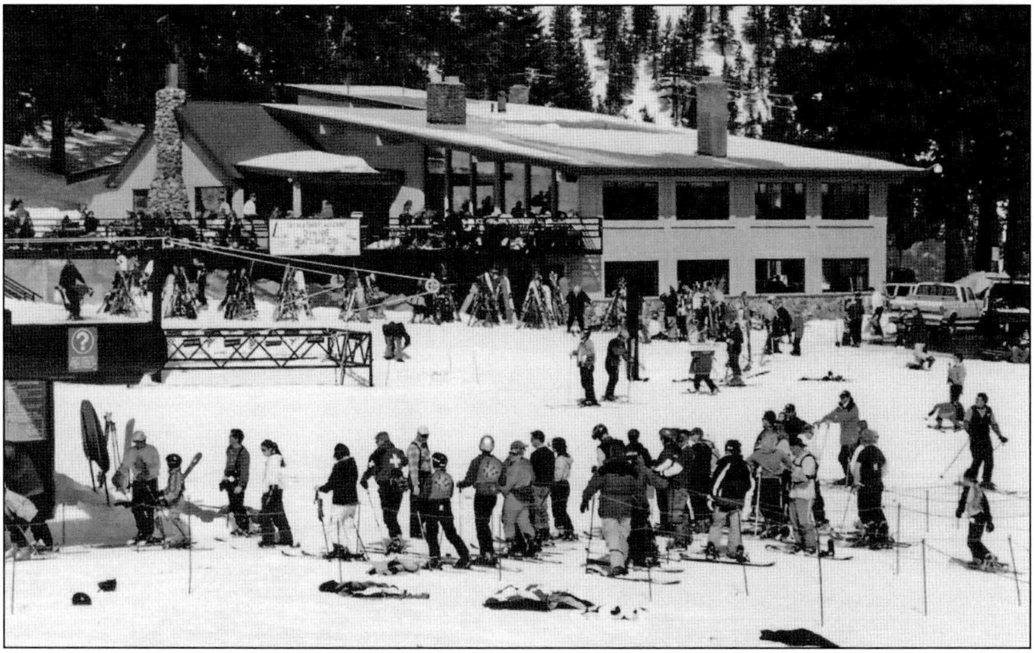

After 1950, business at Sky Tavern dropped off as larger resorts like Squaw Valley and nearby Reno Ski Bowl siphoned off skiers. In 1948, Marce Herz, a local skier and schoolteacher who believed that sports were good for children, started the Junior Ski Program at Sky Tavern. The unique, volunteer-based program continues today, teaching Nevada schoolchildren at a minimal cost, including those who are physically or economically challenged.

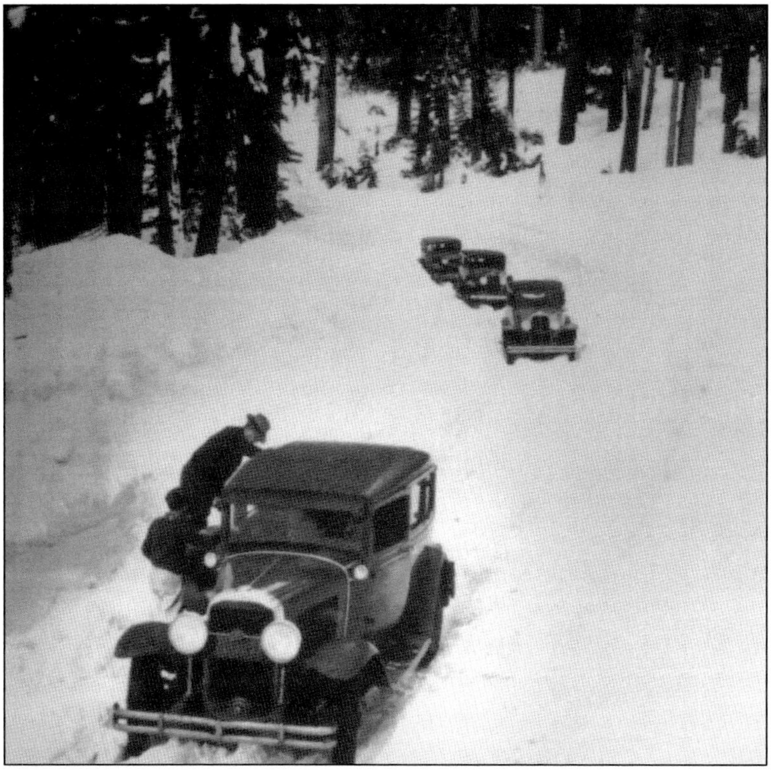

Motorists struggle up Echo Summit on Highway 50 in February 1940. California road crews plowed the road to Twin Bridges, but there was no winter access to South Lake Tahoe. By 1940, an entrepreneur from Twin Bridges installed a rope tow operation there for skiers driving up from Placerville. The tow was powered by the drive wheel from an old Ford Model T.

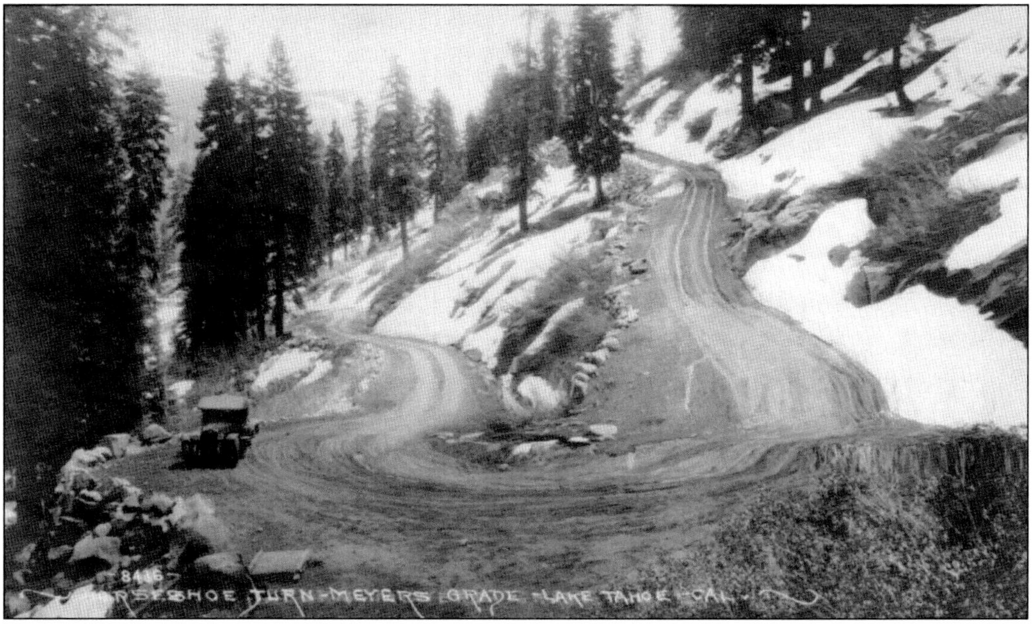


Before World War II, driving Highway 50 (the old Pony Express trail) from Placerville, California, to South Lake Tahoe was a challenge even after winter storms were over. Note this automobile negotiating the Meyers Grade in 1938. During World War II, gasoline rationing forced most skiers to give up long trips to the mountains. (Courtesy Donner Summit Historical Society/ Norm Sayler collection.)

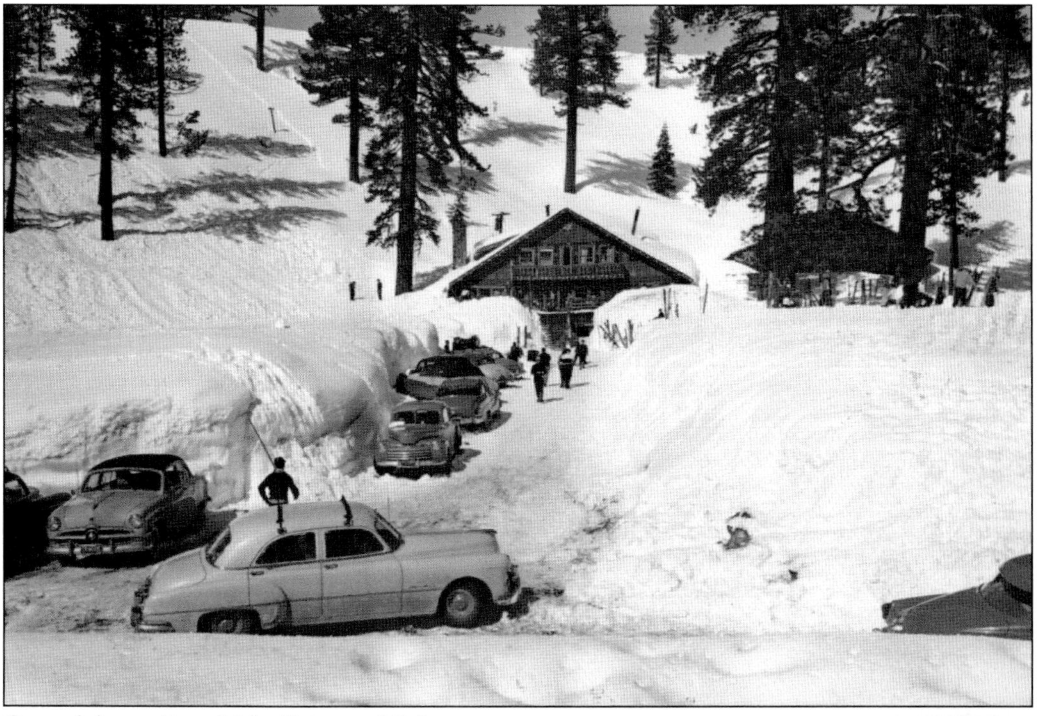

One of the earliest ski facilities on Highway 50 started when Placerville native Fred Baumhoff opened the Strawberry Ski Hut. In 1941, the Edelweiss resort opened up the road near Echo Summit; the lodge was across the highway from the ski lifts. Skiers flocked to the area—just 43 miles from Placerville—in droves. (Courtesy Donner Summit Historical Society/Norm Sayler collection.)

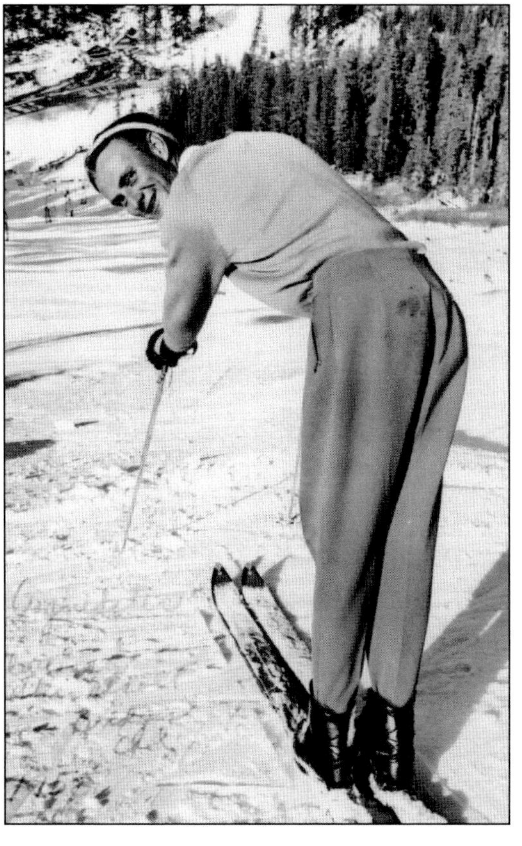

In 1950, Lutz Aynedter was the ski school director at Edelweiss. The 1946 downhill ski champion of Germany, Aynedter taught his students with an accent and a sense of humor. A two-hour lesson cost $2.50. Olympian Vladimir "Spider" Sabich learned to ski at Edelweiss and trained under Aynedter. (Courtesy Donner Summit Historical Society/Norm Sayler collection.)

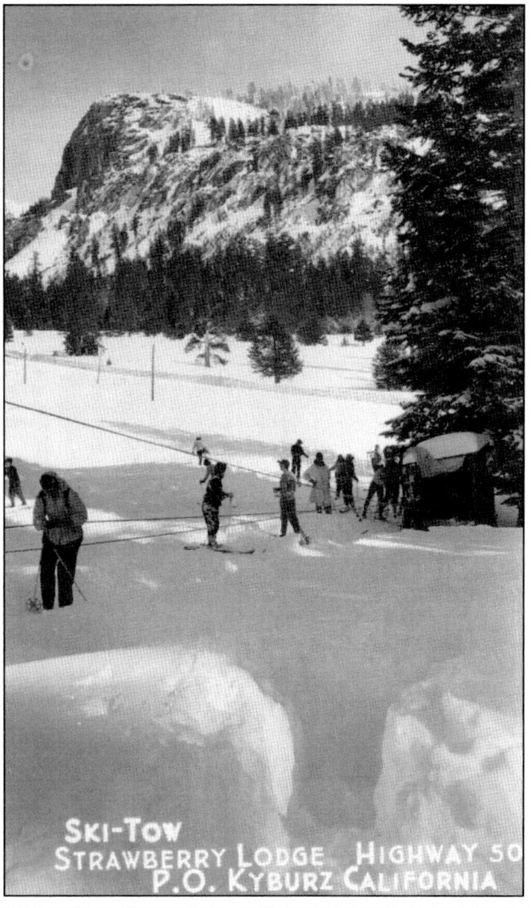


This 1950 image depicts patrons enjoying the Strawberry Lodge below the Edelweiss resort near Kyburz, California. Despite its short ski run of about 200 feet and its paltry snow cover in dry winters, beginning skiers were attracted by the family vibe and prices that were easy on the budget. (Courtesy Donner Summit Historical Society/Norm Sayler collection.)

This café/hotel, built by T.C. Wohlbruck in 1919 to serve motorists, was located at Echo Summit on Highway 50. Over the next several decades, small mom-and-pop ski areas would be established along the road, later to be economically marginalized by larger modern resorts like Sierra Ski Ranch (later Sierra-at-Tahoe) and Heavenly Valley. (Courtesy Donner Summit Historical Society/Norm Sayler collection.)

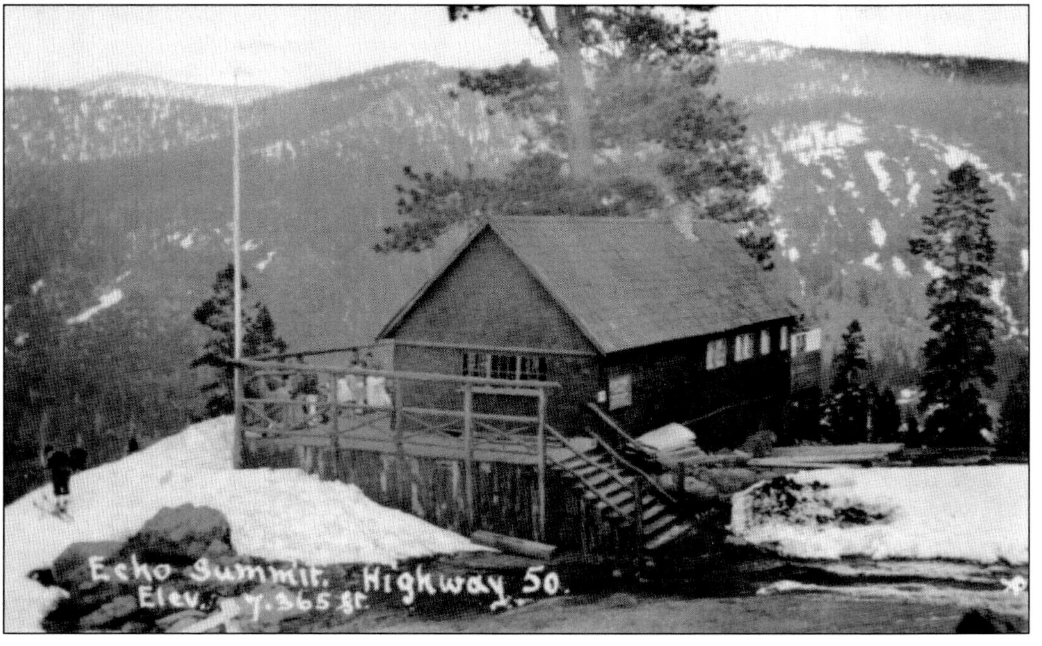

# *Six*

# Postwar Boom in Tahoe Skiing

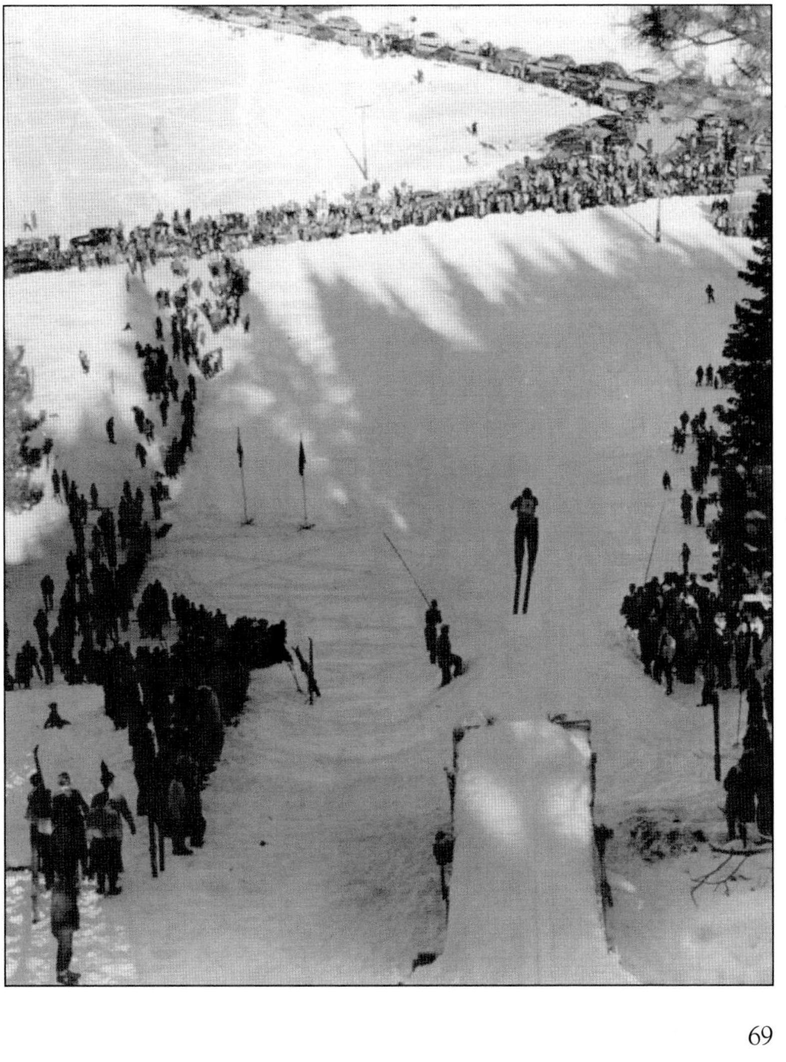

By 1949, the White Hills ski area near Spooner Summit was drawing crowds from around the Tahoe Basin and beyond. White Hills opened with one of the first T-bar lifts in the area and a ski jump. The resort was built by William M. Bliss, a descendant of Duane Leroy Bliss. D.L. Bliss was an iconic pioneer in 19th-century Tahoe and a major player in logging, transportation, and the Comstock mines. (Courtesy Donner Summit Historical Society/Norm Sayler collection.)

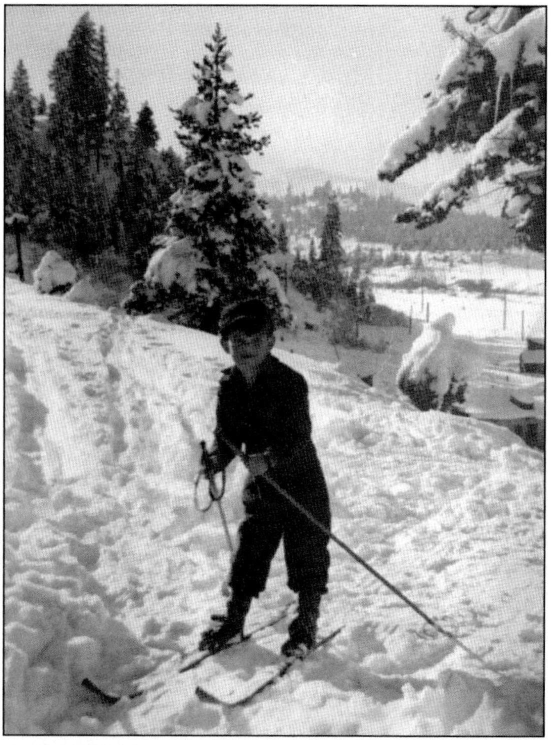

This unidentified boy, photographed near Truckee in 1940, illustrates that skiing was not just for adults—kids loved the sport, too. The ski industry in the Truckee–Lake Tahoe region experienced rapid growth after World War II, when chairlifts replaced rope tows and the end of gasoline rationing led to a more mobile population. Also, antifreeze was finally available, eliminating the need to empty the radiator every night. (Courtesy Craig Beck collection.)

Located at the intersection of Highways 50 and 28, White Hills was open for less than five years before the resort failed because of several years of drought followed by the damaging winter of 1952. Owner William Bliss sold the chairlift to Yosemite's Badger Pass, which was unable to get spare parts for its lift because of the Korean War. Note the cars parked along the roadway. (Courtesy Donner Summit Historical Society/Norm Sayler collection.)

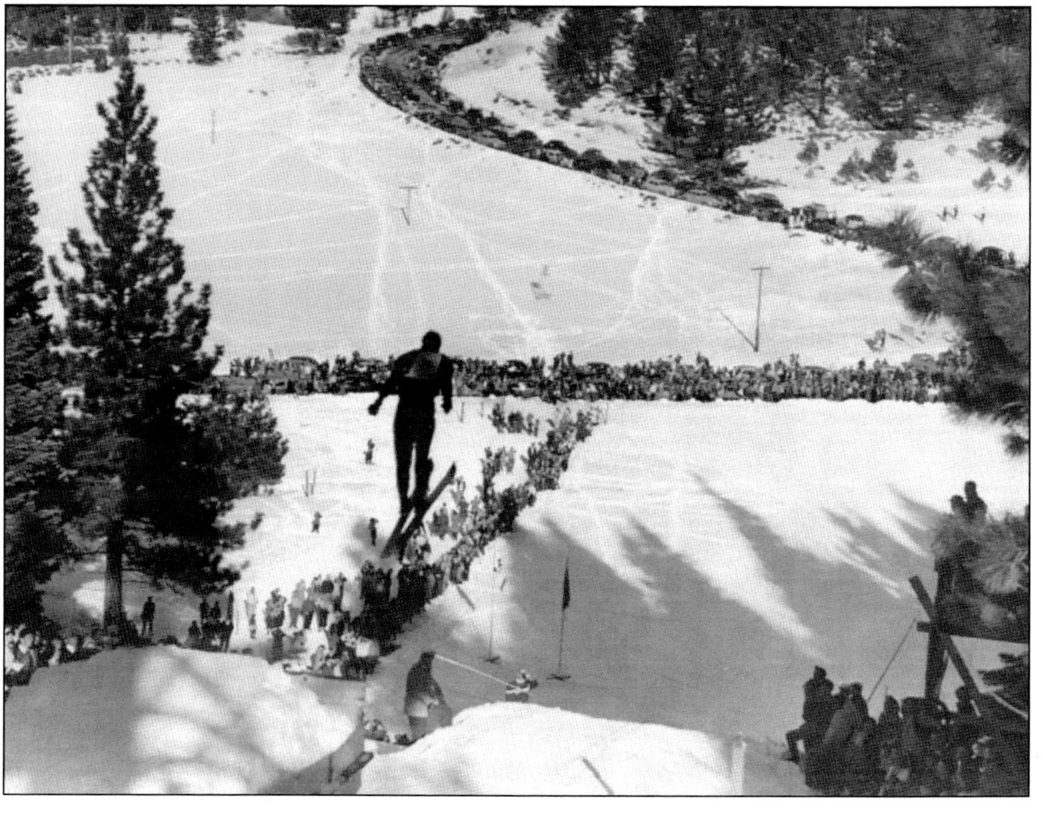

Roy Mikkelsen (left), America's best amateur jumper, poses with an unidentified "bathing beauty" at Sugar Bowl on July 4, 1932, after a two-mile coed cross-country ski race sponsored by the Auburn Ski Club. In the zany contest, many of the younger women wore modified ski outfits featuring shorts and bare legs. Top-ranked jumpers were also invited, including skiing stars like Wayne Poulsen, Andy Blodjer, Sigrid Stromstad, Mikkelsen, and Sig Vettestad. (Courtesy Mark McLaughlin.)

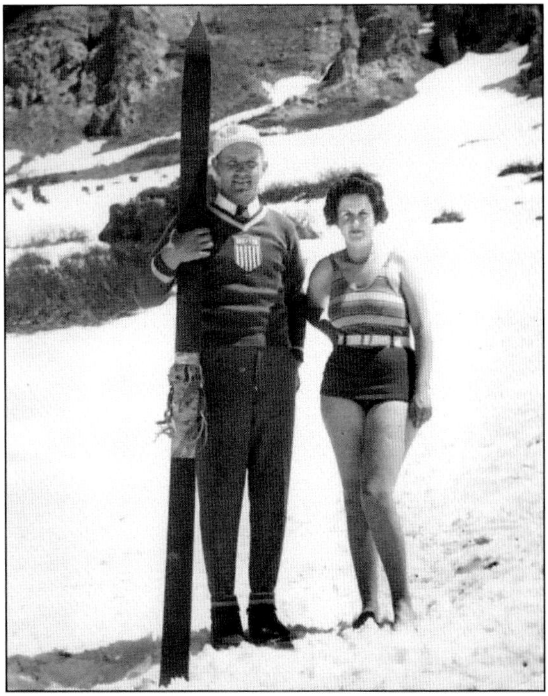

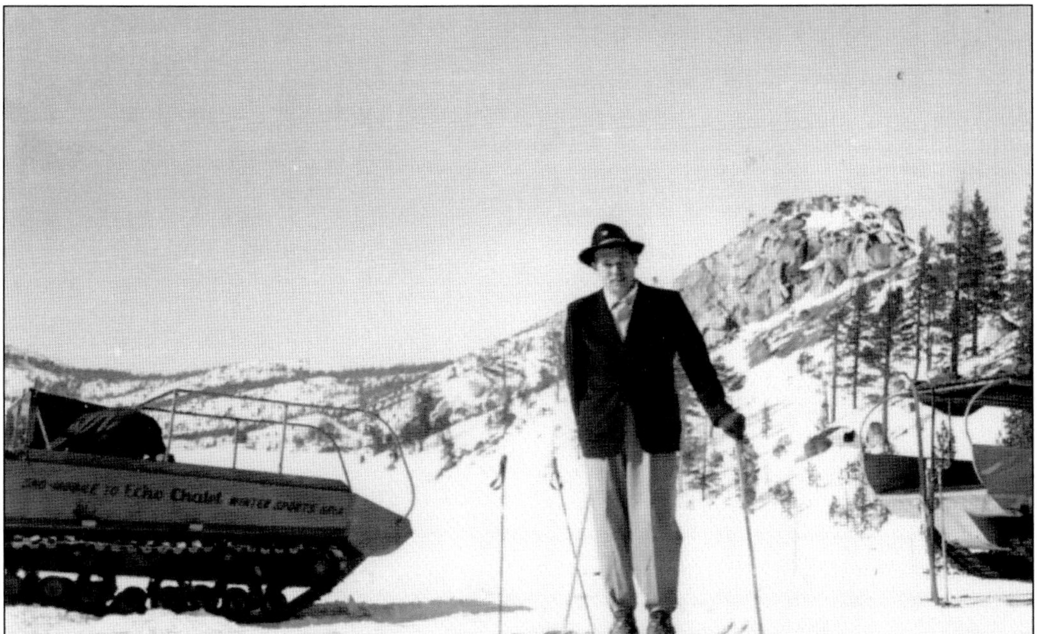

Award-winning ski journalist Carson White poses for a photograph near Echo Summit in February 1952. Founding members of the Oakland Ski Club, White and his wife, Violet ("Vi"), were avid skiers and active in promoting the sport. Carson organized several professional ski journalism groups, while Vi wrote her own newspaper columns. In 1984, Carson White and fellow ski writer Don Thompson set a record by skiing more than 25,000 vertical feet at six different Tahoe resorts in one day. (Courtesy Carson and Vi White collection.)

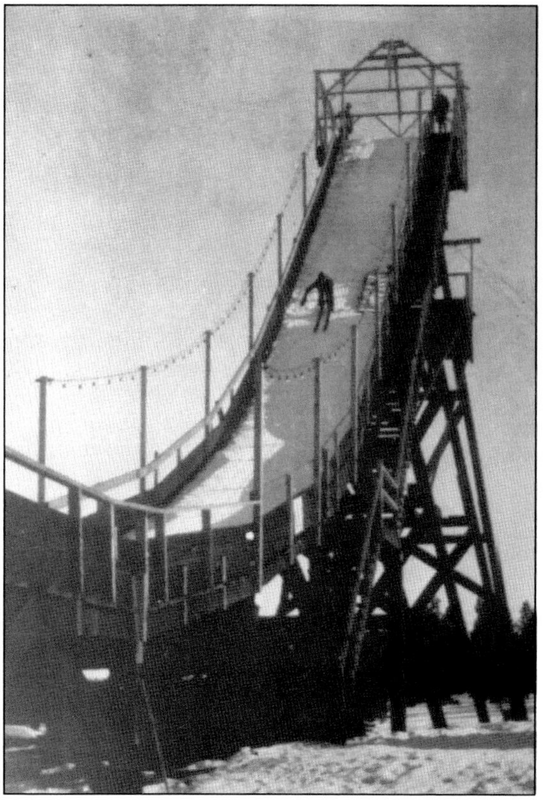

The Hilltop ski jump at Truckee was still going strong in the 1940s. Several prominent alpine ski areas opened in the Tahoe-Truckee region during the 1940s, but jumping remained popular. Truckee's wooden scaffold jump was a busy site for local and regional competitions. (Courtesy Truckee Donner Historical Society.)

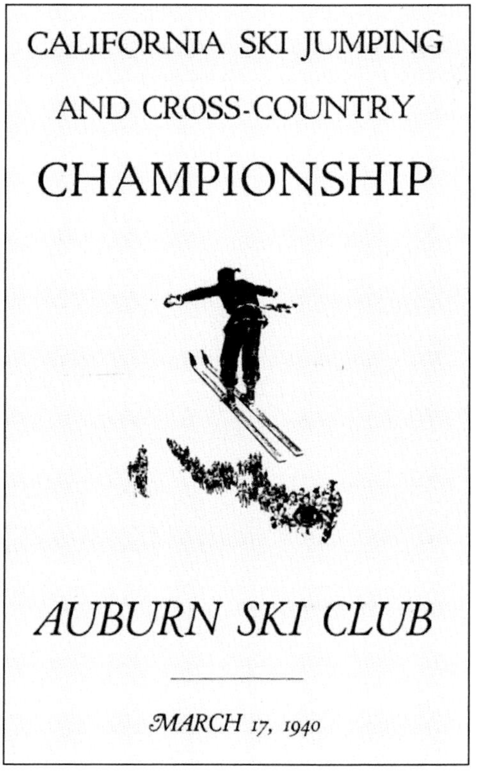


The Auburn Ski Club hosted many competitions, but with America's entry into World War II, the military requested that the Auburn Ski Club help recruit and process skiers for eventual placement in the 10th Mountain Division. During the war, servicemen from the United States, Great Britain, and other allies utilized the Auburn Ski Club's winter park and equipment for recreational use. (Courtesy Mark McLaughlin.)

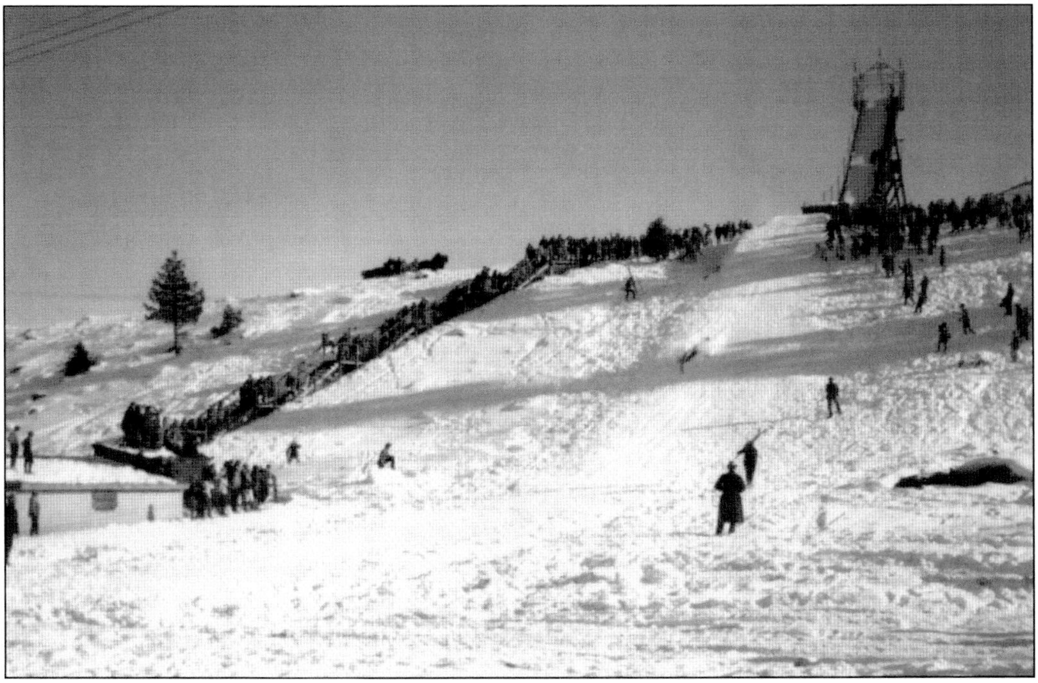

Note the skier crash-landing below Truckee's Hilltop ski jump in the 1940s. Before the construction of the Hilltop jump, there had been a few small wooden launches, but this new version was 140 feet high and built under the direction of professional ski jumper Lars Haugen. It was an impressive structure that the Truckee *Sierra Sun* newspaper called a "dangerous modification." (Courtesy Truckee Donner Historical Society.)

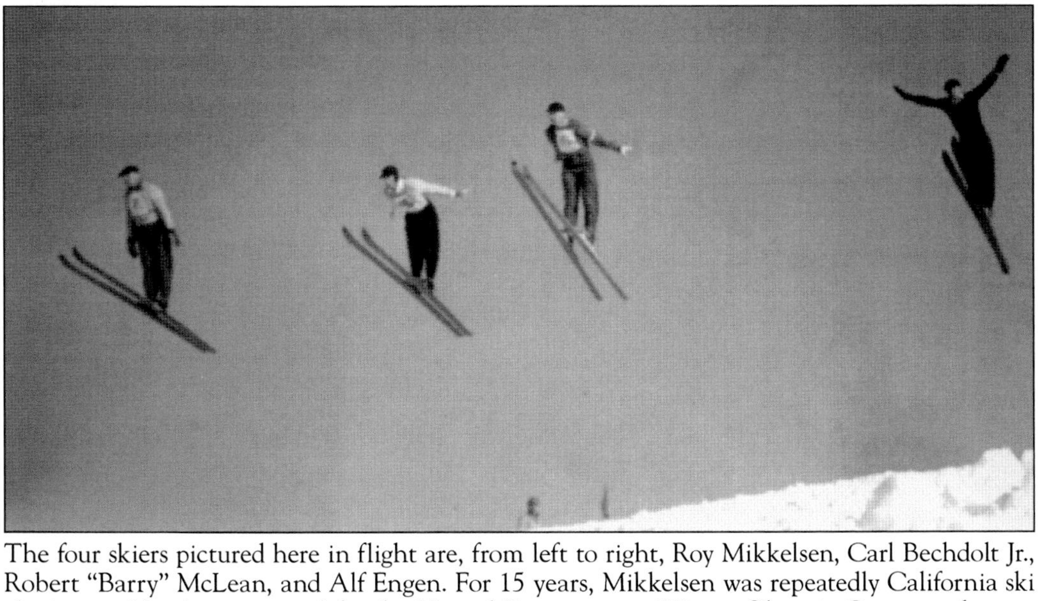

The four skiers pictured here in flight are, from left to right, Roy Mikkelsen, Carl Bechdolt Jr., Robert "Barry" McLean, and Alf Engen. For 15 years, Mikkelsen was repeatedly California ski champion. He also competed for the United States in two Winter Olympic Games and was a strong advocate for the Squaw Valley Olympics. Bechdolt was nearly unbeatable until polio slowed him down. One of three legendary brothers, Engen set several ski-jumping world records in the 1930s. (Courtesy Donner Summit Historical Society/Norm Sayler collection.)

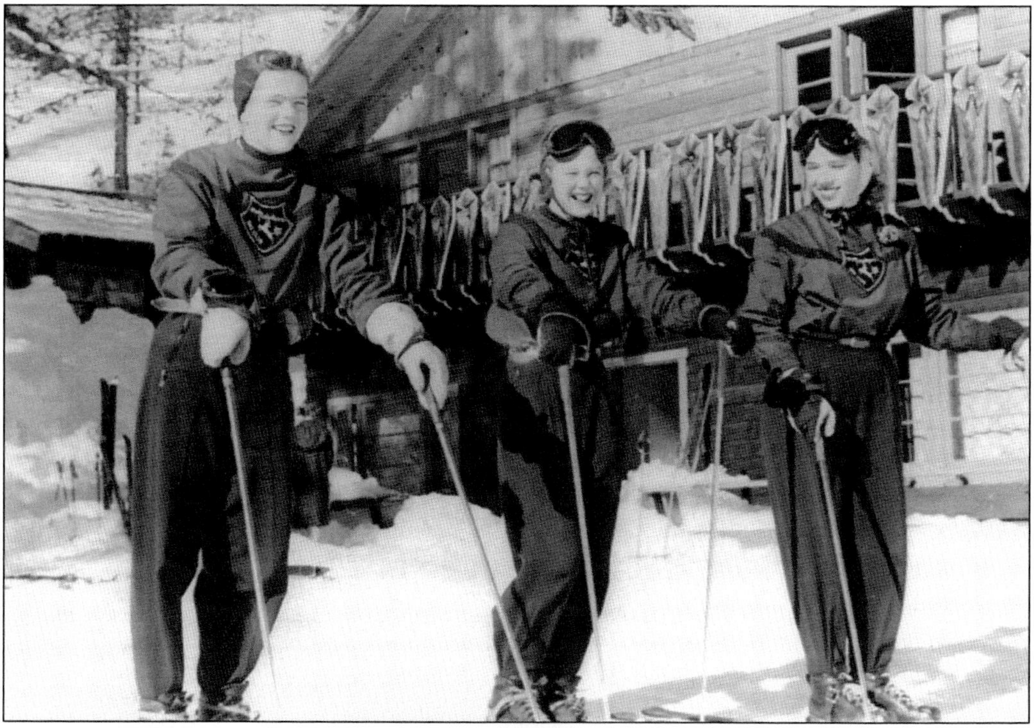

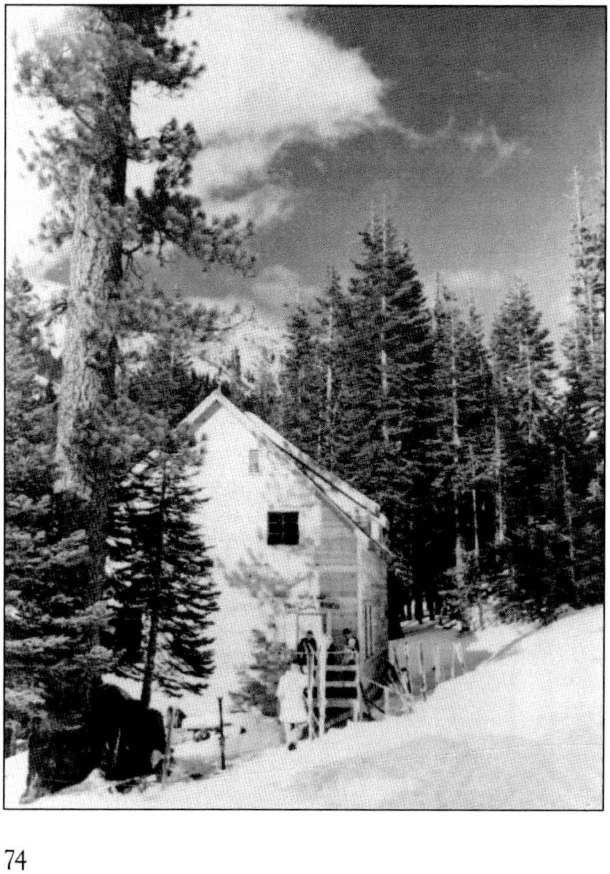

Edelweiss Red Hornet ski team members Cecil Gayner (left), Laurie Wakeman (center), and Judy Roy are pictured here in 1950. Ski teams and clubs proliferated in the 1940s and 1950s. The Edelweiss resort closed in the early 1960s. (Courtesy Donner Summit Historical Society/Norm Sayler collection.)

Two brothers, Ray and Floyd Barrett, started Sierra Ski Ranch in 1946. The owner-operated resort at the top of Echo Summit had two rope tows and about 80 acres of easy terrain. In 1953, employee Vern Sprock and his wife, Bobbie, purchased the ski area from the Barrett brothers. The rope tows and facilities were moved several times to make way for a proposed highway expansion that never happened. (Courtesy Sierra-at-Tahoe Resort.)

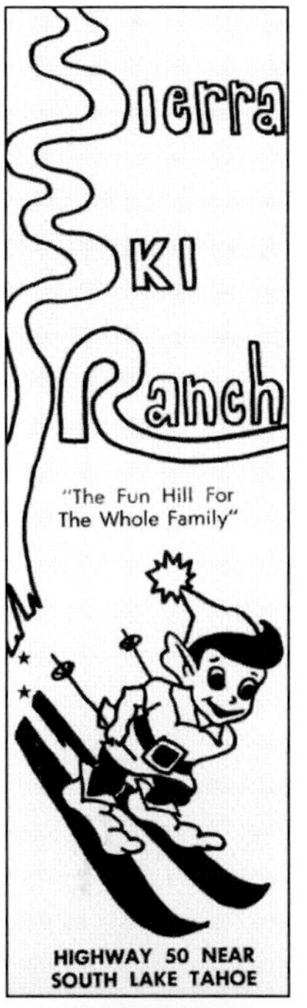


In the late 1960s, Sierra Ski Ranch owner-operator Vern Sprock expanded his resort's skiable vertical and acreage. He also added a chairlift to the existing Poma lift and rope tow and built a 10,000-square-foot lodge. Sprock opened the new and improved Sierra Ski Ranch on Christmas Day, 1968. By the mid-1970s, the ski area was showing a profit, and Sprock kept improving mountain operations and adding more runs. The resort was oriented toward skiing families, and Sprock refused to sell alcohol or encourage consumption on the property. In 1993, Sprock sold the resort to Trimont Corporation, which renamed it Sierra-at-Tahoe. (Right, courtesy Mark McLaughlin; below, courtesy Sierra-at-Tahoe Resort.)

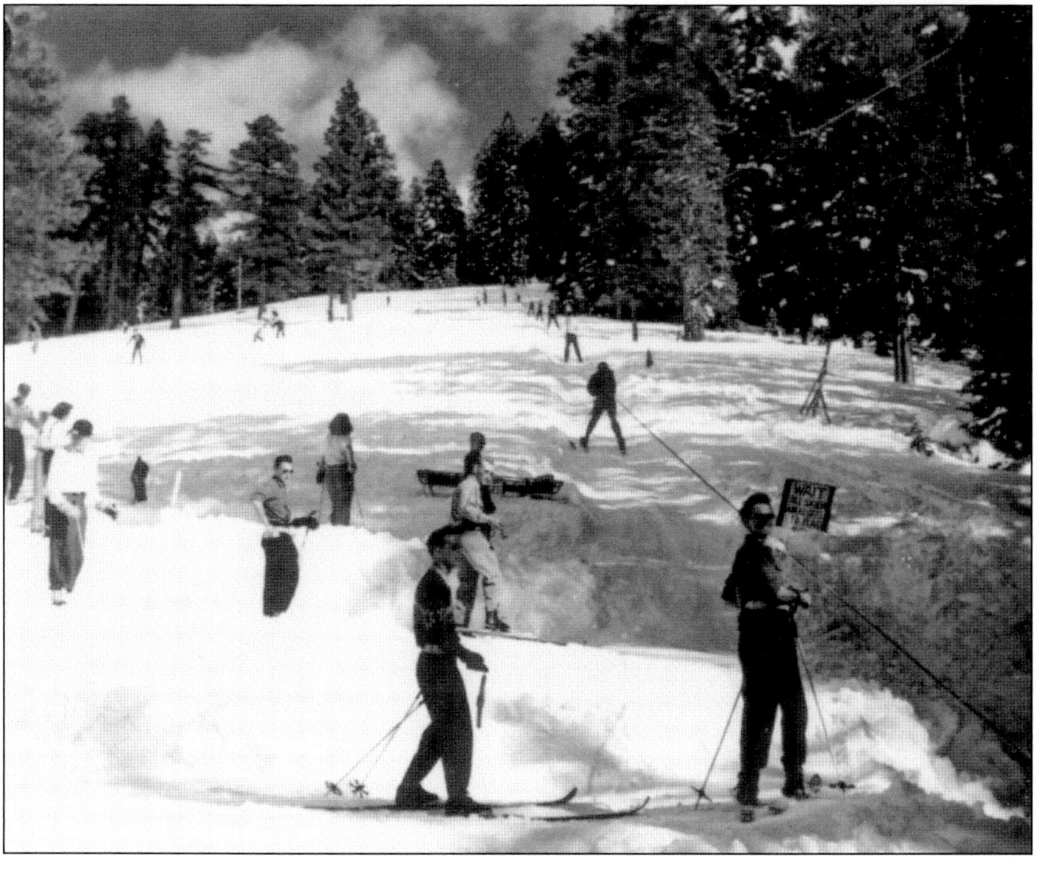

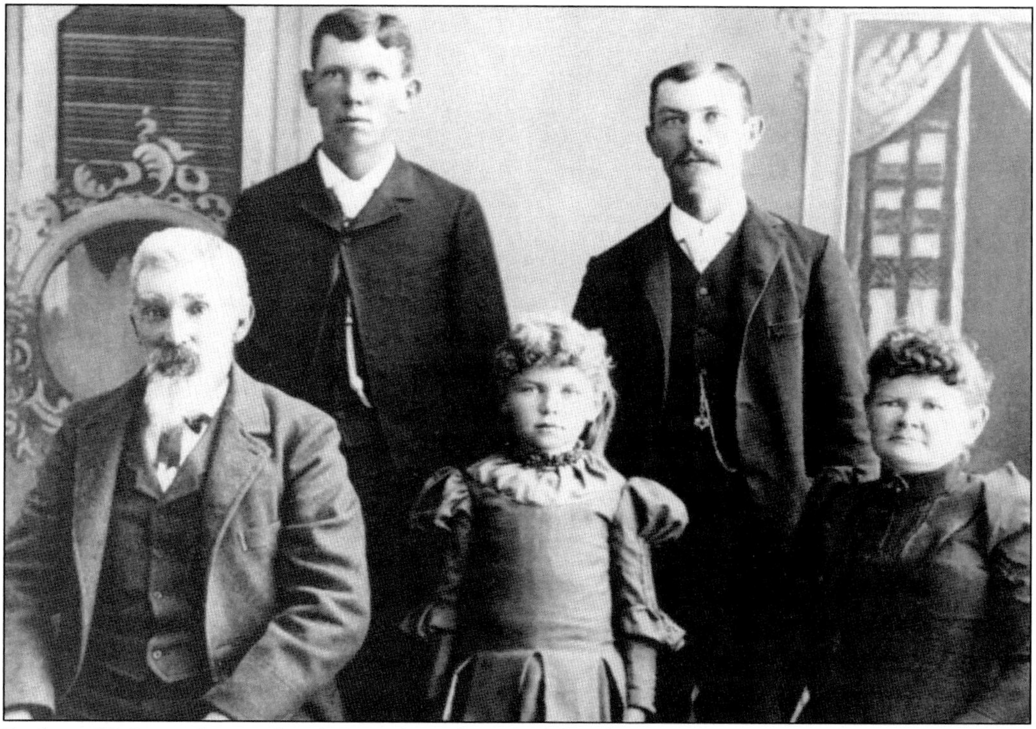

Zachary Kirkwood, seated at left, and unidentified family members gather for a photograph. In 1860, Kirkwood staked a claim to a verdant and picturesque valley south of Lake Tahoe. In the valley, surrounded by towering mountains, Kirkwood established a dairy and herded his cattle and sheep. (Courtesy Kirkwood Mountain Resort.)

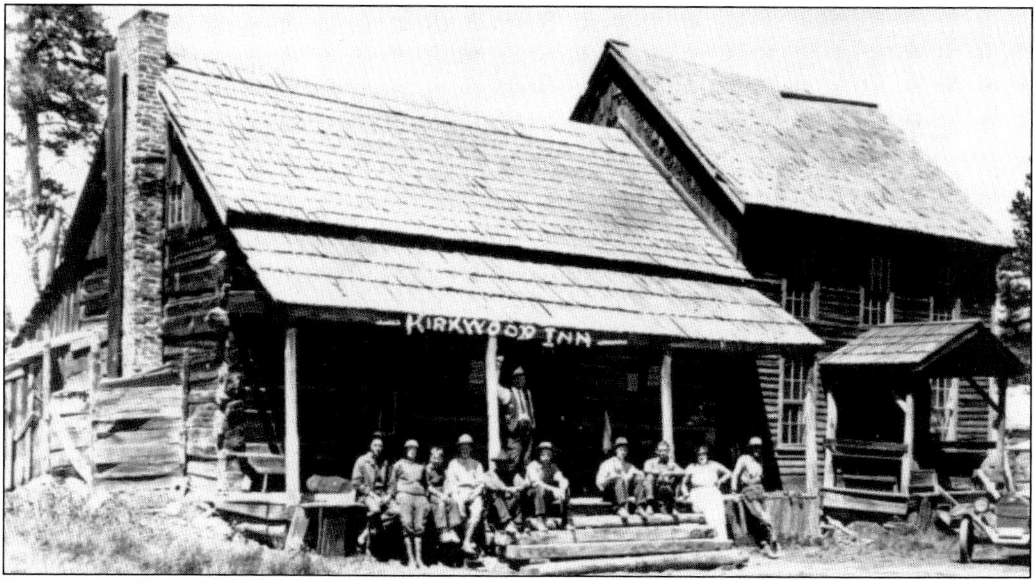


In 1864, Zachary Kirkwood opened the Kirkwood Inn, which soon earned a reputation for its hospitality to travelers and cattle ranchers. Legend has it that the Kirkwood, located near the Mormon Emigrant Trail, was a good place to get bootleg whiskey during Prohibition. (Courtesy Kirkwood Mountain Resort.)

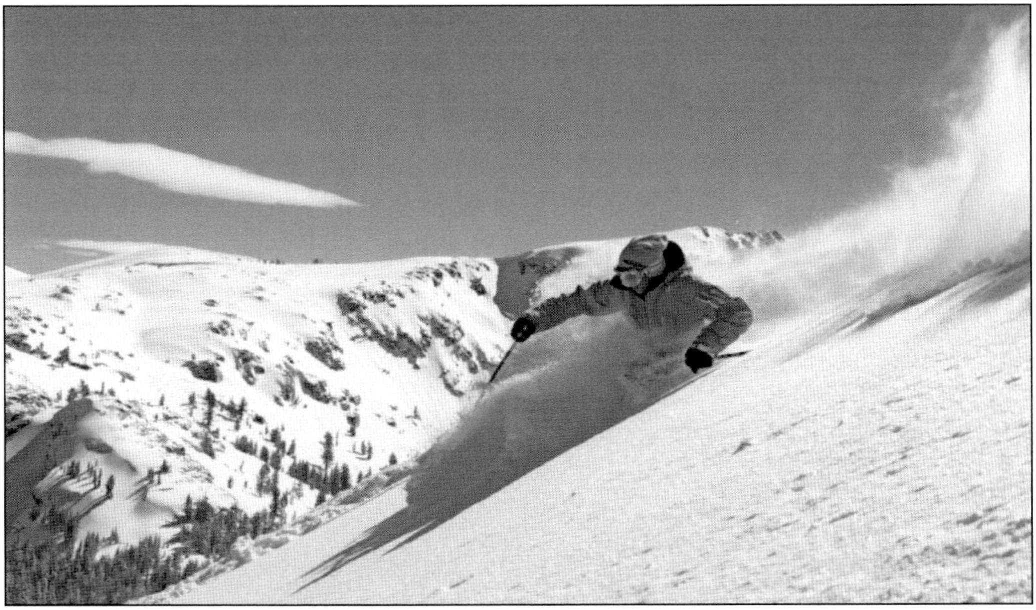

In the late 1960s, businessman Bud Klein recognized the potential for a world-class ski resort at Kirkwood. Access was impossible because Highway 88 was closed in winter, but in 1971, California converted it to an all-weather road, and the US Forest Service issued Kirkwood Meadows, Inc., a permit to construct a ski area. Klein's Kirkwood Ski Resort opened in 1972 with Dick Reuter as mountain manager. Reuter, an avalanche control expert, cut timber and planned runs to maximize skier safety on the rugged mountain. (Courtesy Kirkwood Mountain Resort.)

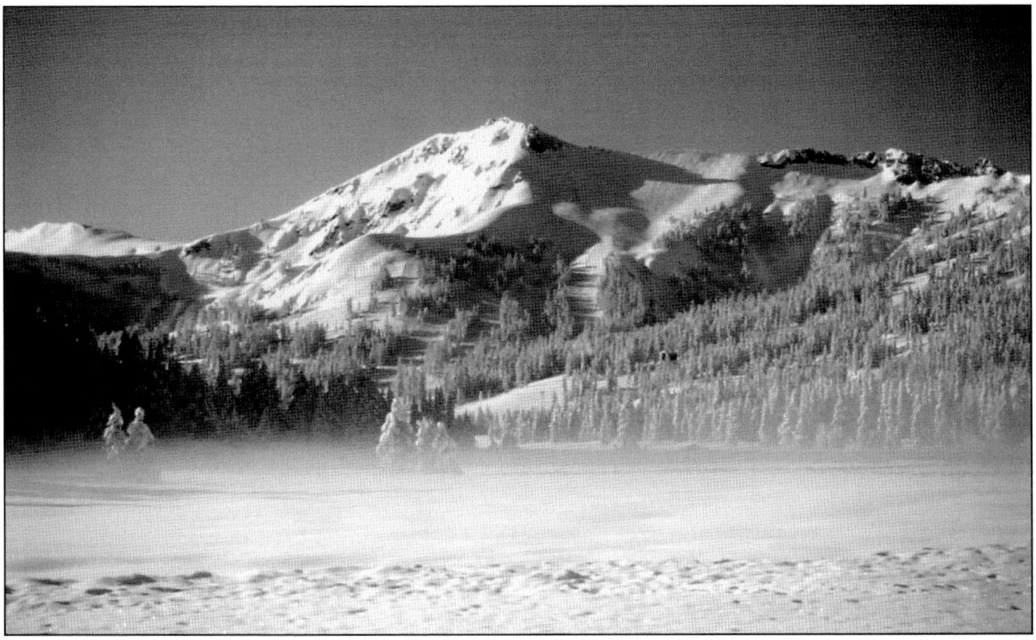

At more than 9,800 feet elevation, Thimble Peak stands tall over the valley meadows near Kirkwood Mountain Resort. Located 35 miles from South Lake Tahoe, the ski area is known for its sense of serenity, peace, and quiet not found at major Lake Tahoe resorts. (Courtesy Kirkwood Mountain Resort.)

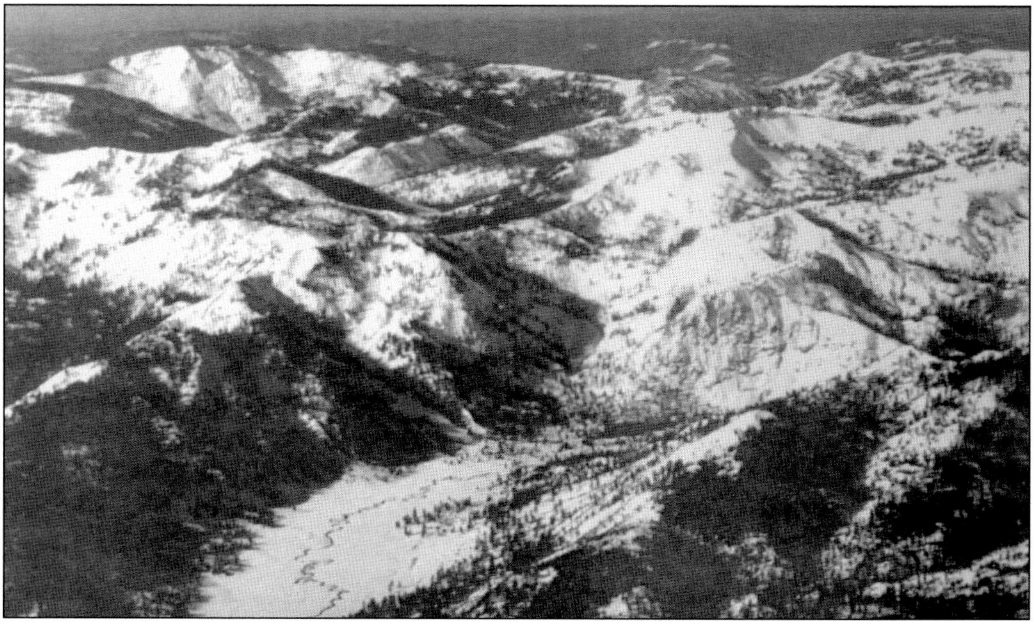

In 1942, Keston Ramsey, an amateur photographer and future developer of the Sky Tavern resort in Nevada, took this aerial photograph of the undeveloped Squaw Valley. The rented plane was piloted by Wayne Poulsen, an avid skier who was in the process of purchasing the valley—for his family home—and access to the mountains to develop the area into a ski resort. Note Squaw Creek flowing through the valley. (Courtesy Keston Ramsey collection.)

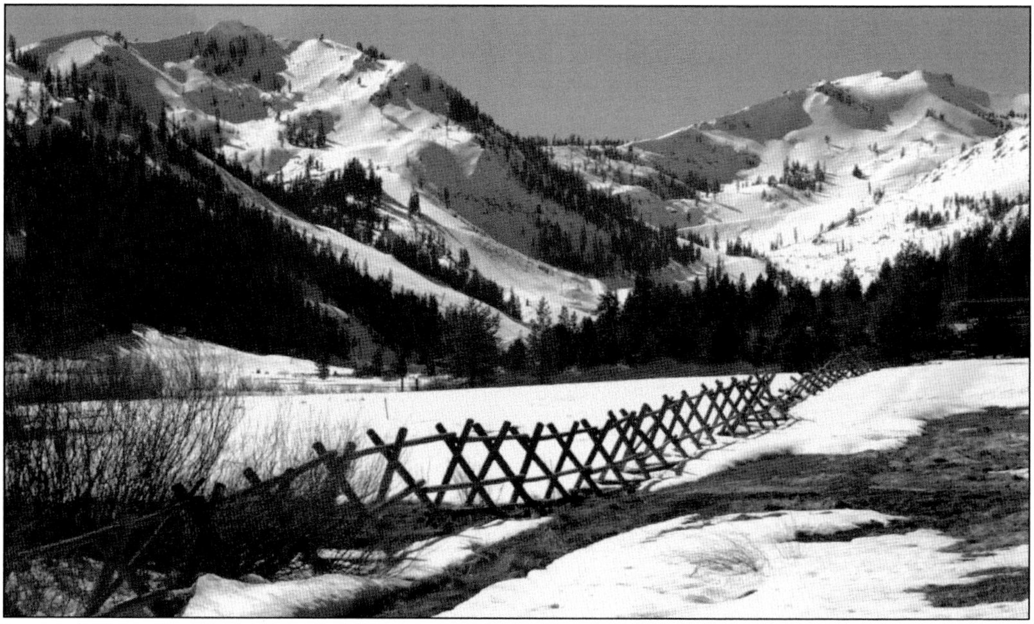

Instead of cattle, the livestock fence in Squaw Valley now corrals horse-drawn snow sleighs in winter and golfers during summer. For thousands of years, the Washoe Indian tribe used the verdant valley as its summer camping and hunting grounds. In 1862, four men settled on federal land there to establish the Squaw Valley Ranch. Each summer and fall season, they harvested more than 125 tons of wild hay. (Courtesy Mark McLaughlin.)

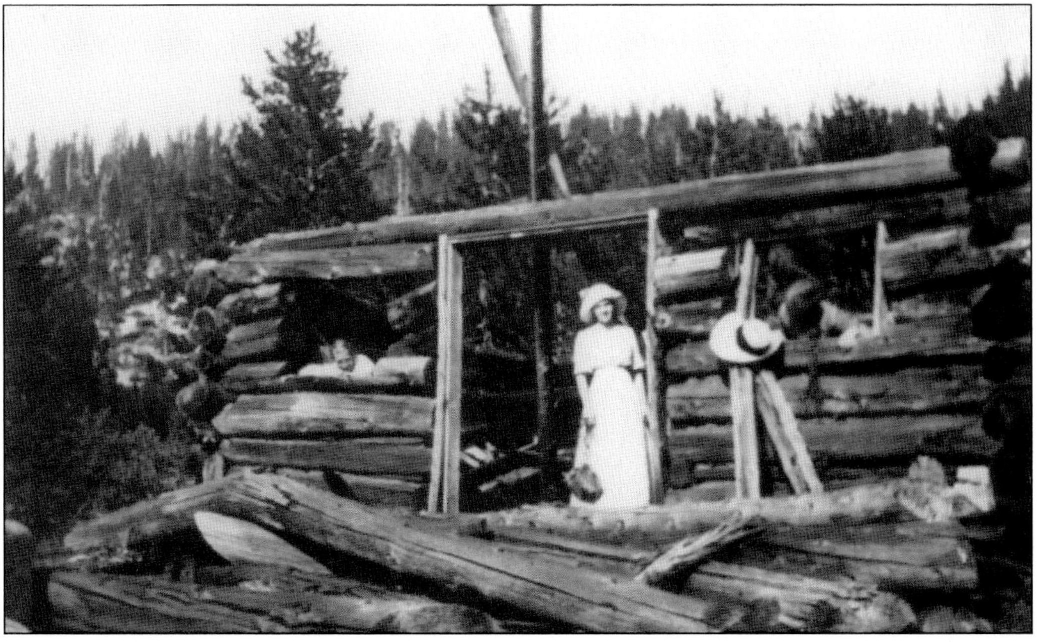

Sisters Marian (left) and Pauline Chamberlain pose in the old remains of the Knoxville Tavern in 1912. In 1863, two prospectors, John Keiser and Shannon Knox, claimed to have discovered silver ore near where Squaw Creek enters the Truckee River. The news spread like wildfire, and the shantytowns of Knoxville and Claraville sprouted virtually overnight. Ore samples proved worthless, however, and the "strike" was quickly over. (Courtesy Richard Hoyt Chamberlain collection.)

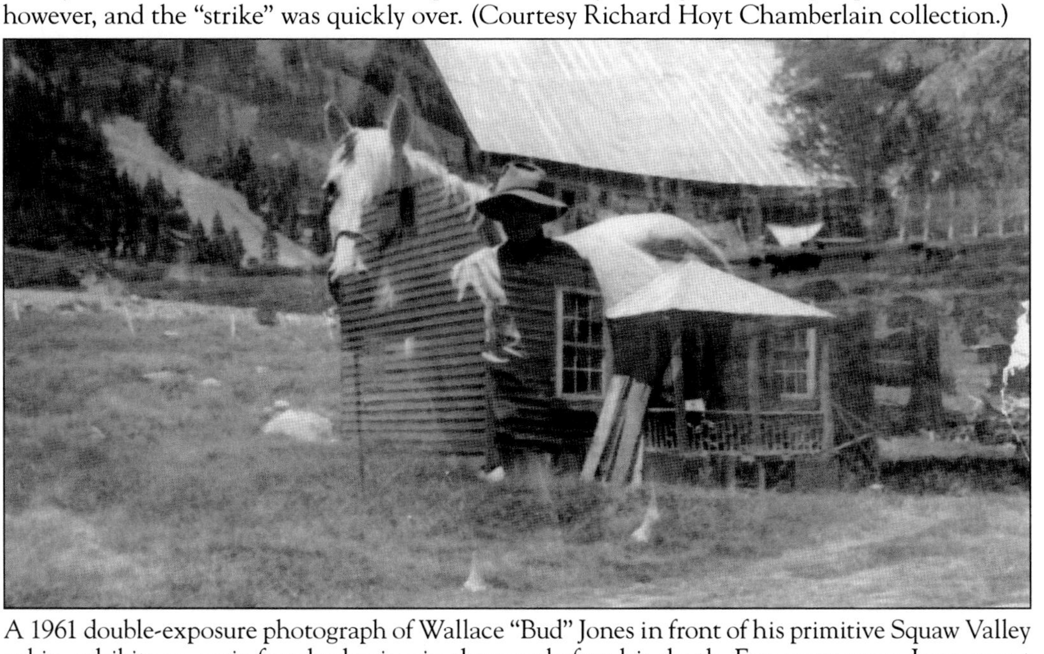

A 1961 double-exposure photograph of Wallace "Bud" Jones in front of his primitive Squaw Valley cabin exhibits an eerie foreshadowing in the year before his death. For many years, Jones spent summers in the valley, where he tended cattle shipped by train from Sacramento to Truckee and then herded south to the valley. The cabin had no plumbing, but Jones enjoyed the solitude. Jones died in the fire when his ranch house burned down on April 1, 1962. (Courtesy Carson and Vi White collection.)

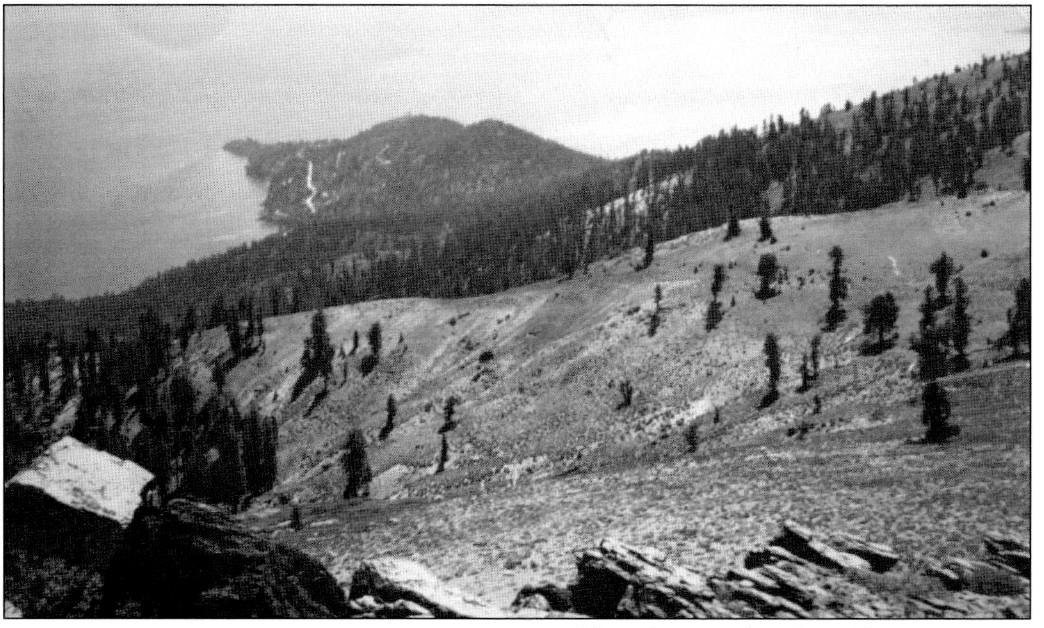

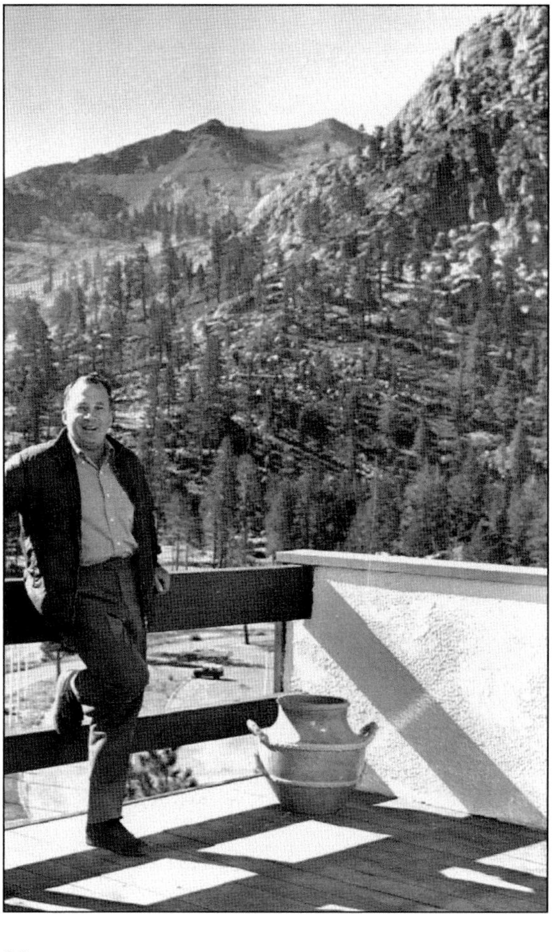

This photograph is from Wayne Poulsen's 1938 survey that studied Rifle Peak for possible development as a Tahoe ski resort. Rifle Peak is a few miles east of the California-Nevada state line, on the north shore of Lake Tahoe. Poulsen planned for a lakeside base lodge with an uphill tram to carry skiers to a lodge near the 9,488-foot peak. Ultimately, Poulsen determined that Rifle Peak was not a viable site. (Courtesy Craig Beck collection.)

Raised in Reno, Nevada, Wayne Poulsen first fell in love with Squaw Valley when he was 16 years old. One of Poulsen's best friends was fellow skier Martin "Marti" Arrougé. Arrougé's father was a Basque sheepherder who spent summers grazing flocks at Squaw Valley. In 1931, Poulsen and Arrougé took an extended fishing trip in the mountains above the valley, which inspired young Poulsen to develop a ski resort there. (Courtesy Truckee Donner Historical Society.)

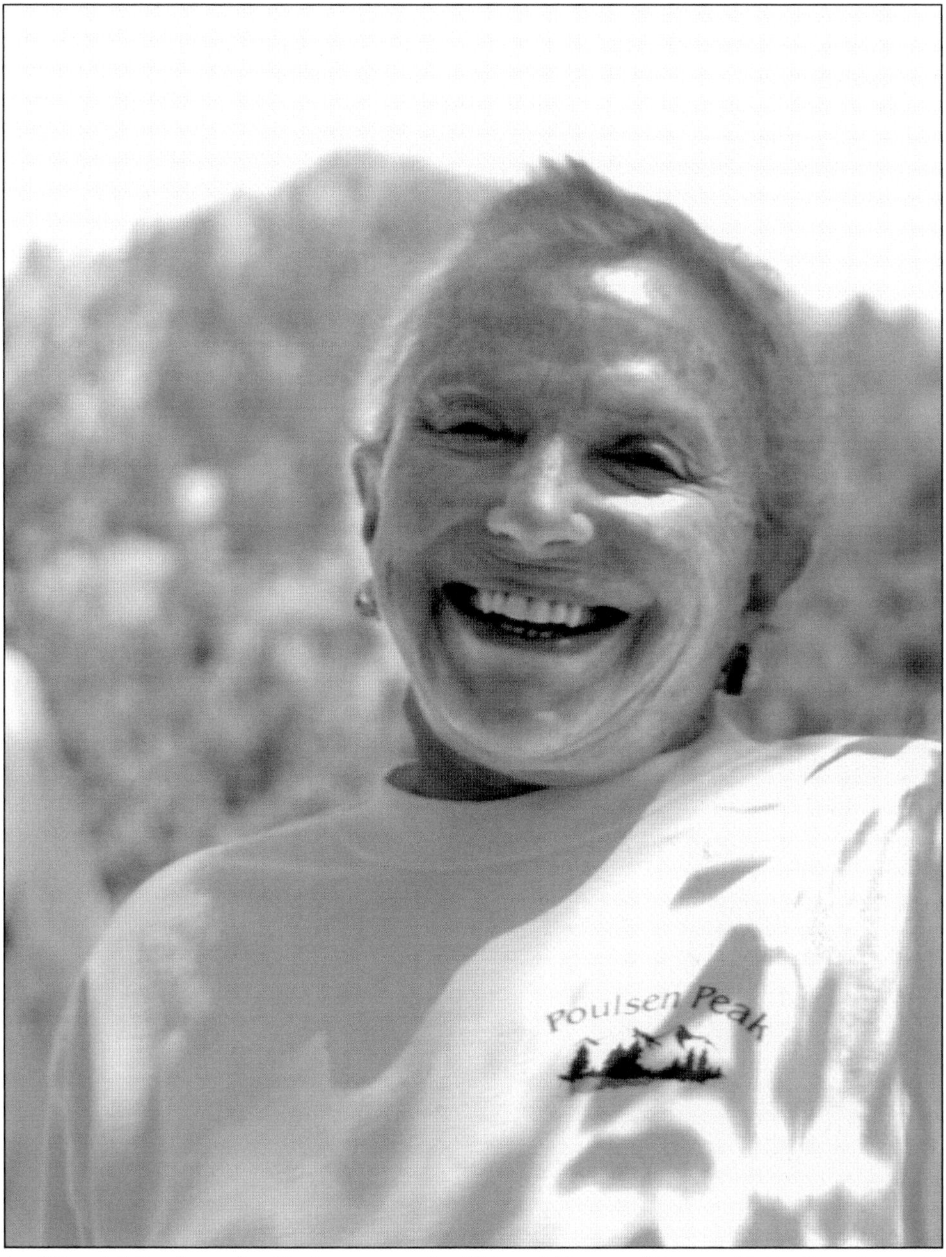


Gladys "Sandy" Poulsen, fondly known as the "Grand Dame of Squaw Valley," is pictured here around 2005. A true pioneer who built the first family home in Squaw Valley with her husband, Wayne, in the 1940s, she raised eight children, two of whom skied well enough to make a US Olympic ski team. Sandy Poulsen once said, "I grew up in New York, in a penthouse, but I ended up living in a tent in Squaw Valley. Yet I could not have been luckier." It is hard to separate the achievements of Sandy and Wayne; their love affair lasted 53 years. In 1969, Sandy was honored by the Far West Ski Association with the Elizabeth "Schatzi" Wood Award, and in 1980, Wayne was elected to the US National Ski Hall of Fame. In May 2005, the US Board on Geographic Names unanimously approved "Poulsen Peak" at Squaw Valley. It is a permanent and deserving honor for a Lake Tahoe pioneer ski family. (Courtesy Mark McLaughlin.)

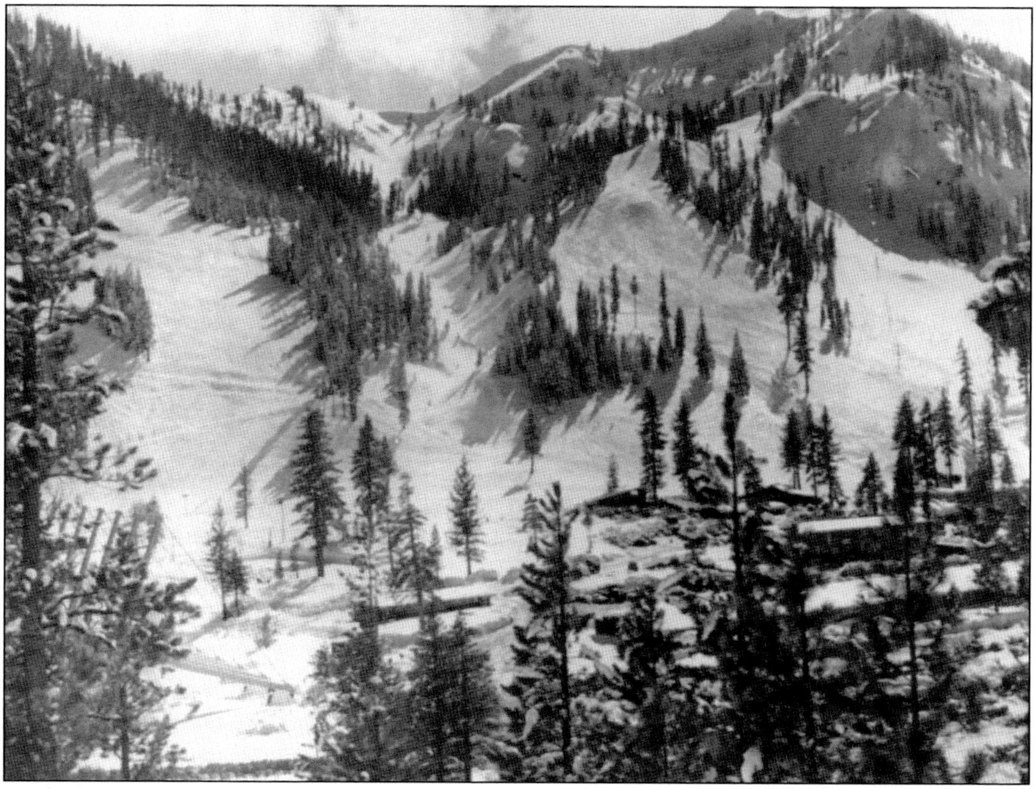

With five peaks, Squaw Valley has famous and challenging terrain, such as KT-22 (far right). KT-22 got its name when Wayne and Sandy Poulsen skied a steep, north-facing slope before the resort's development. As an expert skier, Wayne easily descended the challenging run, but Sandy was too terrified to carve turns down the precipitous pitch. She negotiated the steep run by kick turning and traversing the slope bit by bit. Wayne counted Sandy's 22 kick turns and named the run KT-22. (Courtesy William B. Berry collection.)

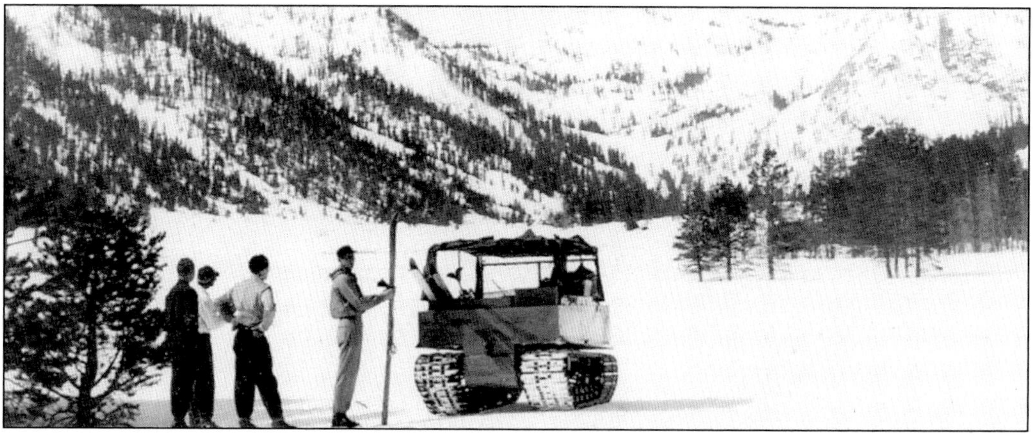

To show off Squaw Valley to friends and potential investors, Wayne Poulsen purchased an Army surplus Weasel to pull everyone along for an effortless and enjoyable tour of the valley. Poulsen, a pilot for Pan American Airways, called his tractor the "Clipper Reindeer" as a tribute to his employer, which often used the word "clipper" in its aircraft names and radio call signs. (Courtesy North Lake Tahoe Historical Society.)

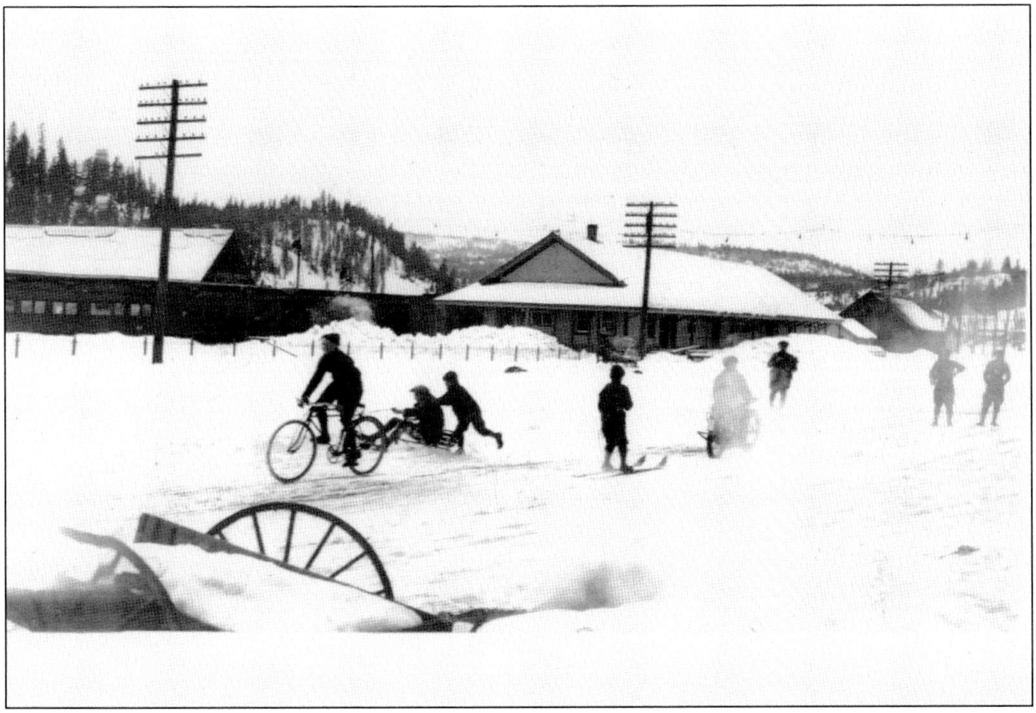

Mechanized skijoring was nothing new to Wayne Poulsen. Skijoring—skiers pulled along by motorcycle, bicycle, horse, and so forth—was a popular pastime in the 1930s, when Poulsen was a young man. In this 1938 photograph, children catch rides behind bicycles and motorbikes in downtown Truckee. (Courtesy Truckee Donner Historical Society.)

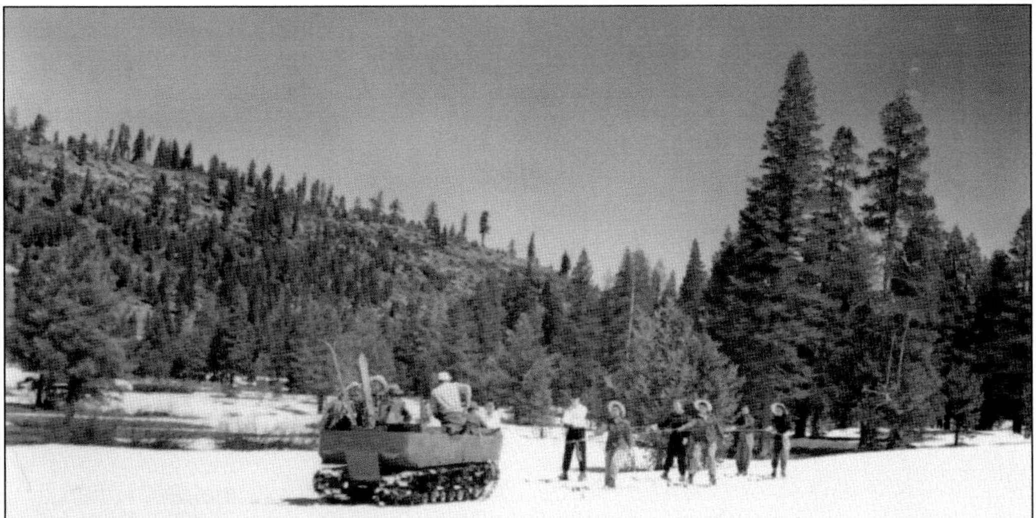

Friends enjoy skijoring behind Poulsen's "Clipper Reindeer" in Squaw Valley in 1948. Poulsen used the tractor as a mechanical horse to pull Olympic-caliber skiers like Friedl Pfeifer and André Roch as they helped to advise on the future ski area's layout and design. At one point, Corty Hill, a principal investor at Sugar Bowl, was interested in the project but then declined. (Courtesy Carson and Vi White collection.)

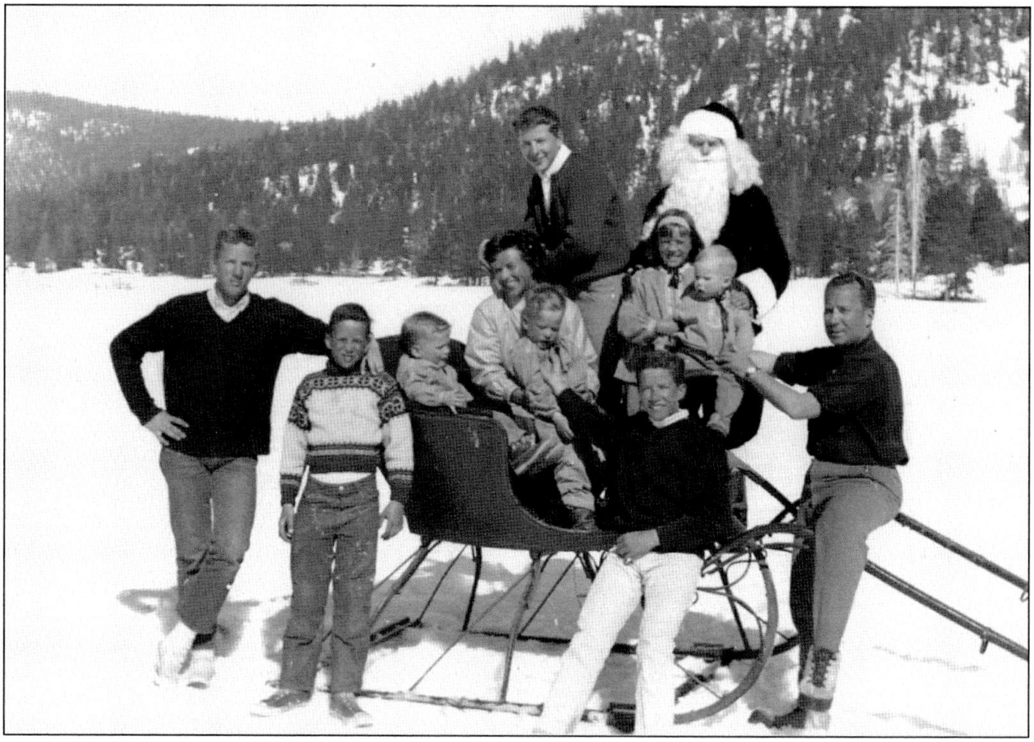

Wayne Poulsen spent half of each month flying for Pan American Airlines, which left his wife, Sandy, alone to raise their eight children. During winter, when the school bus did not show up, Sandy drove the children to Tahoe City or Truckee in an old station wagon. She also took on the roles of ranch boss for the Poulsen livestock operation, postmaster, realtor, and mother to a family of competitive ski racers. (Truckee Donner Historical Society.)

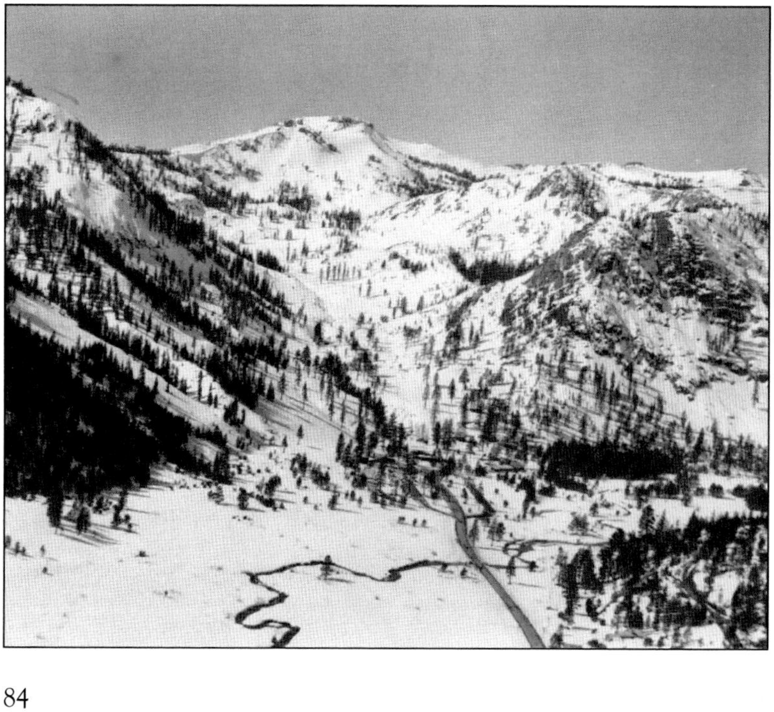

Before the development that came with the 1960 Winter Olympics, Squaw Valley retained its rural character. Wayne Poulsen had big dreams for his Sierra Shangri-la. The forested slopes and rugged granite peaks that surrounded the valley floor made for idyllic scenery and the glaciated alpine terrain offered the best skiing at Lake Tahoe. (Courtesy Bill Briner collection.)

Even before the 1960 Winter Games, skiers were shredding powder at Squaw Valley. As a pilot, Wayne Poulsen pioneered air routes for Pan American over China, Burma, and India. He traveled all over the world but never gave up his dream of building a ski area in Squaw Valley. During World War II, Poulsen purchased nearly 2,000 acres of the valley floor; he now owned the valley, but he needed investment capital to succeed. (Courtesy Bill Briner collection.)

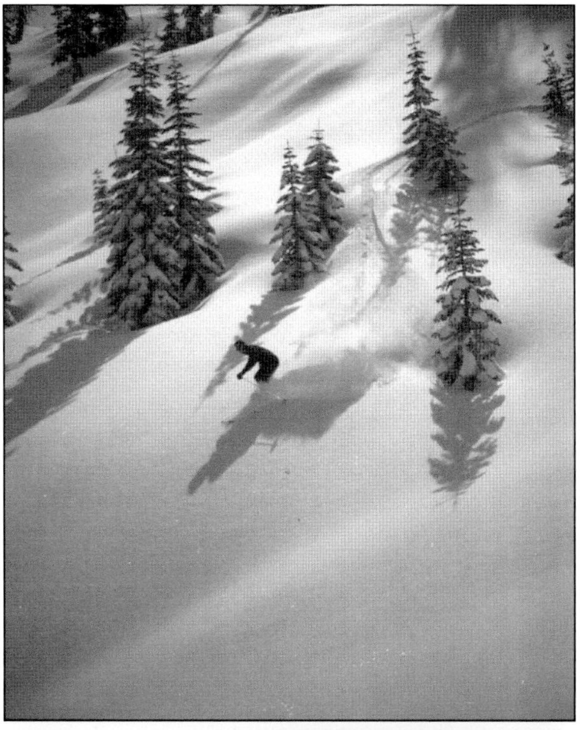

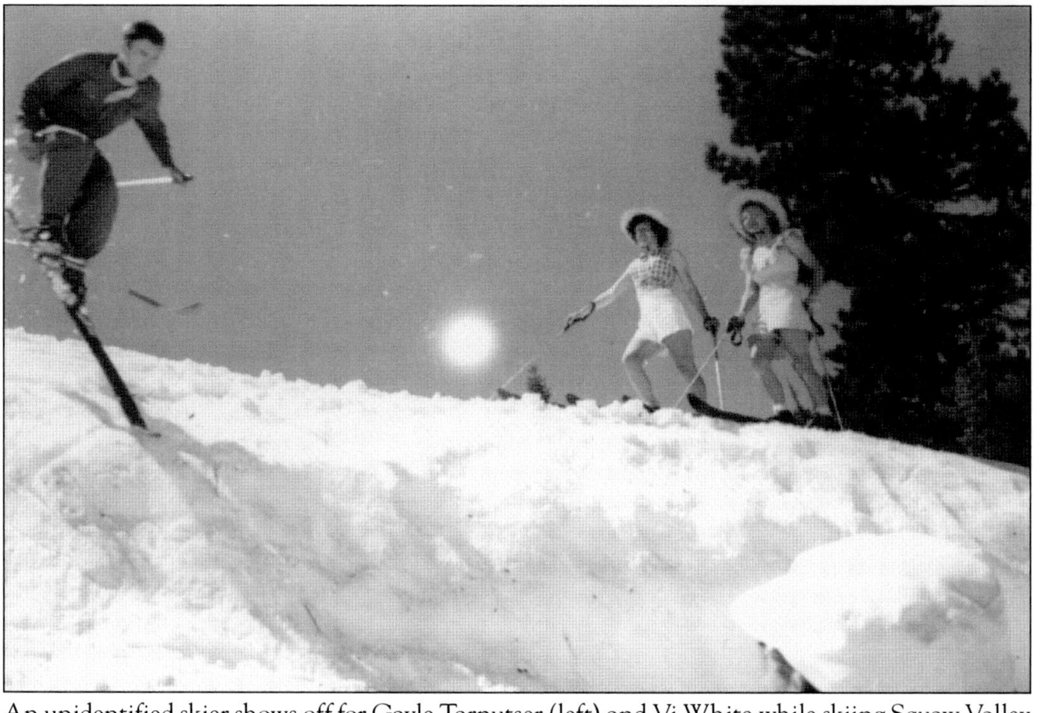

An unidentified skier shows off for Gayle Tarnutser (left) and Vi White while skiing Squaw Valley on April 29, 1949. Squaw Valley's chairlift would not start turning until November 1949, when the resort officially opened, but that did not stop avid skiers from climbing the slopes to enjoy spring skiing in the sun. (Courtesy Carson and Vi White collection.)

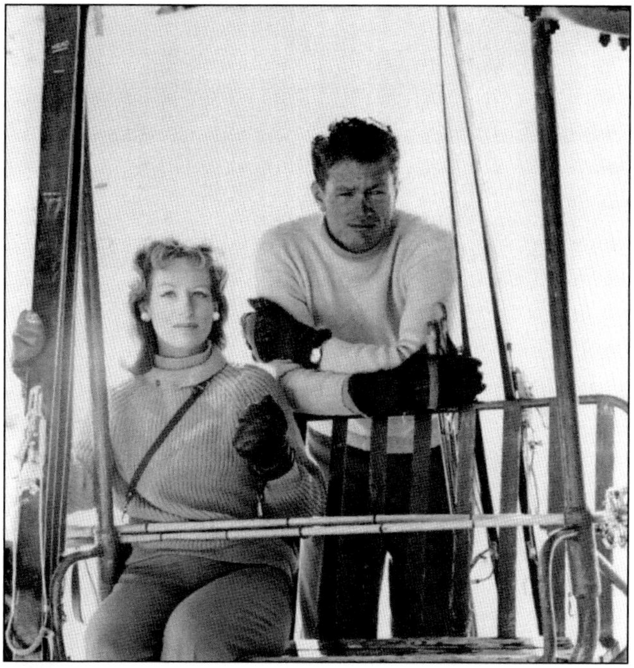

Justine and Alexander Cushing relax at Squaw Valley in 1959. Born to a prominent East Coast family, Alex Cushing was a graduate of Harvard Law School. After serving in World War II, Alex headed west on a ski trip. Still looking for a major investor, Wayne Poulsen heard that Cushing might have access to the kind of money needed to build a ski resort. Poulsen showed Squaw Valley to Cushing, and the two men decided to start a partnership—the Squaw Valley Development Corporation. (Courtesy Donner Summit Historical Society/ Norm Sayler collection.)

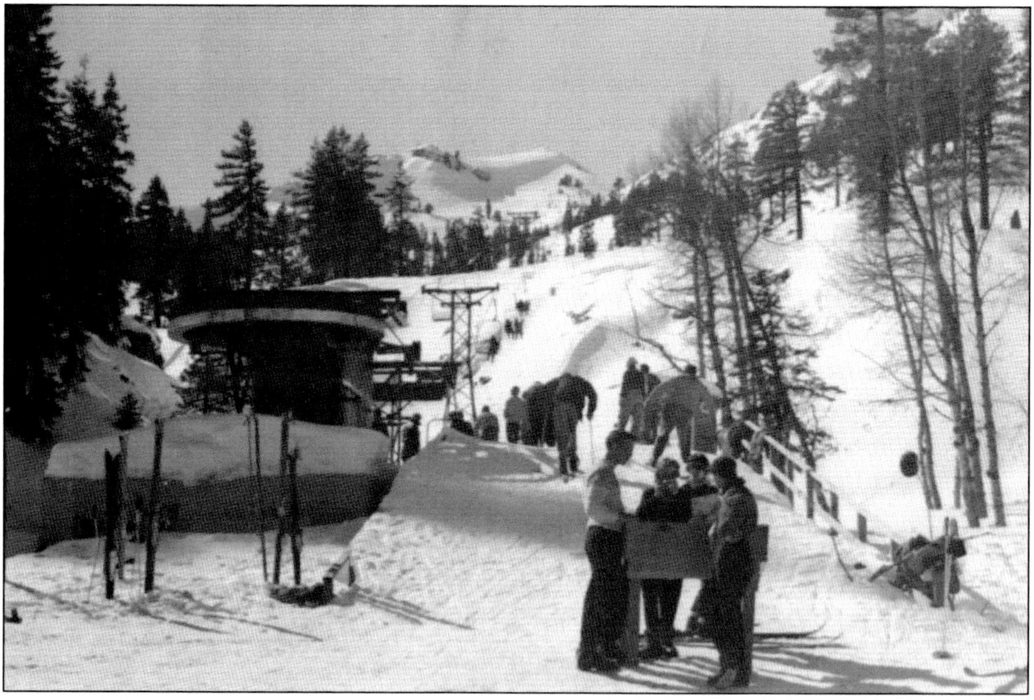

This c. 1950 image shows Squaw Valley in its first year of operation. Upon forming the Squaw Valley Development Corporation in 1948, Wayne Poulsen contributed substantial acreage at the west end of the valley, while Alex Cushing provided about $400,000 in capital. However, due to sharp business and philosophical differences between Poulsen and Cushing, the partnership failed within the year, and Cushing took control of the company. (Courtesy Donner Summit Historical Society/Norm Sayler collection.)

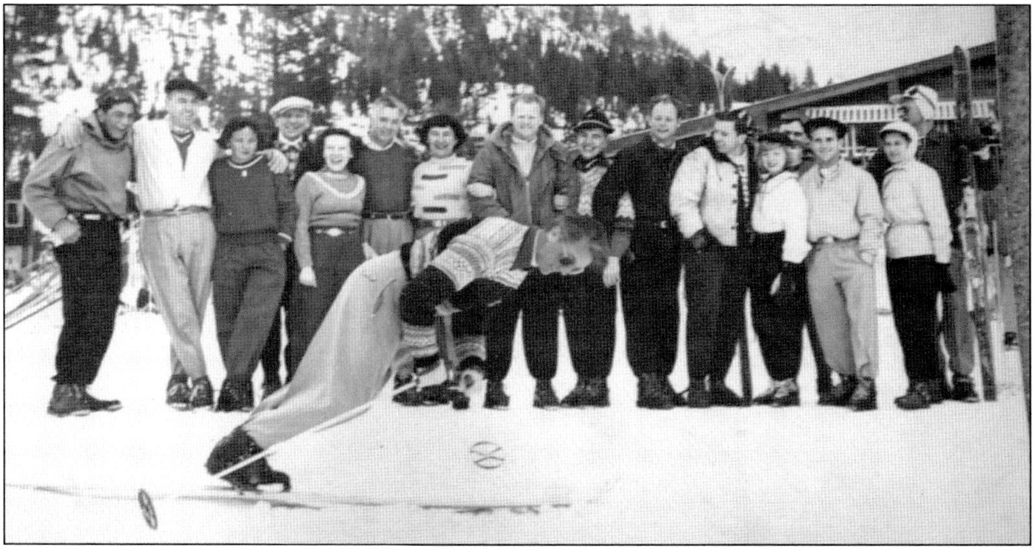

Squaw Valley's first director of its ski school, Emile Allais, entertains his students around 1951. A legendary French Olympic ski champion who had won seven world championships, Allais was considered the world's greatest skier. He was known for an innovative style of instruction that threatened to replace the Arlberg system employed at Sun Valley and other resorts. Allais's presence at Squaw Valley gave Cushing's new operation strong credibility. (Courtesy Nevada Historical Society.)

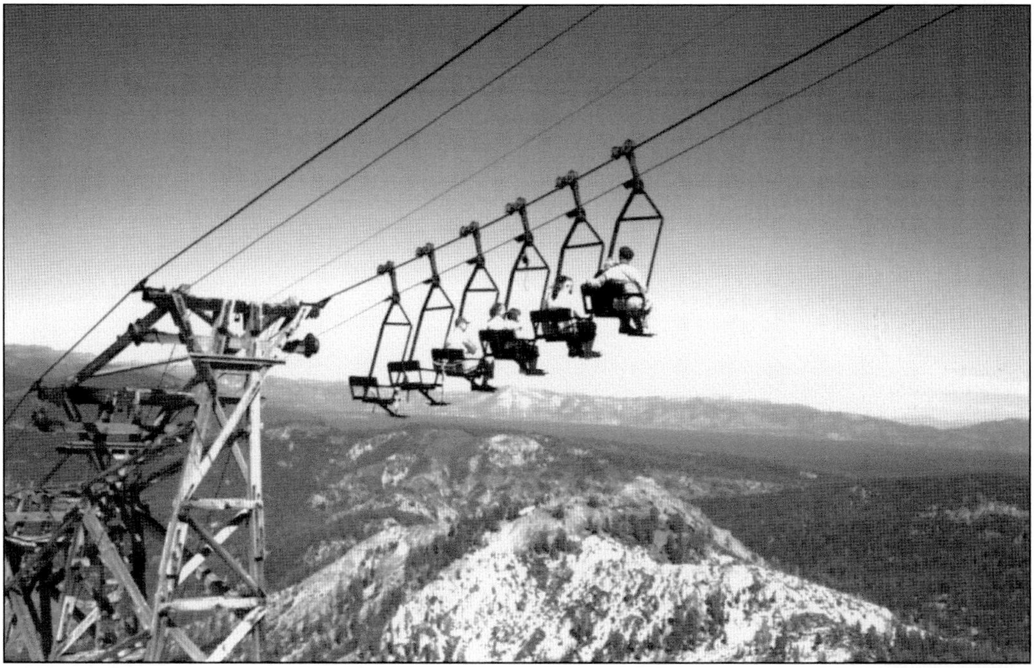

Squaw Valley's jigback tram is pictured here in 1953. Squaw Valley opened with a double chairlift and two rope tows, but owner Alex Cushing—always an innovator—soon had a jigback chairlift system installed. The jigback, based on mining tramway technology, was powered by a gasoline engine and could transport up to 12 people at a time on six double chairs. (Courtesy Bill Briner collection.)

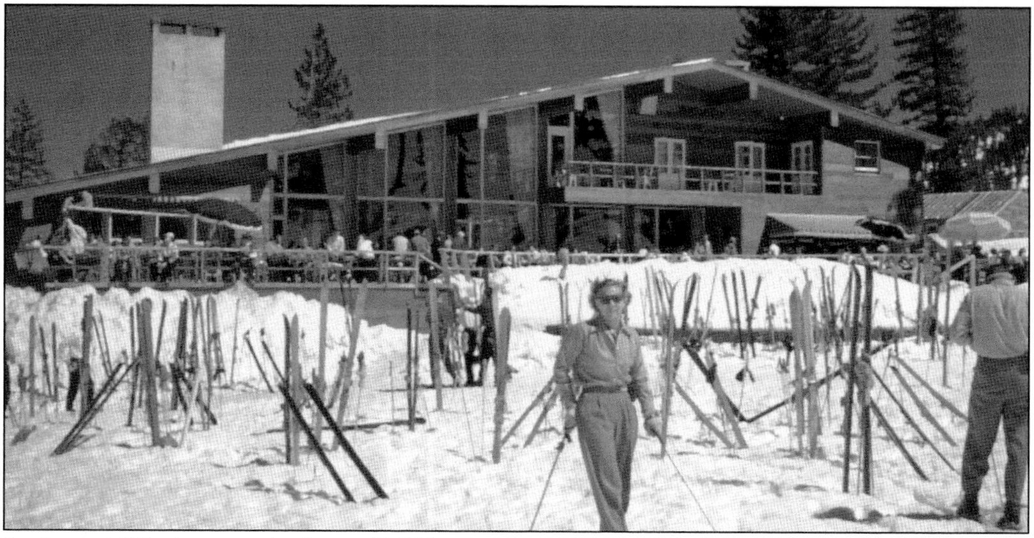

In the c. 1955 photograph above, Vi White poses in front of the original Squaw Valley Lodge; it burned down the following year. Following a work stoppage by union workmen, Squaw Valley owner Alex Cushing hired strikebreakers in the struggle to finish the construction of the facilities. Working feverishly on a deadline, the Harvard-educated lawyer was forced to hook up the plumbing himself. During the gala opening, on Thanksgiving Day, 1949, only one toilet was usable, and dinner was not served until 10:00 p.m. Money was in short supply, and although the resort's opening was generally well-received by skiers and the media, Cushing's company was broke. Despite his hard-nosed approach to business, Cushing was an accomplished piano player and frequent performer in the Squaw Valley Lodge, where he entertained guests. (Above, Carson and Vi White collection; below, Donner Summit Historical Society/Robert Frohlich collection.)

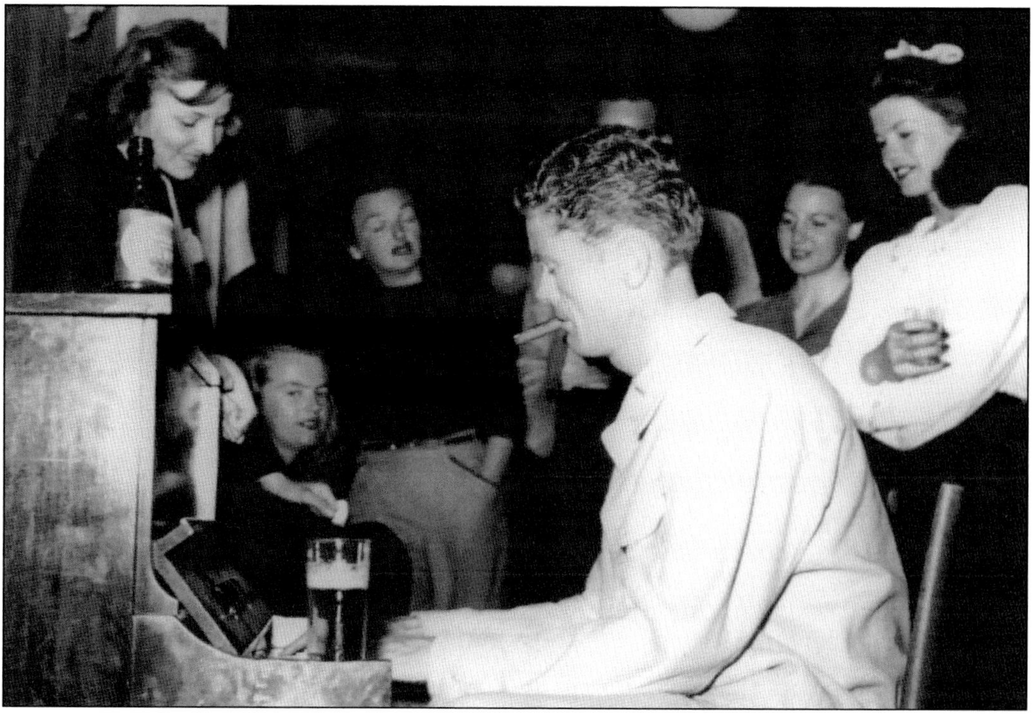

During World War II, Alex Cushing worked in Naval Intelligence as a troubleshooter for the Naval Air Transport Service. Cushing was primarily based in South America and the Pacific. During a prolonged period of intense work with no sleep, he collapsed from exhaustion. When he woke up in Bethesda Naval Hospital, his face was paralyzed; the condition gave him a permanent scowl. (Courtesy Nevada Historical Society.)

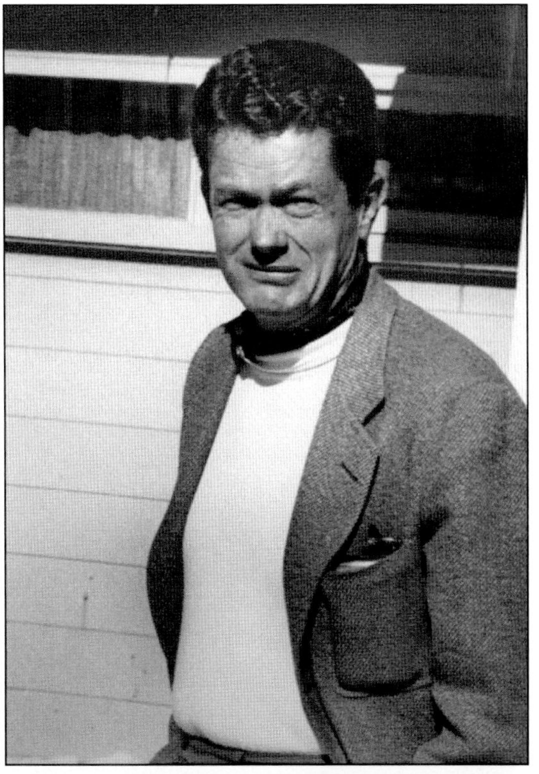

Squaw Valley's second ski school director, Joseph "Jo" Marillac, enjoys some deep powder in 1953. Marillac took over after the first director, Emile Allais, headed to France in 1954 to work at Courchevel. Marillac was a famed mountaineer and French Resistance war hero. In 1955, when Alex Cushing revealed his doubts about hosting the 1960 Winter Olympics at Squaw Valley, Marillac told him, "You have the mountain, have the snow, and you can build the rest." (Courtesy Bill Briner collection.)

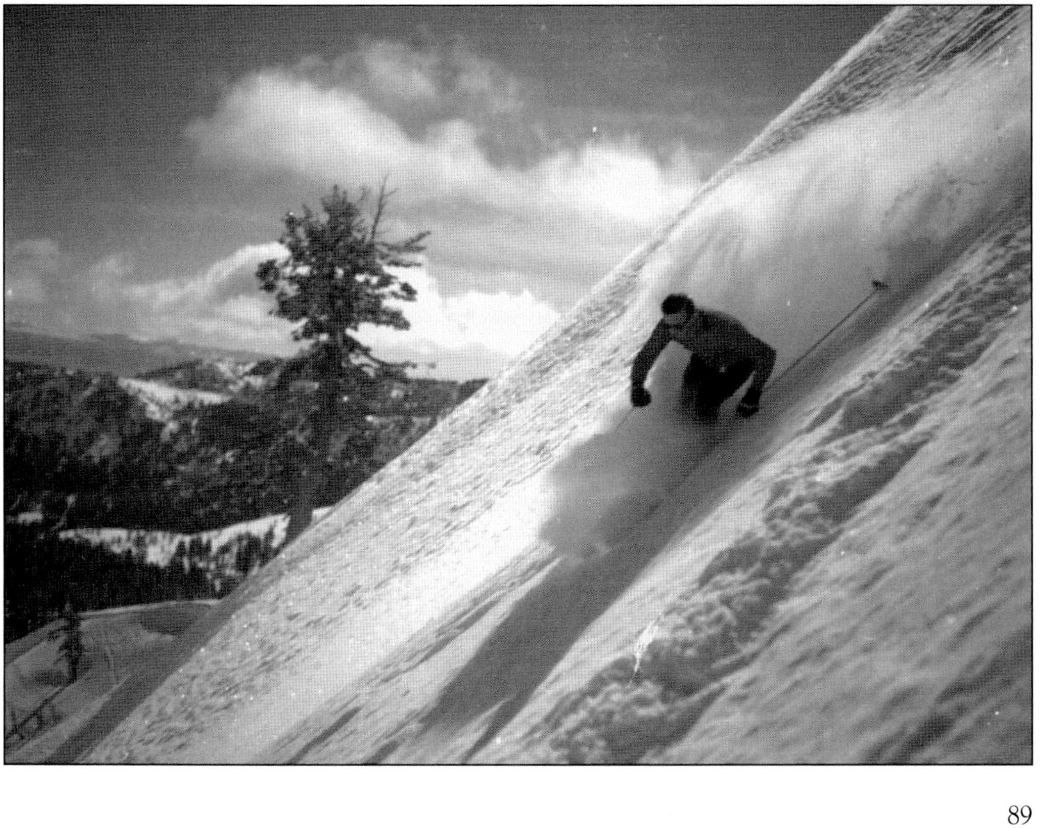

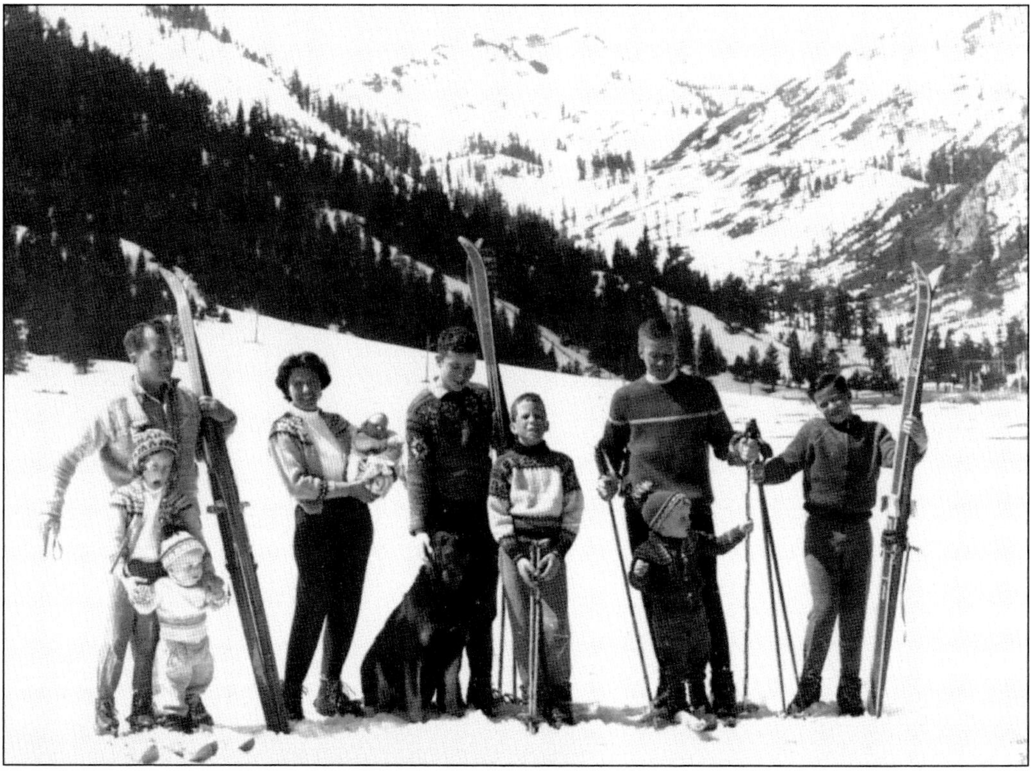

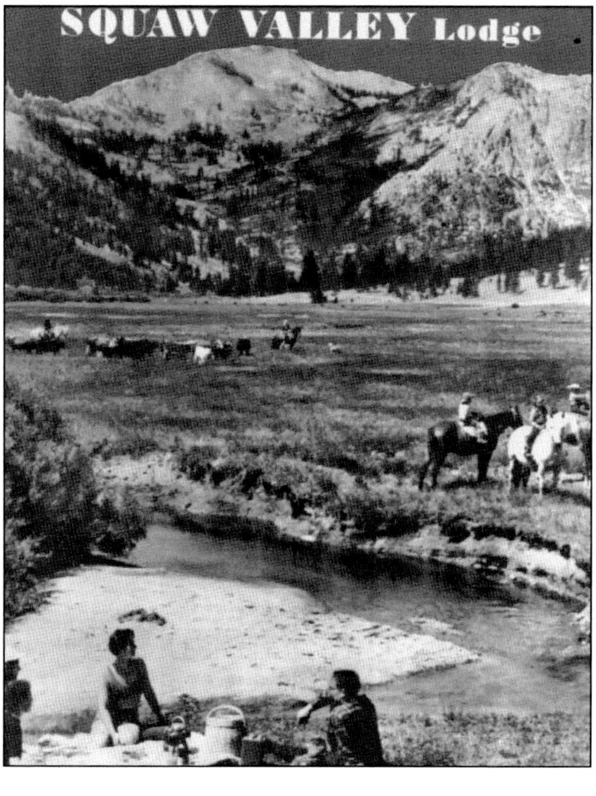


The Poulsen family, pictured above in Squaw Valley around 1960, are, from left to right, Wayne (with Sandra and Glenn in front of him), Sandy (holding Russell), Christopher, Eric, Wayne Jr., Craig (in front of Wayne Jr.), and Lance. When the Alex Cushing–Wayne Poulsen partnership broke up, Wayne and Sandy formed Squaw Valley Land and Livestock Company, a real estate business that sold parcels for ski chalets. To develop the valley into a real community, they set aside parcels for public purposes and built Papoose, a children's ski area. Wayne Poulsen lost his boyhood dream of building a ski resort at Squaw Valley, but Cushing's successful bid to host the 1960 Winter Olympic Games brought recognition, increasing the value of his land. (Above, courtesy Truckee Donner Historical Society; left, courtesy of Donner Summit Historical Society/Norm Sayler collection.)

*Seven*

# A Heavenly Valley and Nevada Game On!

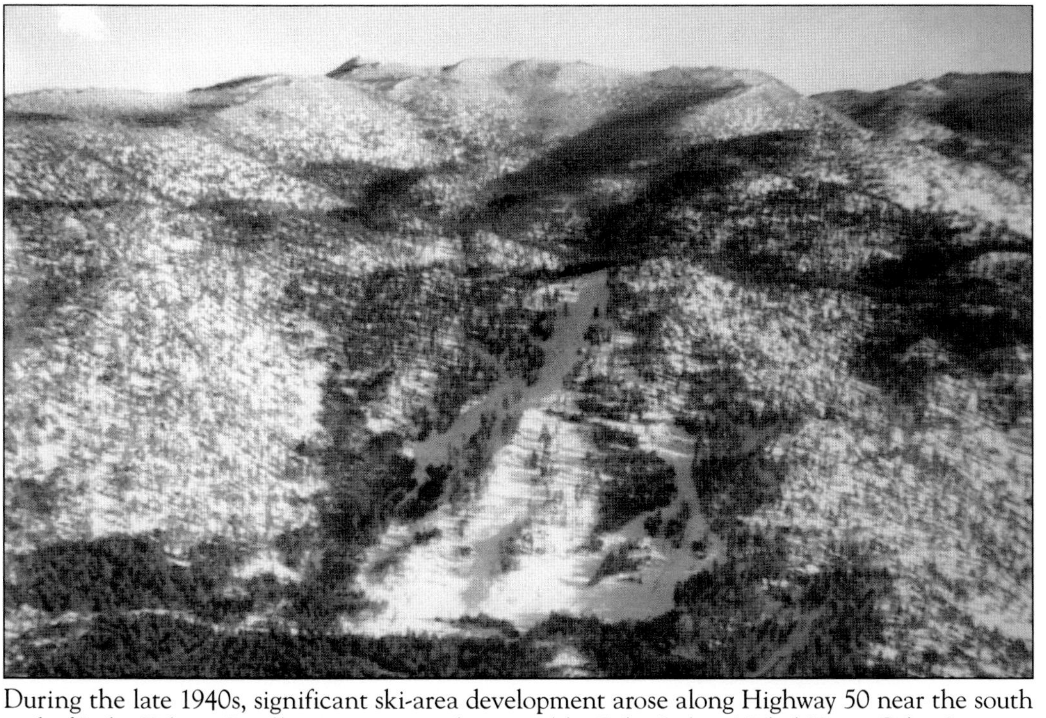

During the late 1940s, significant ski-area development arose along Highway 50 near the south end of Lake Tahoe. Small owner-operated resorts like Echo Lakes, Nebel Horn, Echo Summit, and the Edelweiss attracted skiers from Placerville and Sacramento. In 1947, Lee and Daisy Miller established the Bijou Skiway Park at South Lake Tahoe. The fledging operation was sold to businessman Chris Kuraisa and his wife, Dottie, in 1954, and they renamed it Heavenly Valley. (Courtesy Nevada Historical Society.)

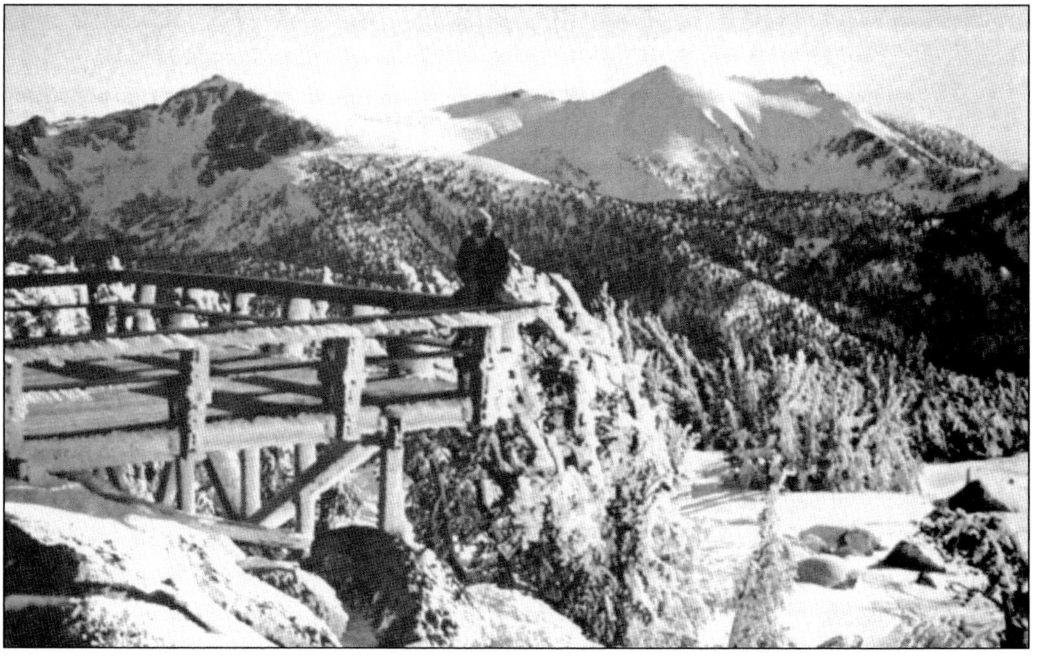

After Kuraisa bought the Bijou Skiway, he formed a partnership with three South Shore casino operators and moved the operation further up the mountain. They installed a 4,000-foot double chairlift over the Gunbarrel run at the base of the mountain. Soon, more chairlifts were added, including one that reached the top ridge at 10,000 feet. The resort could now boast of a 3,600-foot vertical rise and astonishing views of Lake Tahoe. (Courtesy Donner Summit Historical Society/ Norm Sayler collection.)

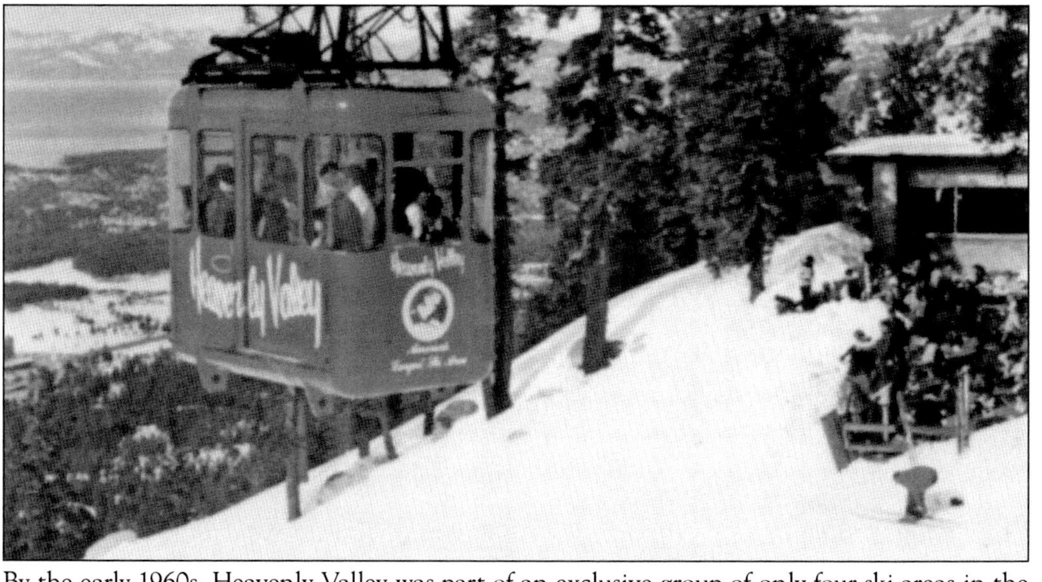


By the early 1960s, Heavenly Valley was part of an exclusive group of only four ski areas in the United States with vertical rises in excess of 3,000 feet. The other three were Sun Valley, Idaho, and Aspen and Vail, in Colorado. In 1962, Heavenly installed a 25-passenger aerial tramway, the largest in America at the time. The glass-enclosed cabins protected skiers and opened the mountain to year-round sightseeing. (Courtesy North Lake Tahoe Historical Society.)

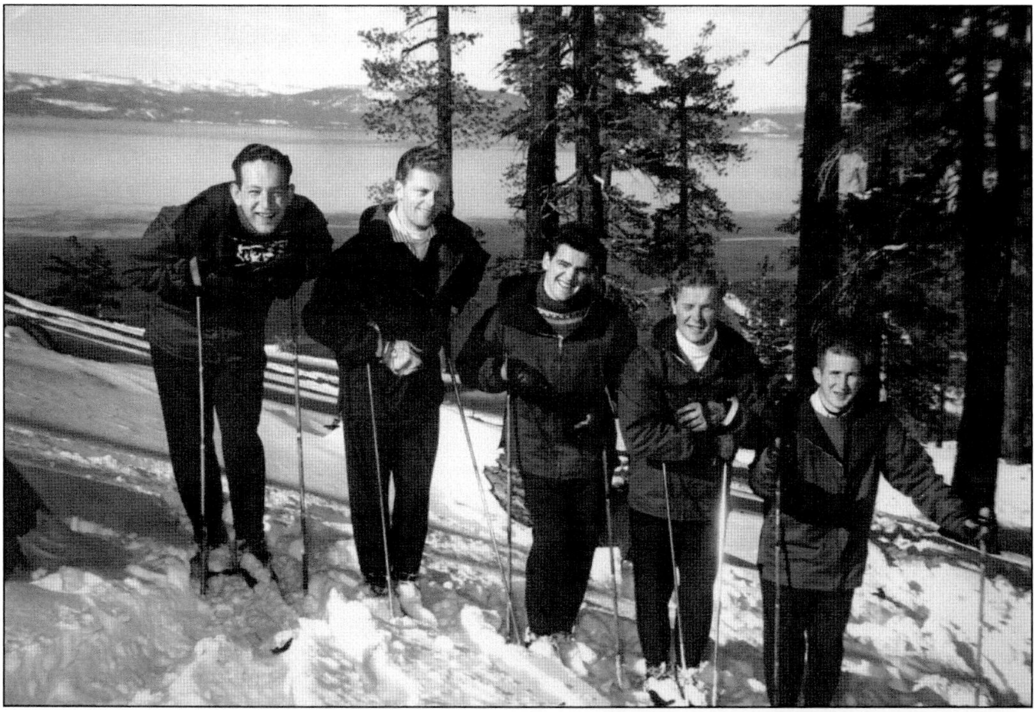

From 1956 to 1958, Stein Eriksen (second from left; the other skiers are unidentified) was Heavenly Valley's ski school director. Eriksen took home gold and silver medals in the 1952 Oslo Olympics. In 1954, he won three gold medals at the World Championships in Sweden, becoming the first alpine skier in the world to win triple gold at a world championship. (Courtesy Nevada Historical Society.)

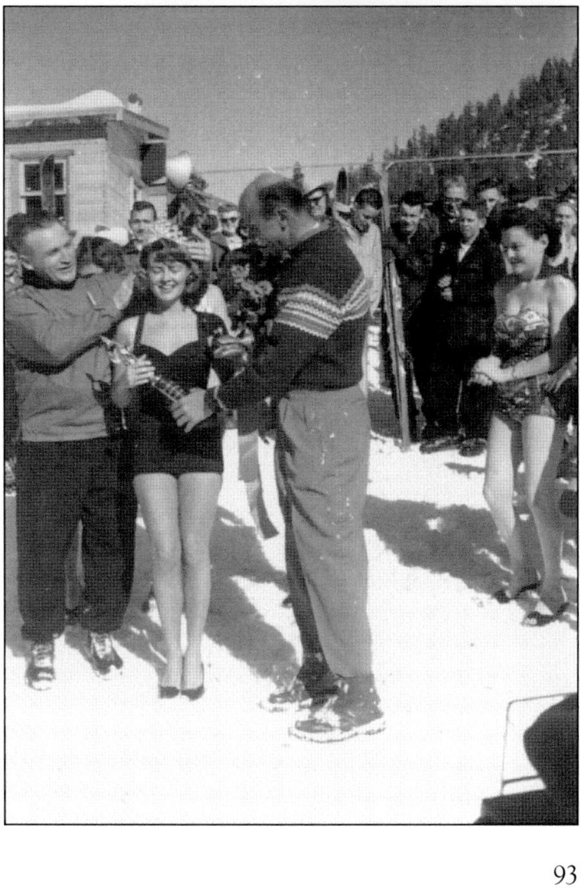

In this c. 1960 photograph, George Cannon (left) and Heavenly Valley owner Chris Kuraisa crown an unidentified snow queen. (Courtesy Carson and Vi White collection.)

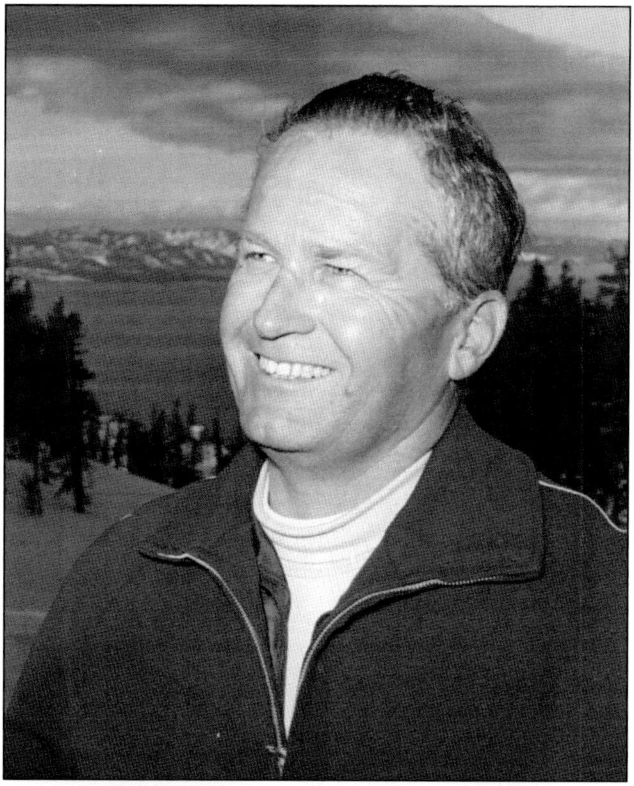

In 1964, San Francisco tax attorney Hugh Killebrew purchased a substantial interest in Heavenly Valley. Killebrew quickly expanded the resort across the state line into Nevada with two chairlifts that accessed northeast-facing slopes. By 1967, Heavenly Valley could call itself "America's Largest Ski Area." (Courtesy Donner Summit Historical Society/ Robert Frohlich collection.)

During his tenure as ski school director, Stein Eriksen began to promote Heavenly Valley with popular swimsuit beauty pageants such as the "Miss Snow Fun" competition. Later, international ski races like the World Cup brought national television coverage that showcased the ski area's varied terrain and views of Lake Tahoe. (Courtesy Carson and Vi White collection.)

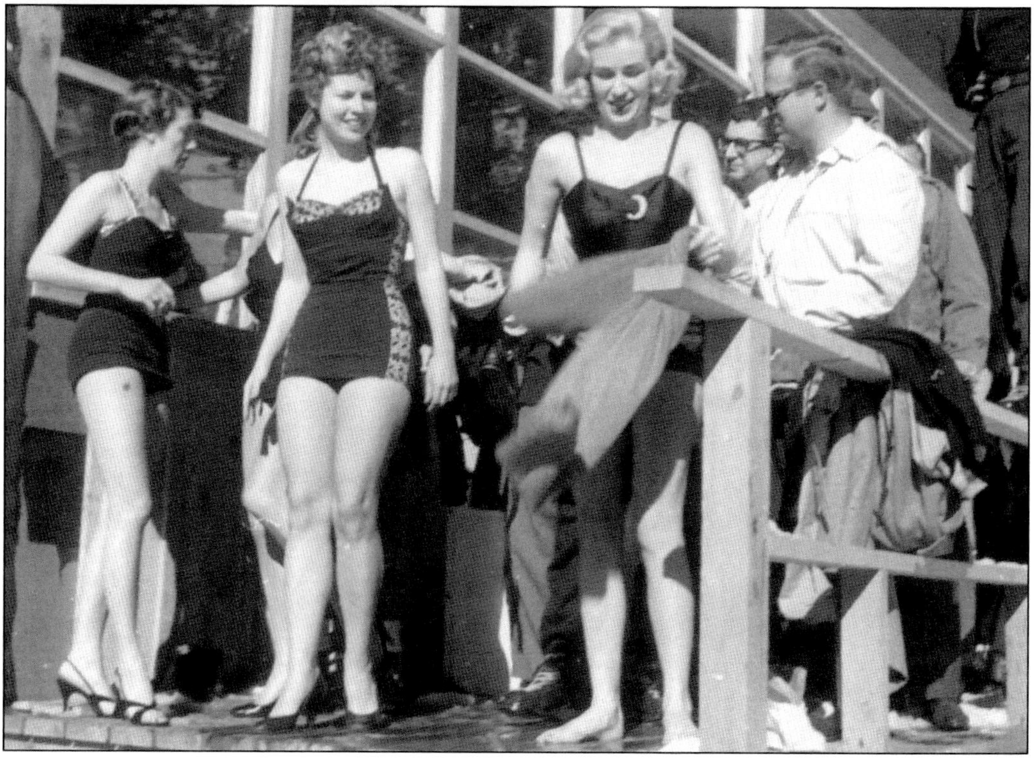

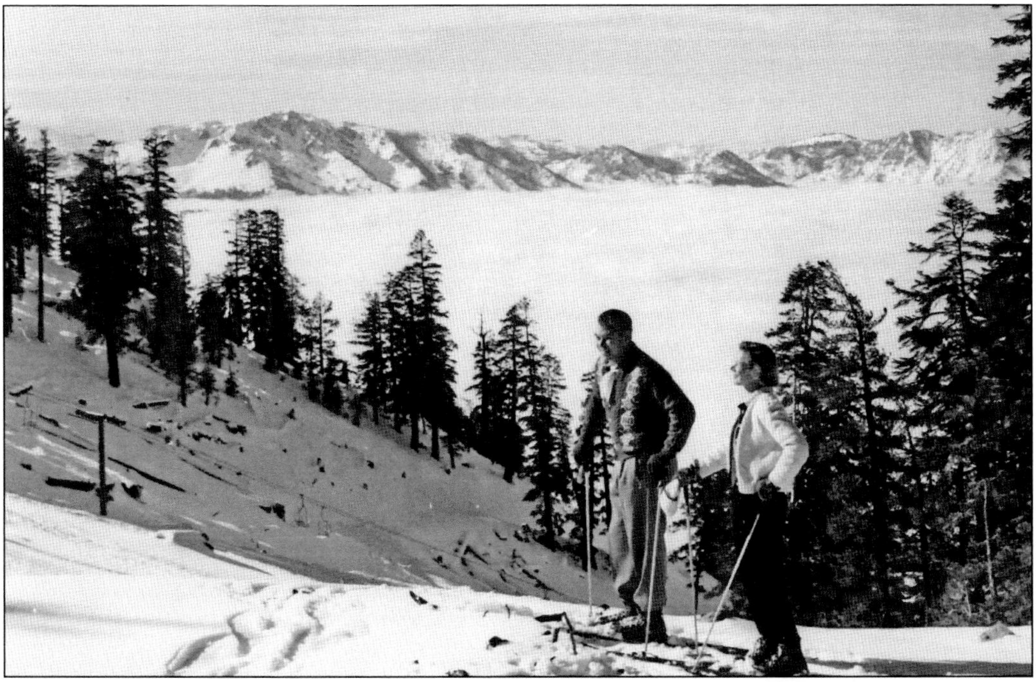

Carson and Vi White ski above the clouds at Heavenly Valley in January 1960. To protect its business against winter seasons with poor snow conditions, the huge resort installed the largest snowmaking system in the West and now boasts 4,800 acres of skiable terrain. (Courtesy Carson and Vi White collection.)

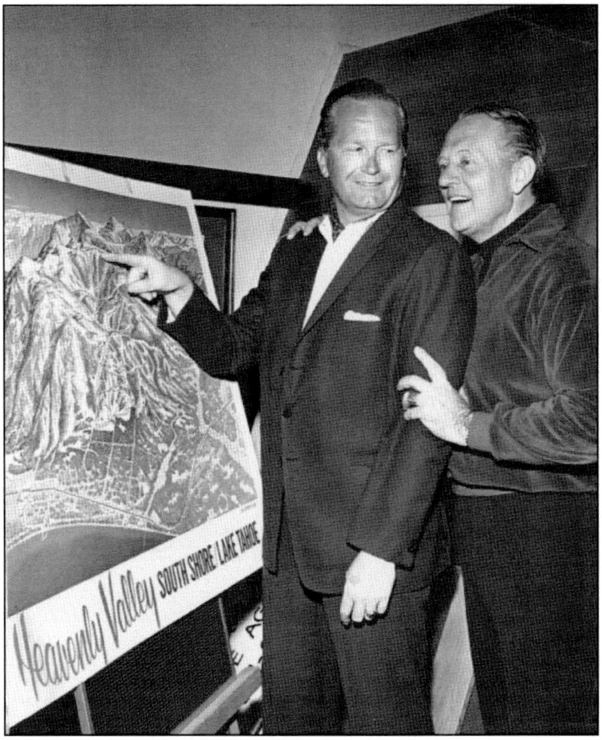


Hugh Killebrew (left) shows entertainer Art Linkletter the plans for Heavenly Valley improvements and expansion. Killebrew was killed in a plane crash in August 1977, and resort operations were taken over by his son William. After a two-year drought in the late 1970s, William Killebrew followed his father's plan to install an extensive snowmaking system to guarantee a profit during dry winters. (Courtesy Donner Summit Historical Society/ Norm Sayler collection.)

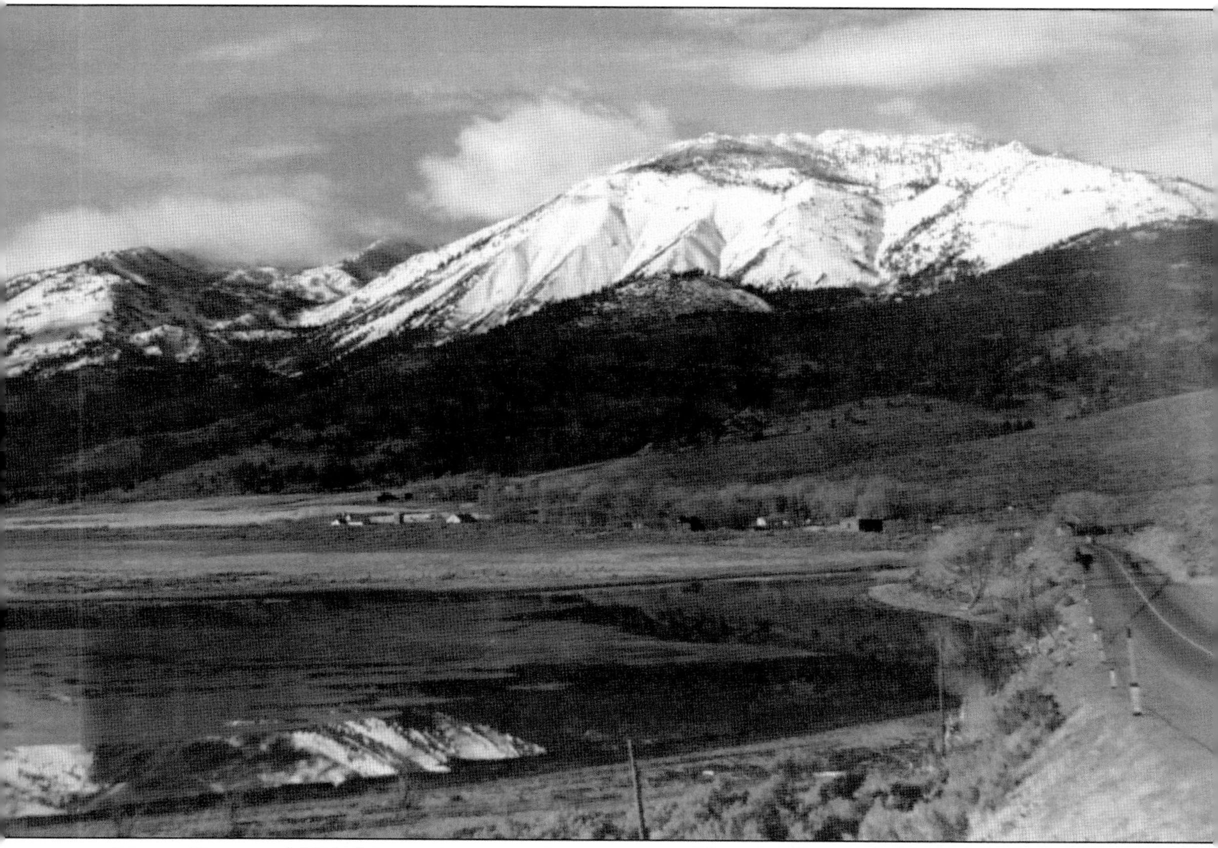

Mount Rose and Slide Mountain tower above western Nevada. Because of its proximity to Reno, the area has drawn skiers like a magnet since 1930. Just as World War II ended, the Sky Tavern Lodge opened on the Mount Rose Highway where winter plowing stopped and the road became a dead end. The highway, which connects Reno with Lake Tahoe, was only open during the summer months. Early skiers climbed above the Sky Tavern and cut trails through the trees to open up the terrain. Men like Warren Hart, Wayne Poulsen, and Edward Heath set up small rope tows to offer skiers an easier way up the hill. (Courtesy Craig Beck collection.)

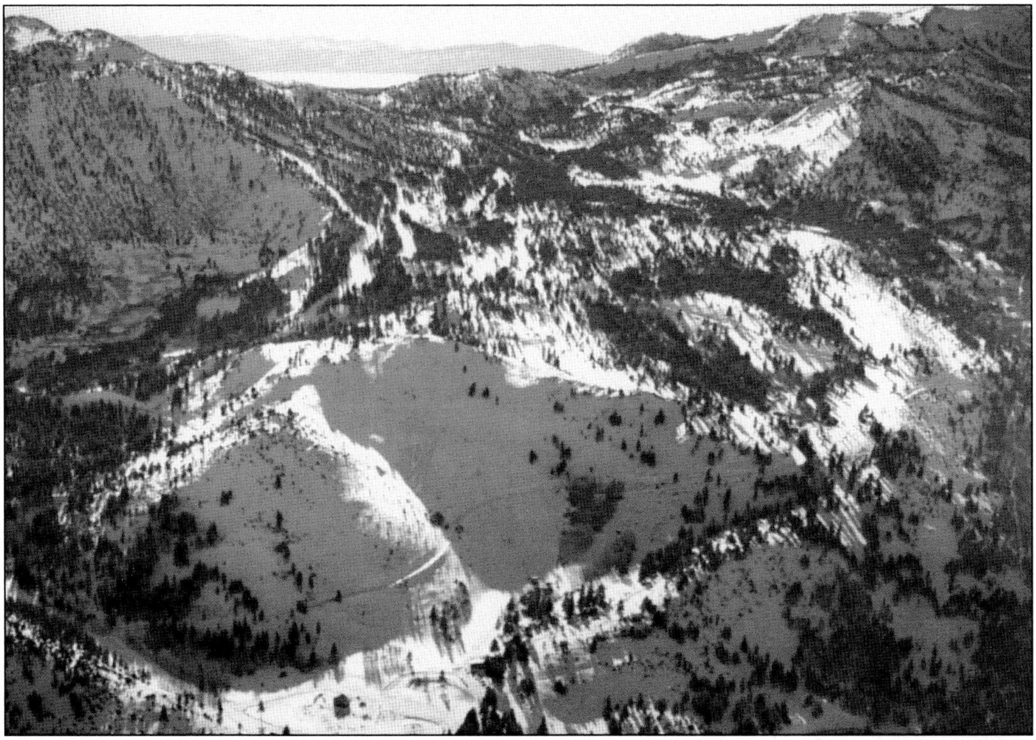

During the 1950s, the Reno Ski Bowl was established on Slide Mountain, next to Mount Rose. An ancient volcano, the Mount Rose summit is 10,776 feet, while its neighbor Slide Mountain tops out at 9,698 feet. Due to the high elevation, snow that falls in the region each winter is drier and lighter than at many other Lake Tahoe resorts. (Courtesy Craig Beck collection.)

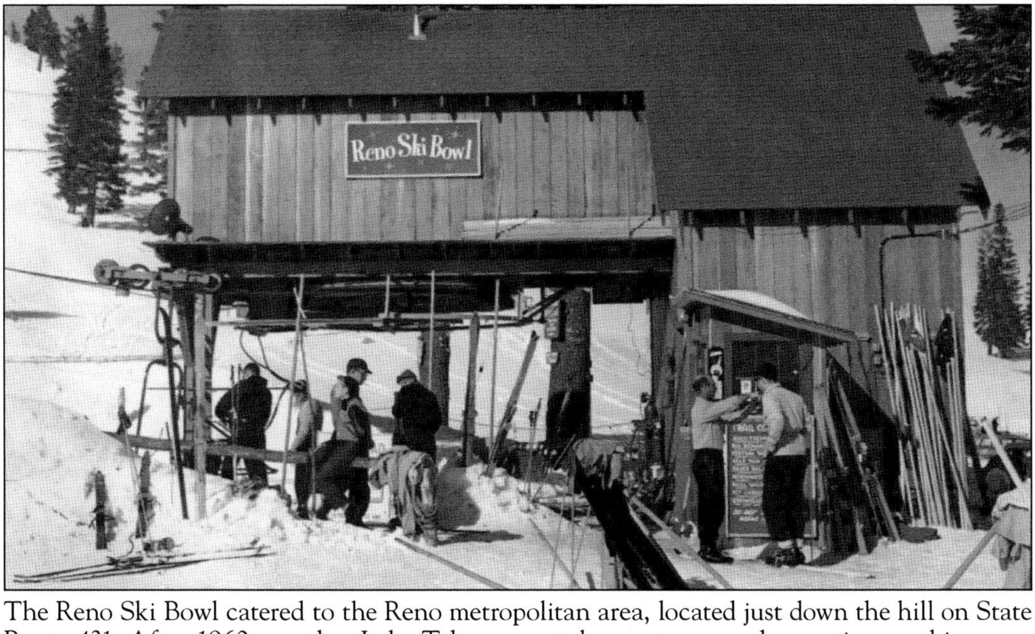


The Reno Ski Bowl catered to the Reno metropolitan area, located just down the hill on State Route 431. After 1960, as other Lake Tahoe resorts began to expand operations and improve infrastructure, pressure increased to modernize the "Bowl." (Courtesy Mount Rose Ski Tahoe.)

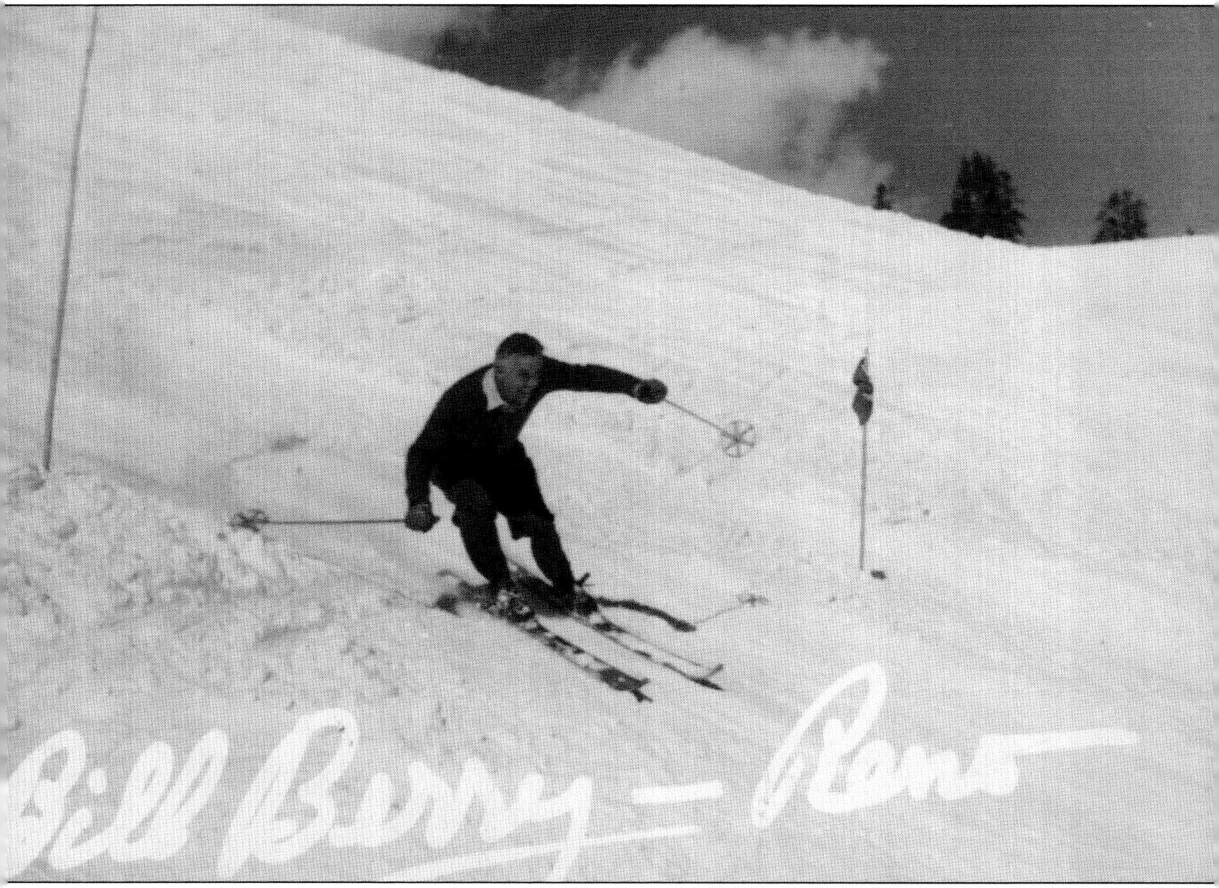


Ski historian and longtime Reno resident William "Bill" Berry slices through slalom gates at the Reno Ski Bowl in 1960. The Reno Ski Bowl was constructed on the east side of Slide Mountain and was once connected to nearby Sky Tavern by a chairlift. In the early 1960s, the Reno Ski Bowl evolved into the Slide Mountain Ski Area, and the north face of Slide Mountain became the Mount Rose Ski Area in 1964. The two resorts operated independently until 1987, when they merged to become Mount Rose Ski Tahoe. The resort has the highest base of any ski area in the Lake Tahoe region, and although it is prone to windy conditions, it rarely rains there. (Courtesy Donner Summit Historical Society/Robert Frohlich collection.)

After 1960, Tahoe's ski industry expanded again. Avid skiers like Art Linkletter (left), ski cartoonist Eric Johnson (center), and William "Bill" Briner recognized the region's potential. Linkletter was active in Tahoe skiing and had financial capital. Briner was hired as an instructor when Squaw Valley opened. As a professional photographer, Briner worked with Squaw Valley owner Alex Cushing to promote the ski area. Later, as a Placer County supervisor, Briner participated in discussions for future resorts. (Courtesy Donner Summit Historical Society/ Norm Sayler collection.)

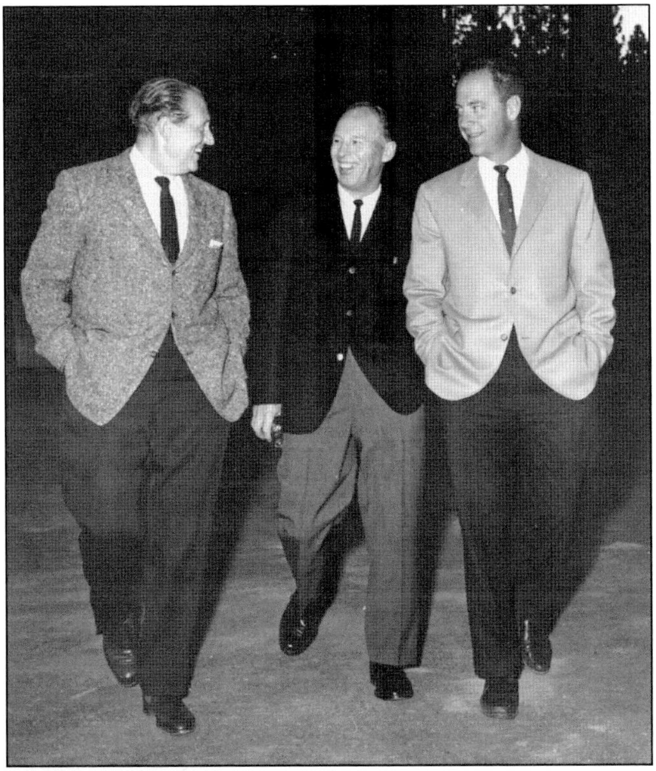

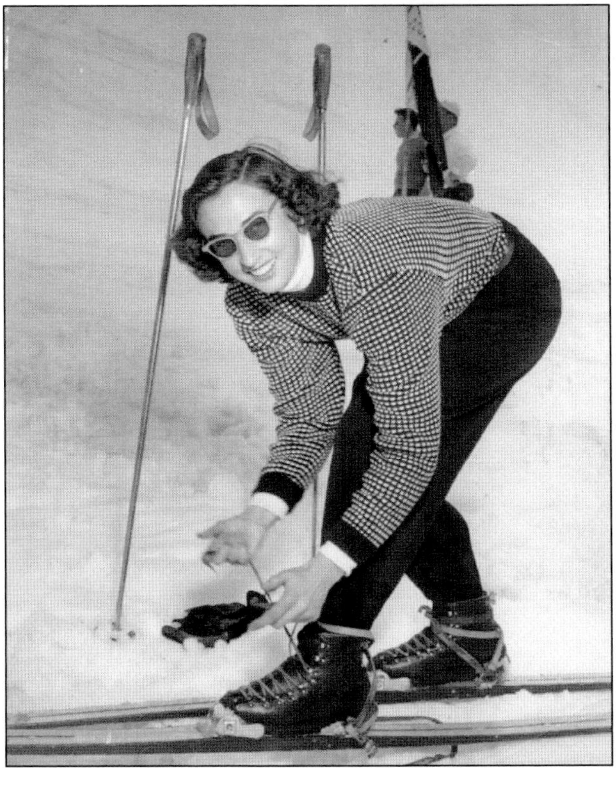

Ski equipment improved during the 1950s, but technology was still a far cry from what modern skiers and snowboarders enjoy. This unidentified stylish skier from 1955 is lacing up her leather boots that are held in the toe piece by long leather thongs, which kept skis tied firmly to a skier's ankles. Modern skis have automatic brakes that stop the board from sliding downhill when bindings release. (Courtesy Donner Summit Historical Society/Norm Sayler collection.)

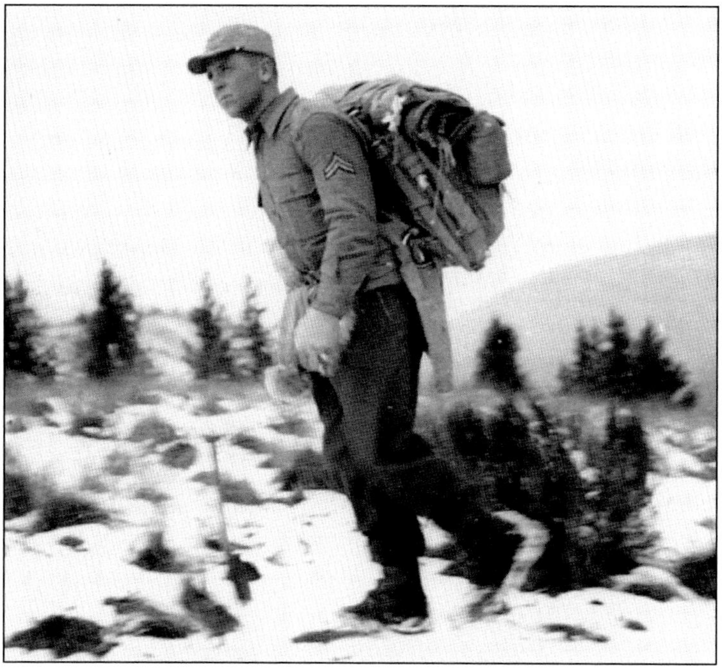

There is a strong connection between Reno, the University of Nevada, and skiing in the Mount Rose area. Like many local residents, Chelton Leonard, shown here training for the 10th Mountain Division in 1943, learned to ski in western Nevada. After his service in World War II, he coached the University of Nevada ski team for 10 years and was appointed chief gatekeeper for all alpine races during the 1960 Winter Olympics at Squaw Valley. (Courtesy Chelton Leonard collection.)

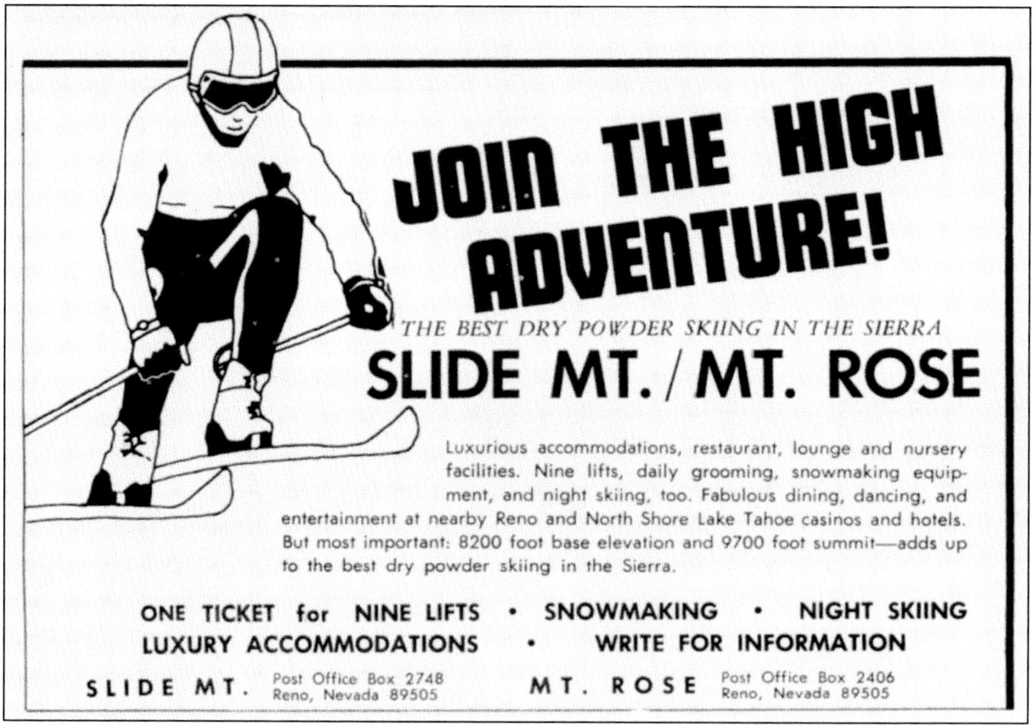


In December 1930, a small group of skiers met in the basement of a Reno shoe store to form the Reno Ski Club. Five years later, the club sponsored the first annual Mount Rose Downhill Race, held at the nearby Galena Creek ski course. According to ski journalist William Berry, "The ladies' [downhill] race had only two contestants, who covered the course in a round-about-way in 14 minutes." (Courtesy Donner Summit Historical Society/Norm Sayler collection.)

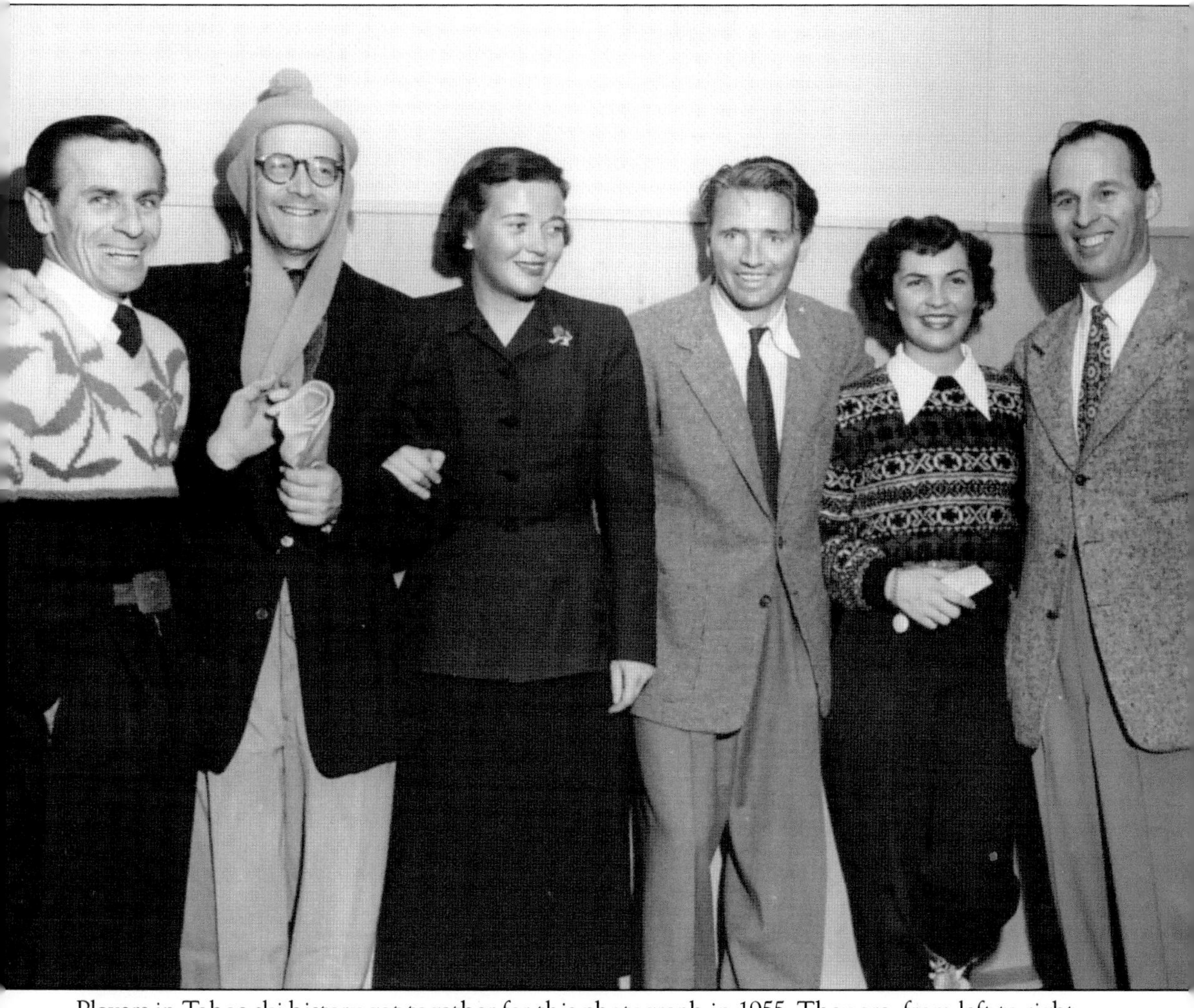

Players in Tahoe ski history got together for this photograph in 1955. They are, from left to right, Larry Gratz Powers, Paul Speegle, Dodie Post, Emile Allais, Shirley Russell, and Eric Johnson. Powers and Allais ran influential ski schools at Donner Ski Ranch and Squaw Valley respectively. Dodie Post Gann, born and raised in Reno, raced for the Reno Ski Club. She won the prestigious Silver Belt at Sugar Bowl and the challenging Silver Dollar Derby at Mount Rose. Gann was captain of the 1948 US Olympic ski team and team manager of the 1956 US women's Olympic alpine team. Gann, chosen by Allais as one of only four ski instructors hired for the first season at Squaw Valley, was the first woman elected to the University of Nevada, Reno, Hall of Fame and is a member of the US Ski Hall of Fame. Speegle humorously emceed many ski club banquets, while Johnson was a talented cartoonist and member of the Oakland Ski Club. Russell was crowned Oakland Ski Club Ski Queen in 1952. (Courtesy Donner Summit Historical Society/ Norm Sayler collection.)

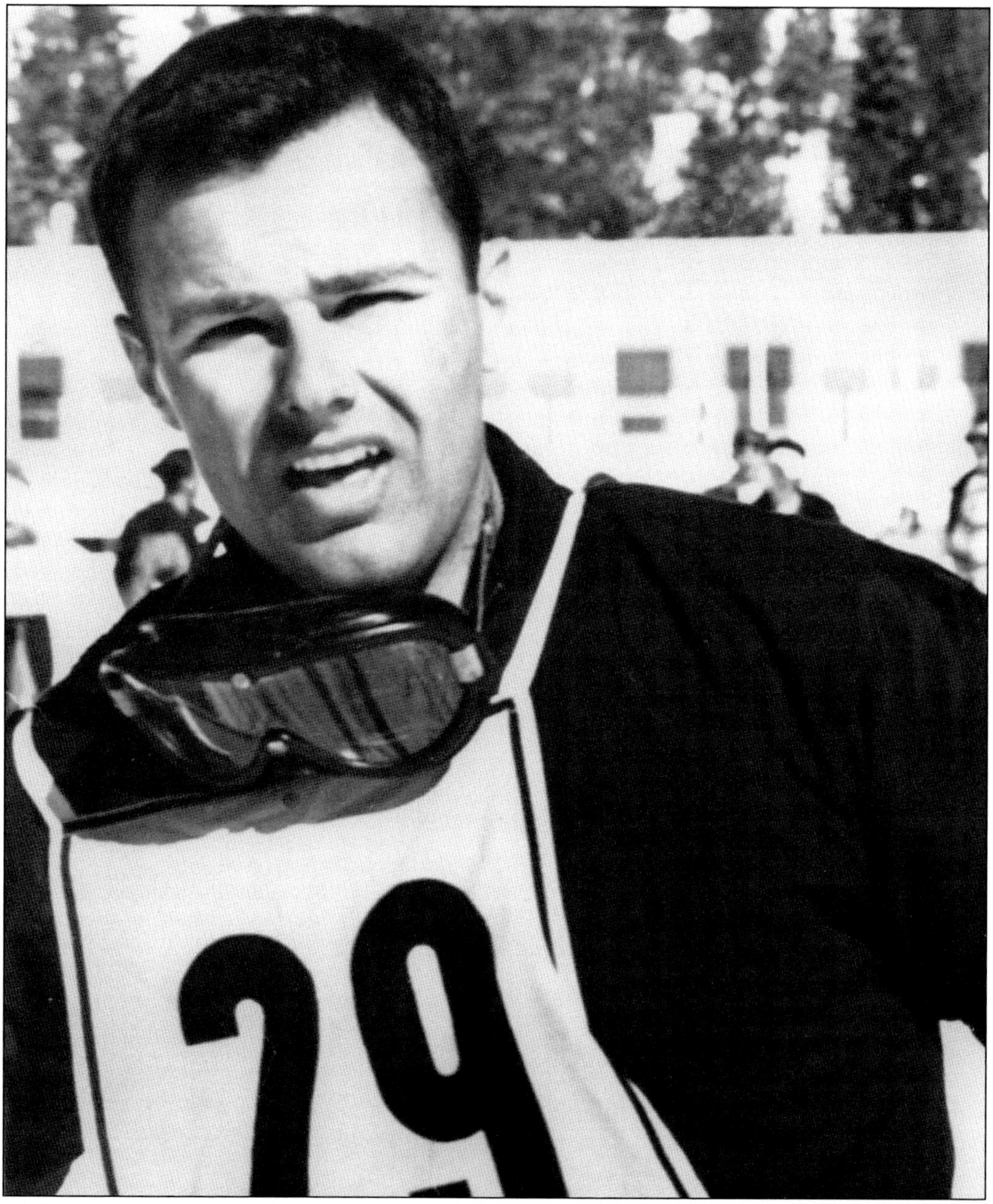

Dick Dorworth, a world-class mountaineer and alpine and speed skier, was born in Reno and raised at Zephyr Cove, Nevada, near South Lake Tahoe. While at the University of Nevada in the 1950s, he won an award as the best four-event skier (alpine, slalom, jumping, and cross-country). Dorworth competed in the 1959 National Ski Championships at Squaw Valley, placing second in slalom and third in alpine combined. In 1962, he was named to the All American Ski Team and the US Olympic training team. The next year, Dorworth set a world speed-skiing record of 106.8 miles per hour. His good friend from Lake Tahoe, Steve McKinney, later set multiple world records and eventually reached nearly 125 miles per hour. Dorworth taught and coached skiing until the mid-1990s while also becoming one of America's legendary mountain climbers. (Courtesy Nevada Historical Society.)

*Eight*

# Bring on the Winter Olympics!

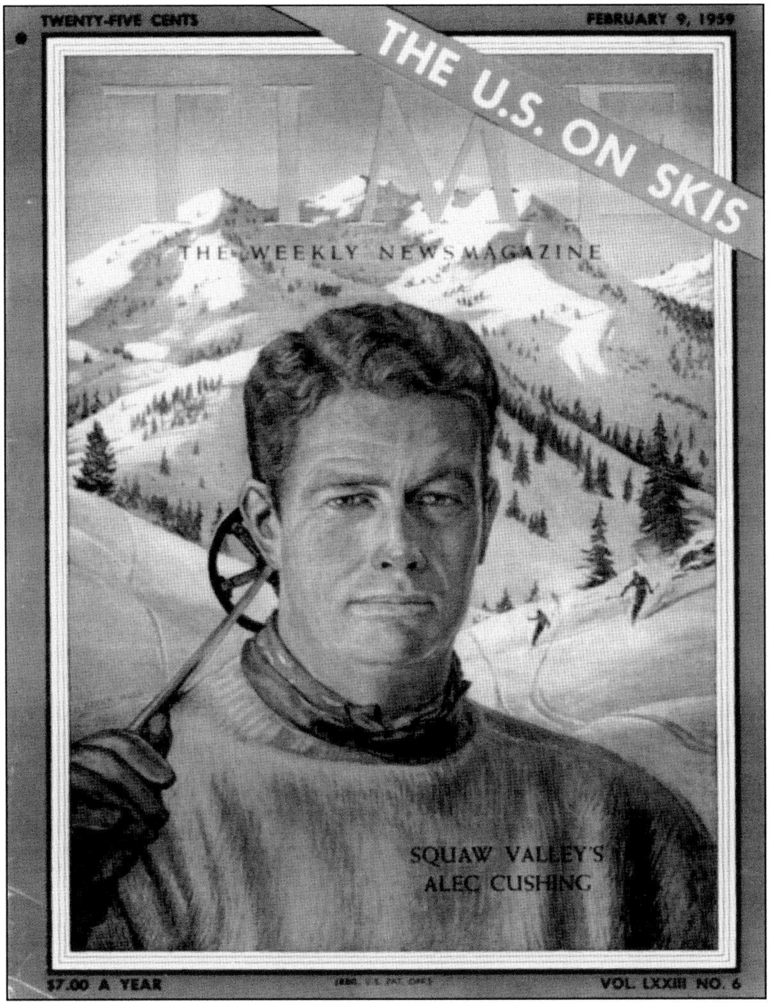


When Alexander Cushing, president of Squaw Valley Ski Corporation, came out of nowhere to boldly snatch the 1960 Winter Olympic Games away from Innsbruck, Austria, the news generated shock and disbelief. Cushing employed savvy marketing tools and marshaled strong public and political support to perform a minor miracle that steered the VIII Winter Games to a little-known alpine valley near Lake Tahoe, California. (Courtesy Squaw Valley USA.)

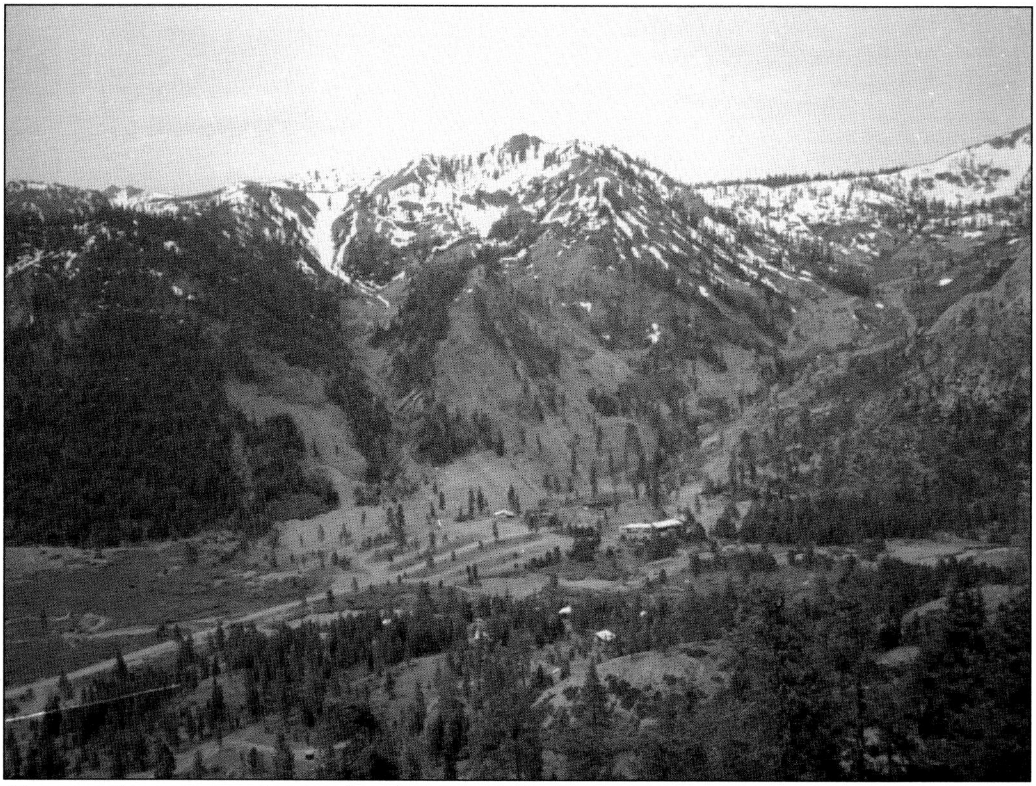

Choosing the remote and undeveloped Squaw Valley to represent America's bid was a risky decision that led International Olympic Committee president Avery Brundage to observe that the US committee "had obviously taken leave of their senses." John Garland, a US Olympic delegate, told Alex Cushing, "I think you are on a wild goose chase." (Courtesy Bill Briner collection.)

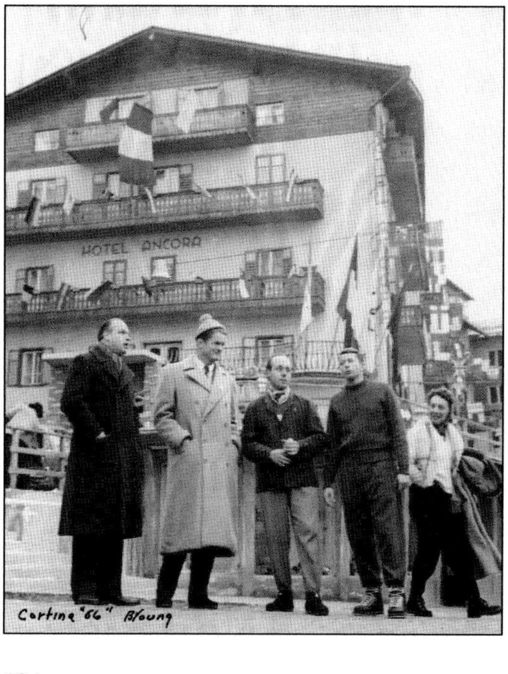


Despite all the naysayers, Cushing pushed ahead with his proposal to land the 1960 Winter Olympic Games. Cushing, second from left among unidentified Olympic committee delegates in Cortina, Italy, pointed out that Squaw Valley was located in the heavy Sierra snow zone. He also pointed out to the non-European countries in South America and the Pacific Rim that since 1891, all but one Winter Olympics had been held in Europe. (Courtesy Donner Summit Historical Society/Norm Sayler collection.)

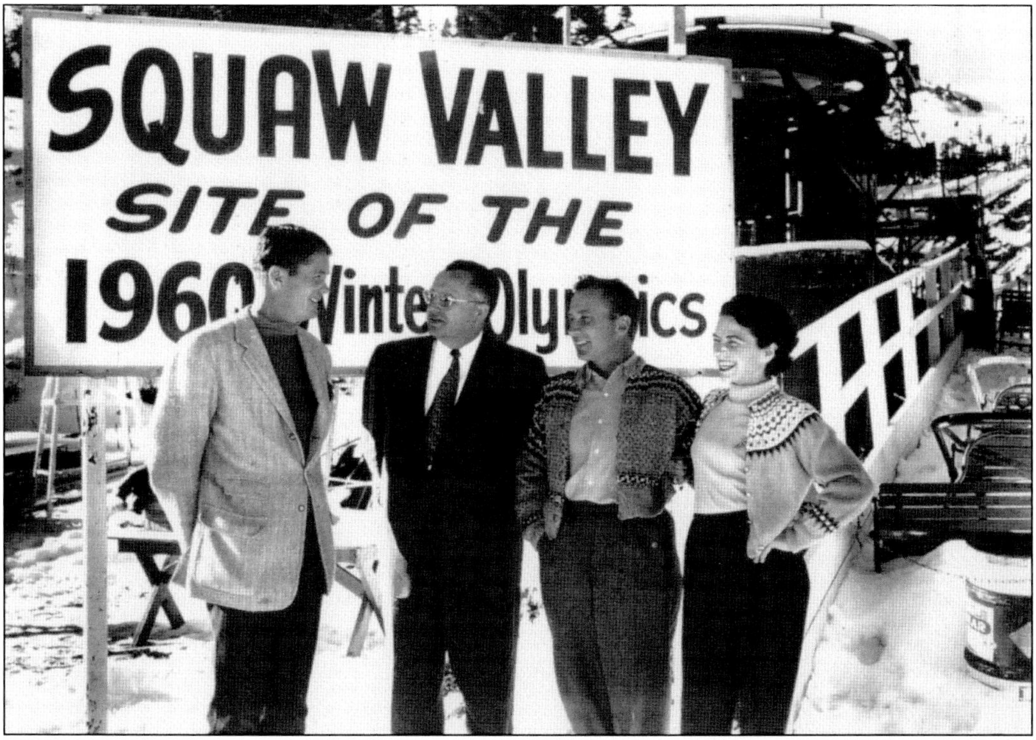


Despite the acrimonious breakup of their business partnership, Alex Cushing and Wayne Poulsen displayed professional enthusiasm in welcoming the Olympics. Pictured here are, from left to right, Cushing, California state senator Harold "Biz" Johnson, and Wayne and Sandy Poulsen. Senator Johnson and California's governor, Goodwin Knight, pushed through legislation that guaranteed $1 million to support Cushing's efforts—a small down payment on the ultimate $16-million price tag. (Courtesy Donner Summit Historical Society/Norm Sayler collection.)

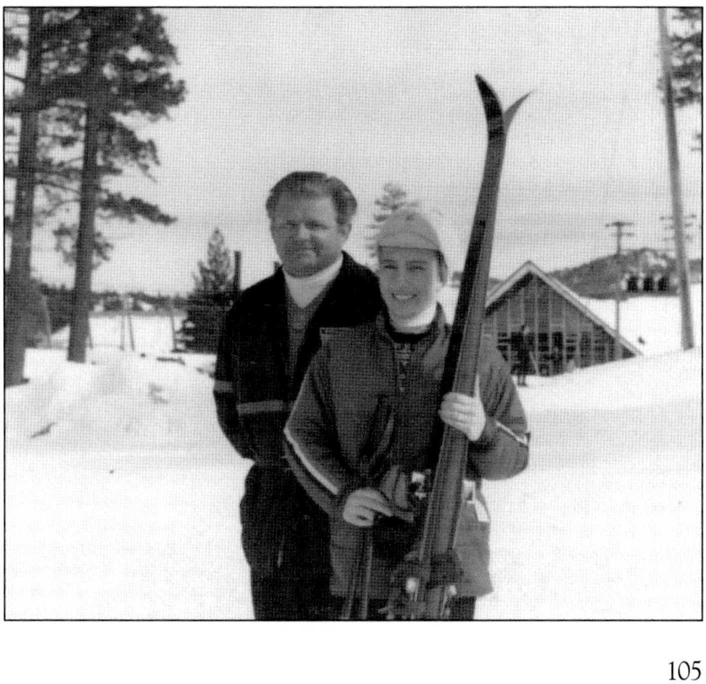

French-born Joseph "Jo" Marillac, shown here with budding ski champion Starr Walton (right), helped Alex Cushing convince the Europeans that Squaw Valley was a suitable venue for Olympic-caliber winter sports. As a noted skier, mountaineer, and respected World War II hero, Marillac's opinion was influential among European delegates. When the International Olympic Committee protested that Squaw Valley could not host an Olympics, Marillac said, "I'm here to tell you we can." (Courtesy Carson and Vi White collection.)

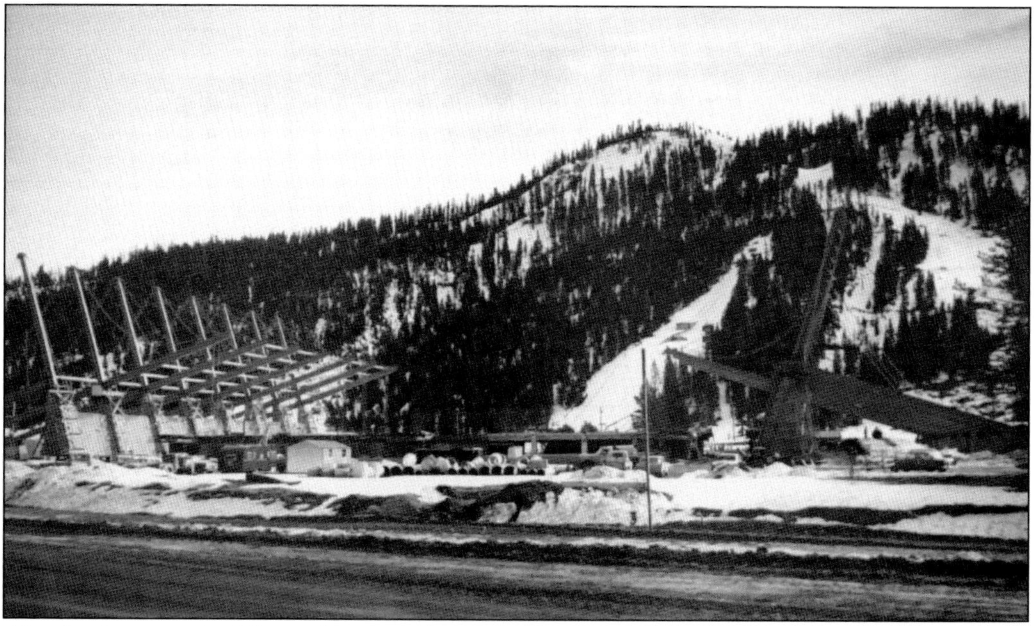

Alex Cushing got the Winter Olympics, but now Olympic-scale infrastructure and facilities had to be built from scratch and within four years. An Olympic Village was erected—the first and only time one was built adjacent to event venues. The Blyth Memorial Arena was a key structure. The arena had a design similar to a suspension bridge, with steel support cables that allowed sections to move. Blyth could seat 9,000 spectators, with unobstructed views of the figure skating and hockey competitions. (Courtesy Nevada Historical Society.)

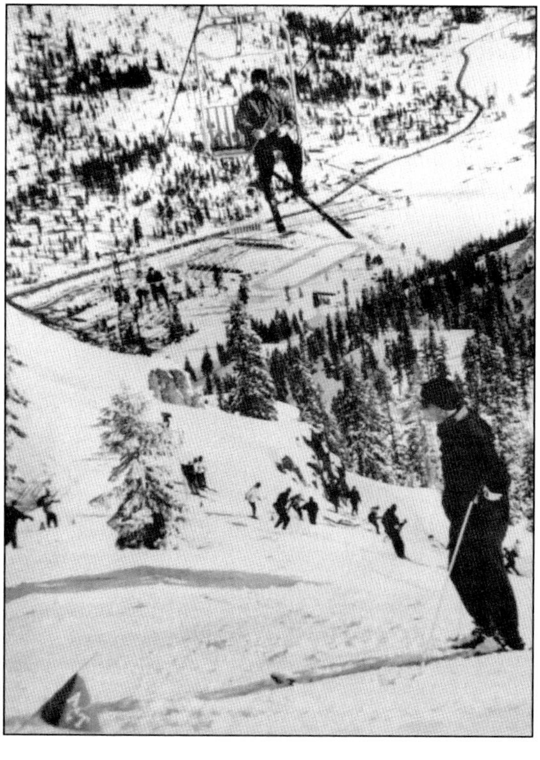

In 1957, construction began on three new double chairlifts to augment the existing system. With the addition of new lifts and ski runs, Squaw Valley suddenly became the largest ski center in the Western Hemisphere. Excitement for the upcoming Olympics inspired more than 2,000 visitors a day to drive into the valley to check out the new state-of-the-art facilities. (Courtesy Nevada Historical Society.)

For the 1960 Winter Olympic Games, three ski jumps were engineered on the lower slope of Little Papoose Peak—at 40, 60, and 80 meters. Germany's Heini Klopfer, a member of the International Ski Federation Jumping Committee, designed the jump profiles. When skiers hit the take-off point, they flew at nearly 60 miles per hour. (Courtesy Carson & Vi White collection.)

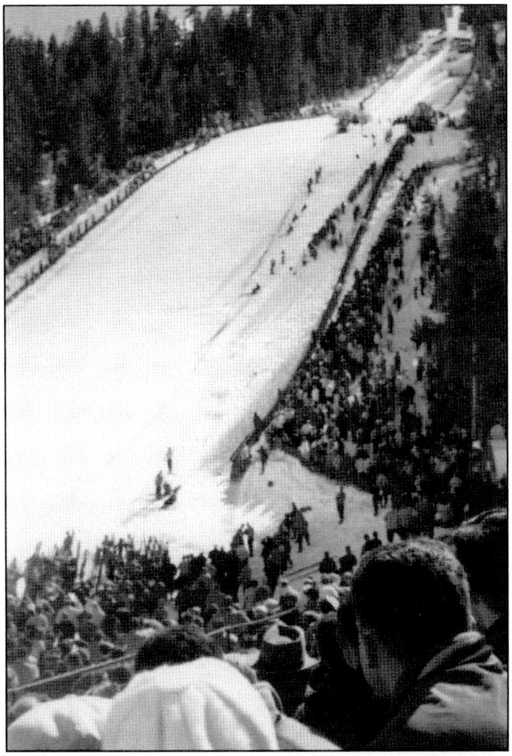

By the time Olympic organizers began to lay out cross-country competition venues, key terrain in Squaw Valley had been lost to private developers. Instead, Nordic events were held on the west shore of Lake Tahoe, near Tahoma (foreground). The 1960 Olympics were the first to host a biathlon, in which athletes ski a cross-country course and target shoot with rifles, as an official event. The 1960 Olympics were also the first time cross-country trails were mechanically groomed. (Courtesy Bill Briner collection.)

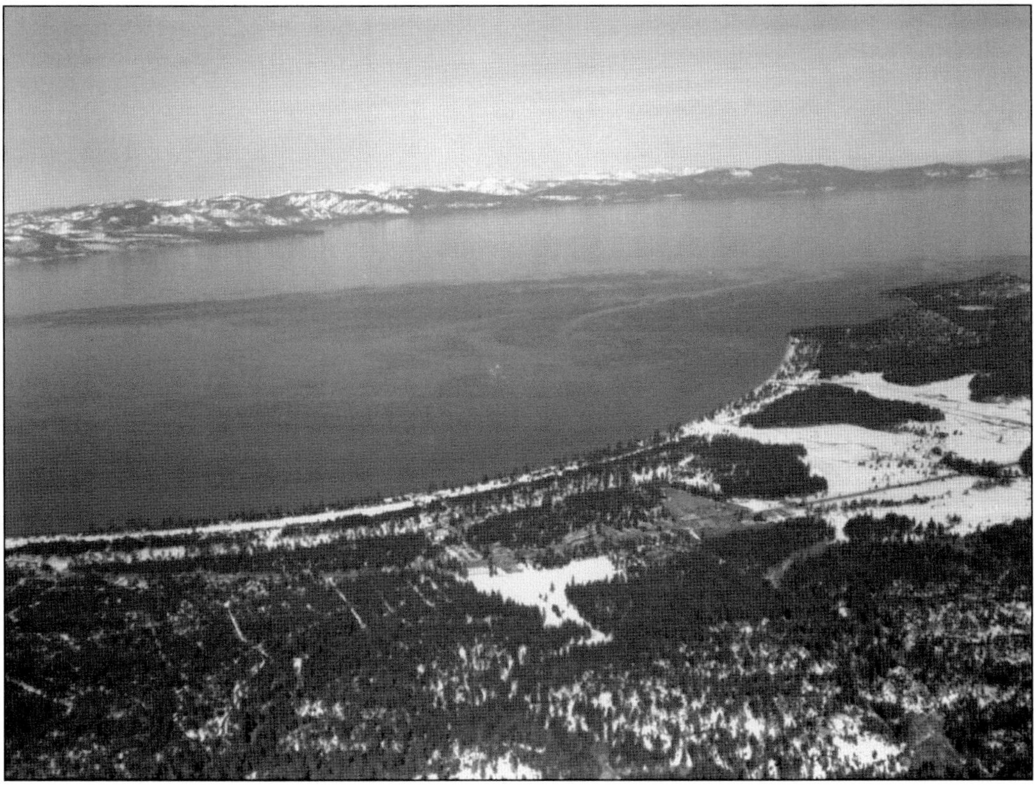

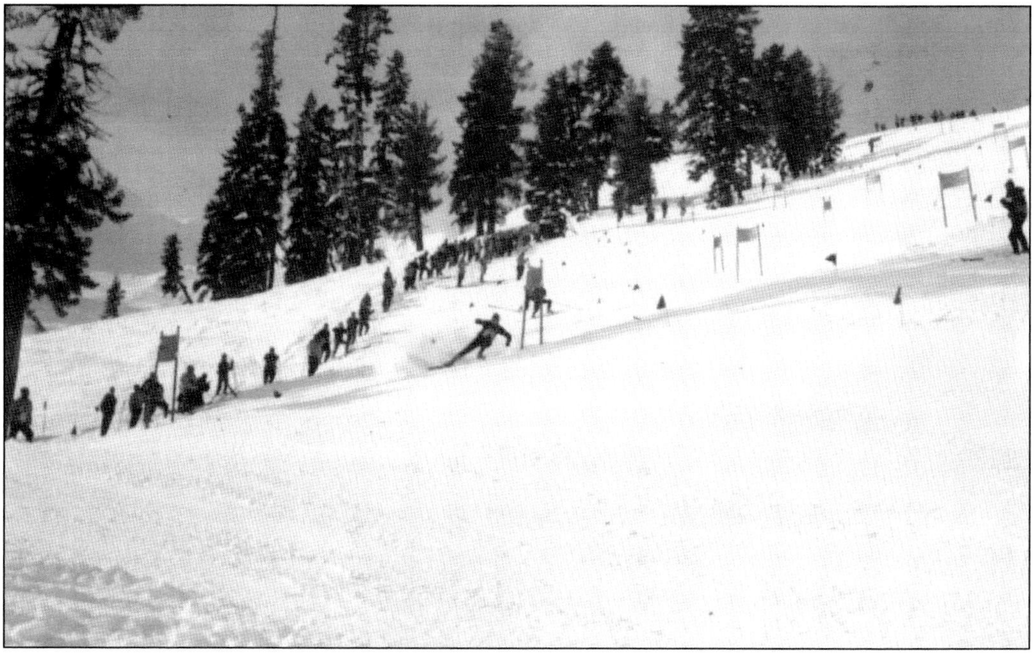

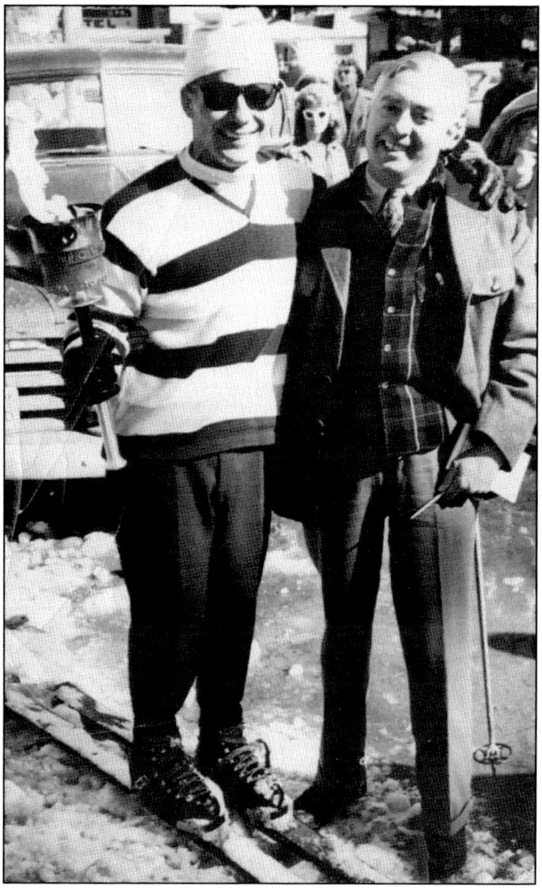

The alpine ski courses were designed under the expert supervision of Wilhelm "Willy" Schaeffler, a University of Denver ski coach and technical advisor for Olympic-level competitions. Although some critics attacked the alpine skiing venues on technicalities, the races were exciting and challenged the athletes. (Courtesy Carson & Vi White collection.)

Norm Sayler (left) is pictured with ski journalist William Berry after Sayler skied down from Donner Pass with the 1960 Olympic torch. Sayler passed the torch to cross-country skiers recruited from students at Tahoe-Truckee High School. So many people wanted to participate in the Olympic pageantry that the flame was hand-relayed to Squaw Valley by local residents. As the torch was passed, community pride soared at hosting the VIII Winter Games. (Courtesy Donner Summit Historical Society/Norm Sayler collection.)

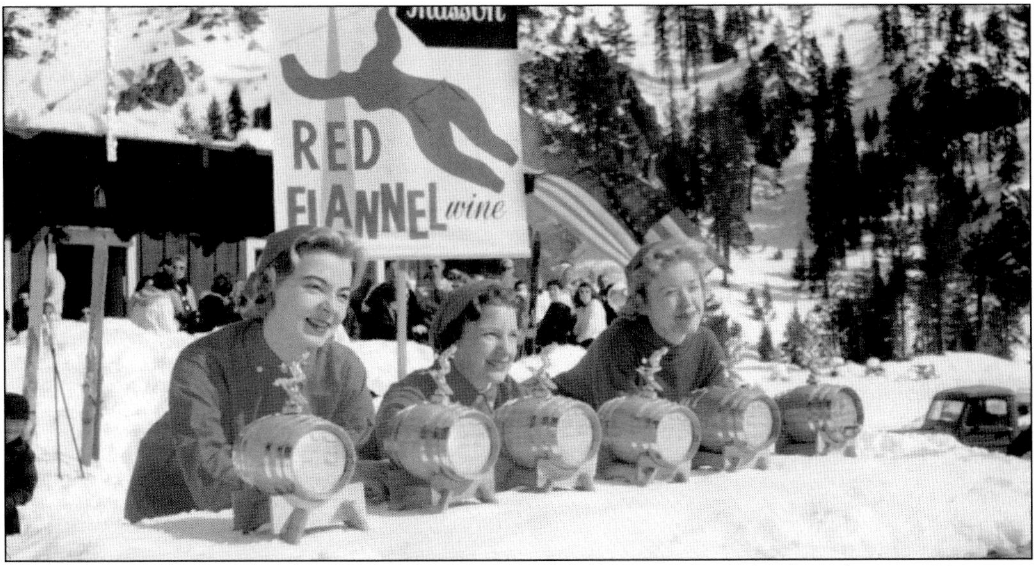


As a side attraction to the 1960 Winter Games, a winery sponsored the Barrel Stave Olympics. Early skis in California were often made from short, slightly curved slats designed for wooden barrels. Inspired by those early roots, Babette Haueisen, a longtime Tahoe ski instructor, and future Olympian Starr Walton brought the Olympic flame into Squaw Valley on barrel staves. The trophies for the Barrel Stave Olympics consisted of a large-banded cask topped with a statuette skiing on barrel staves. (Courtesy Mark McLaughlin.)

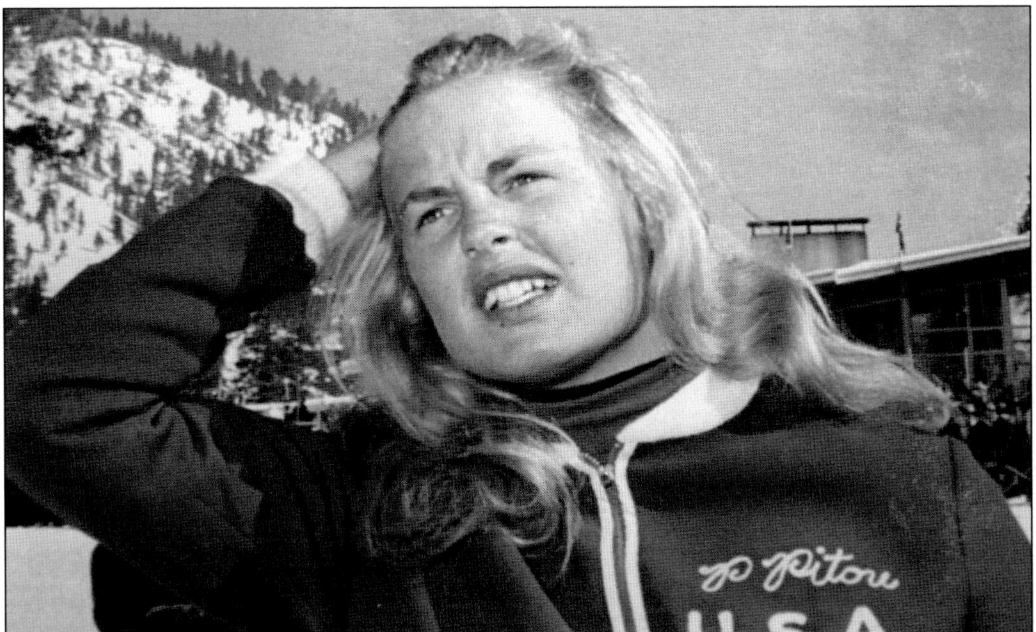


Penelope "Penny" Pitou, a 21-year-old from New Hampshire, grimaces after she missed a gold medal by 1.1 seconds. Because the US men's alpine ski team was decimated by injuries, Pitou was America's best chance in the Olympic downhill races. Despite a bad chest cold, she won a silver medal in the women's downhill and another silver in giant slalom. Pitou became the first American—male or female—to medal in the Olympic downhill event. (Courtesy Craig Beck collection.)

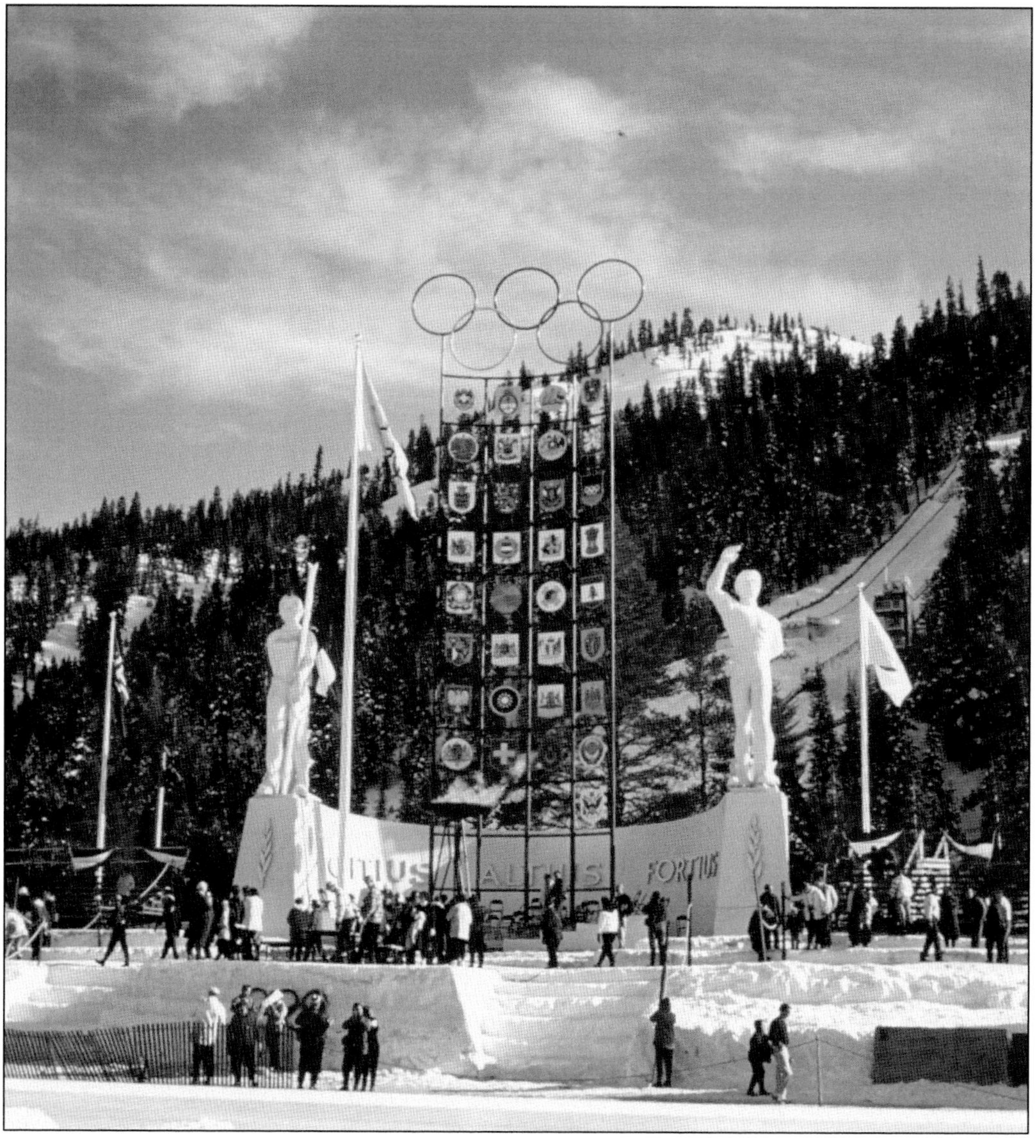

As the first Winter Games held on the west coast of North America, the 1960 Olympics were considered a great success. Never before had the games been shown live on television, and mechanized equipment was used for grooming both alpine and cross-country ski venues. In previous years, results from competitions could take hours to calculate and post, but in 1960, a mainframe computer crunched the numbers in a minute. Fully automated electronic timing in all sports increased accuracy, and mechanical refrigeration was used to freeze the speed skating oval for the first time; 1960 was also the first time women were allowed to compete in speed skating. When race officials asked CBS to replay the videotape to review a skier's possible missed gate, instant replay was invented. New equipment and techniques changed the sport of skiing when, for the first time, French racer Jean Vuarnet used metal/plastic/wood composite skis and an aerodynamic tuck position to win a gold medal in the alpine downhill event. (Courtesy Bill Briner collection.)

# *Nine*

# Lake Tahoe's Skiing Then and Now

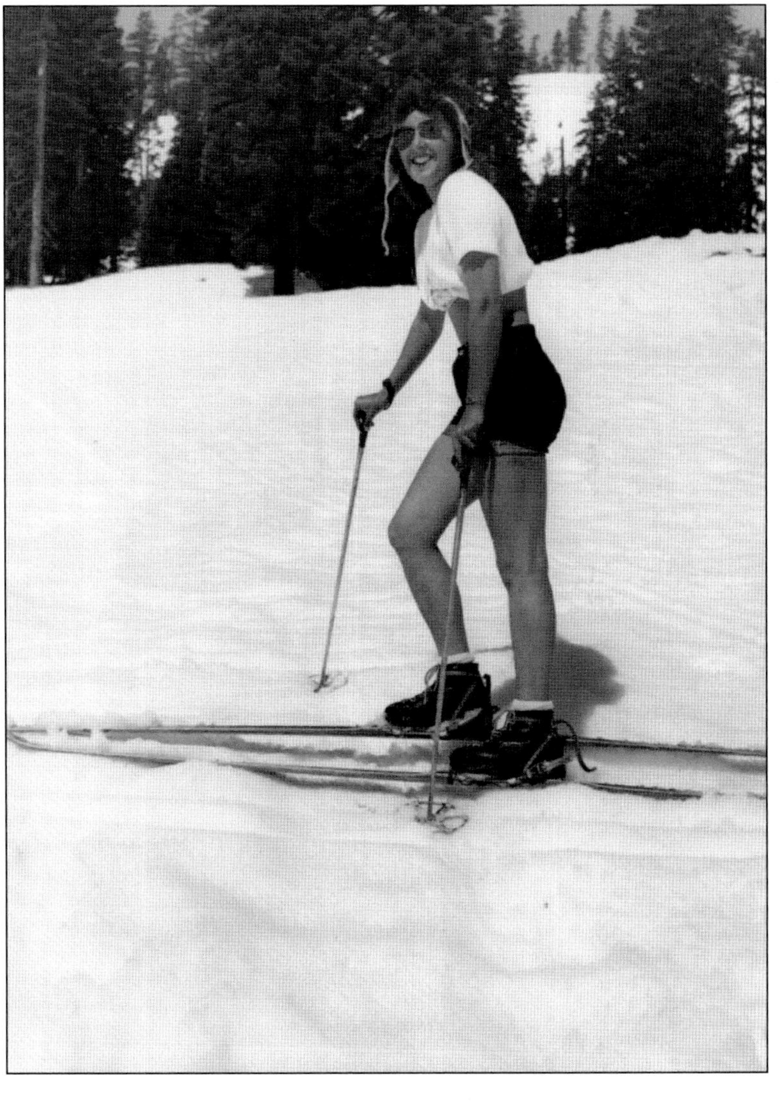

The 1960 Squaw Valley Winter Olympic Games propelled Lake Tahoe into the global limelight and spurred tremendous growth in winter sports—especially alpine skiing. The post-Olympics period launched several new ski areas in the North Tahoe region, including Alpine Meadows, Ski Incline (now Diamond Peak), Homewood, and the Tahoe Ski Bowl (the latter two are now combined as Homewood Mountain Resort). Winter tourism quickly grew upon the completion of Interstate 80, linking Sacramento with Reno. (Courtesy Donner Summit Historical Society/Norm Sayler collection.)

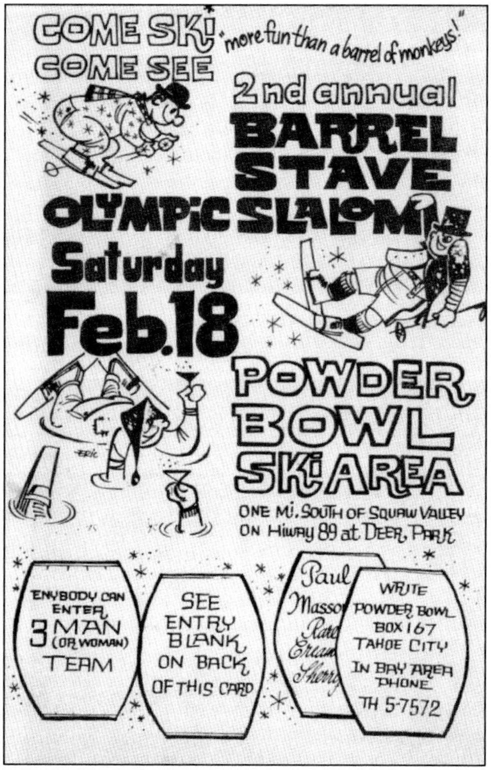


Now defunct, the Powder Bowl ski area (near the bottom of Alpine Meadows Road) opened in 1961. Until larger resorts eclipsed it, the Powder Bowl was legendary for wacky and zany events like the annual Barrel Stave Olympics, which pitted racers on short skis against each other. Often promoted and fueled by wineries or liquor distributors, skiing events at Deer Park were well attended by locals and always entertaining. (Courtesy Donner Summit Historical Society/Norm Sayler collection.)

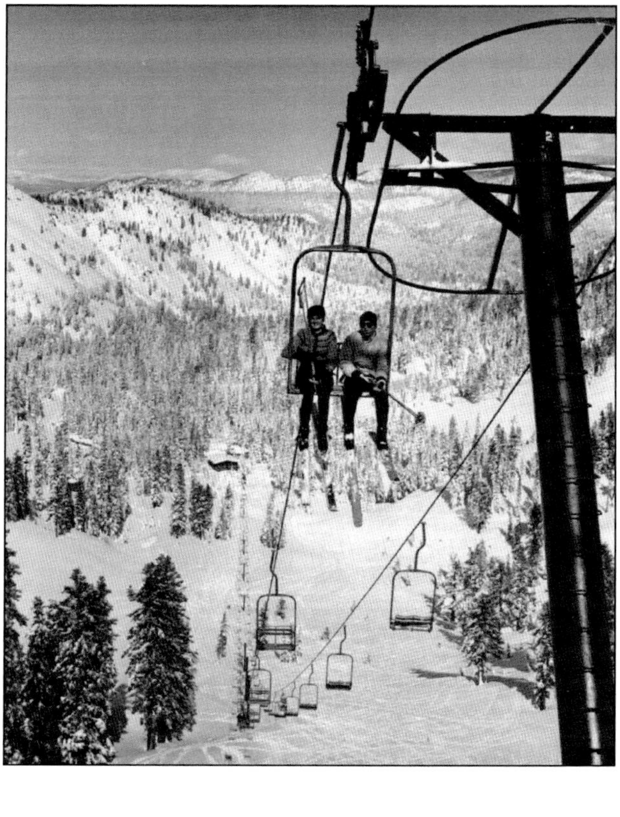

The Alpine Meadows ski area opened with three chairlifts on December 28, 1961. Founded by John Reilly, a successful businessman and skier, Alpine originated as a family-oriented ski resort. Reilly hired Harvard Business School graduate Peter Klaussen to help design the slopes and build an access road connecting the valley to Highway 89. (Courtesy Donner Summit Historical Society/ Norm Sayler collection.)

TV entertainer Art Linkletter (right), pictured with an unidentified fan, often skied Alpine Meadows. In 1960, a group of San Francisco families pooled their resources to open the wide-open powder bowls and abundant tree skiing just south of Squaw Valley. In December 1963, ski instructor Werner Shuster was hired by Luggi Foeger, director of Alpine's ski school. Shuster intended to work one season but ended up taking over the school and staying for another 40 years. Tahoe skier Darian Boyle is pictured below at Alpine Meadows. (Right, courtesy Donner Summit Historical Society/ Norm Sayler collection; below, courtesy Keoki Flagg.)

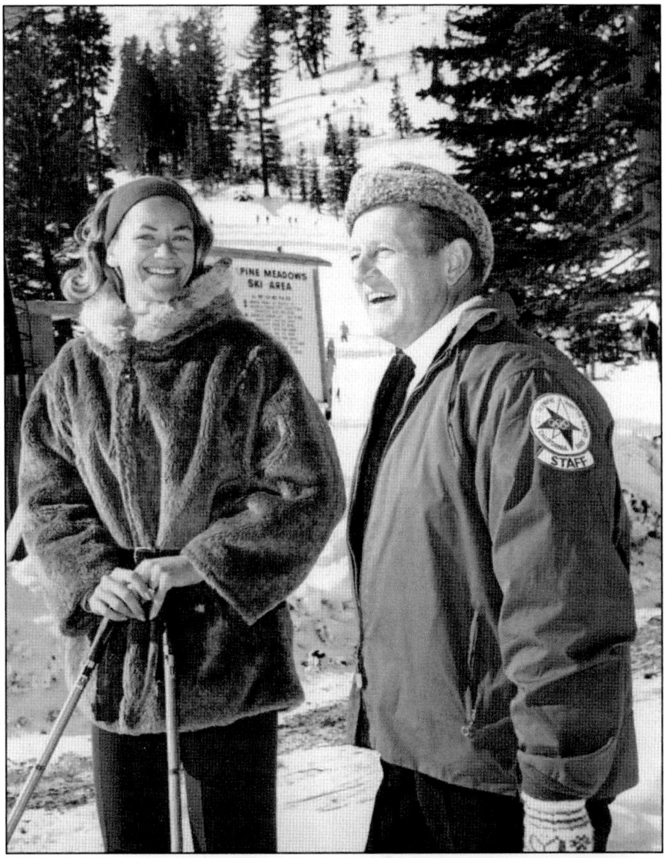


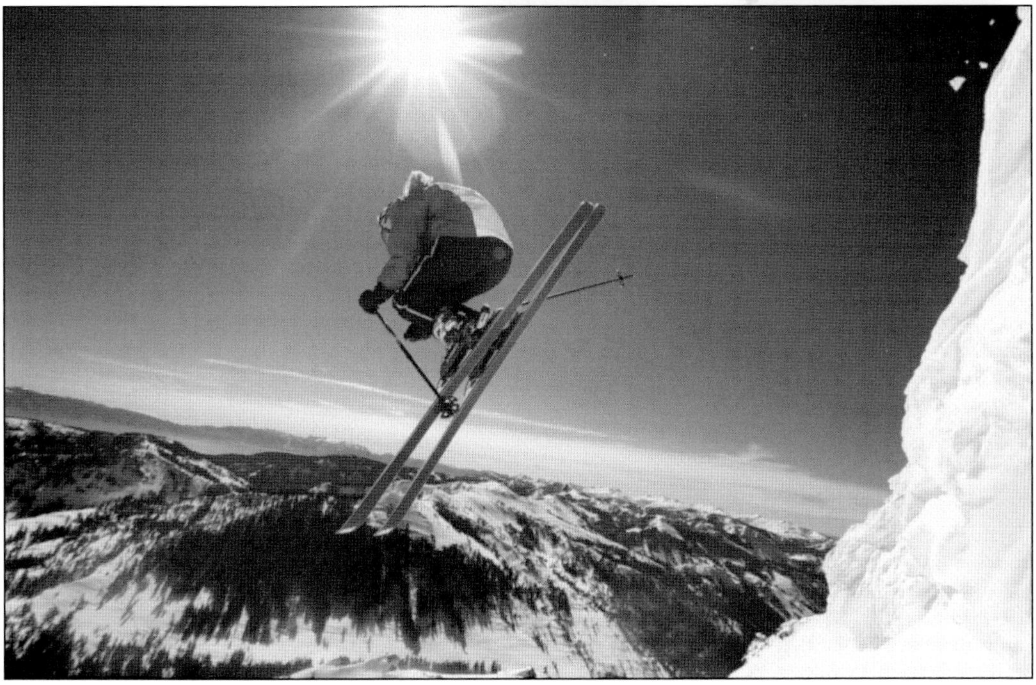

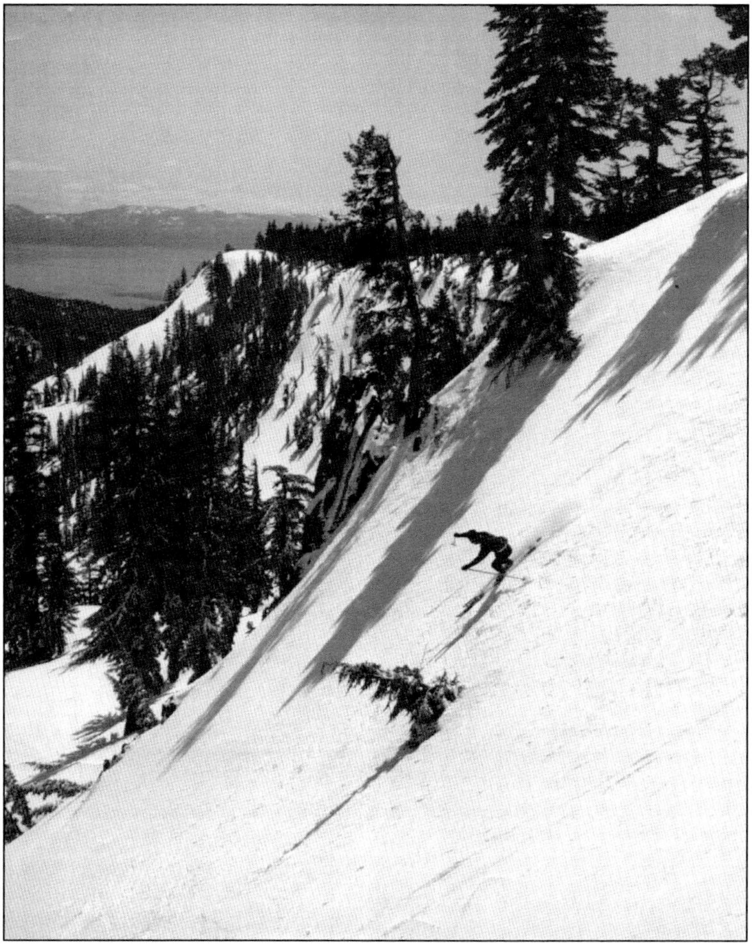

Designed by skiers for skiers, Alpine Meadows offered an alternative to its fast-paced neighbor Squaw Valley USA. During the 1940s, Wayne Poulsen, the primary landowner and original partner with Alexander Cushing in the Squaw Valley Development Corporation, had considered developing Alpine Meadows, but Poulsen thought that an access road into Alpine would be too dangerous due to avalanche hazards. Squaw Valley and Alpine Meadows merged in October 2011. (Courtesy Donner Summit Historical Society/Norm Sayler collection.)

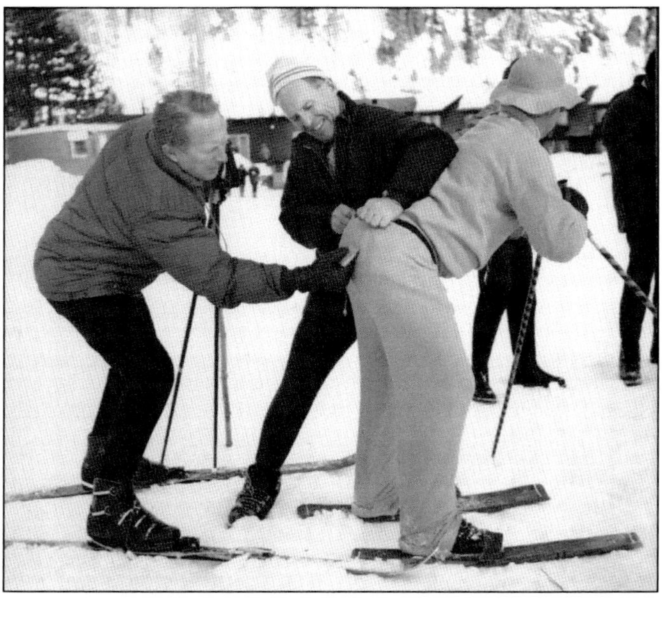

Tahoe resorts have had a long history of innovative skiing events and programs. In this image from the Deer Park Powder Bowl in the early 1960s, a contestant in a barrel-stave racing competition gets some help with his equipment from TV personality Art Linkletter (left) and an unidentified assistant. (Note the racer's short skis.) Alpine Meadows has long been involved with programs like the Tahoe Adaptive Ski School, which helps disabled individuals hit the slopes using adaptive equipment. (Courtesy Donner Summit Historical Society/ Norm Sayler collection.)

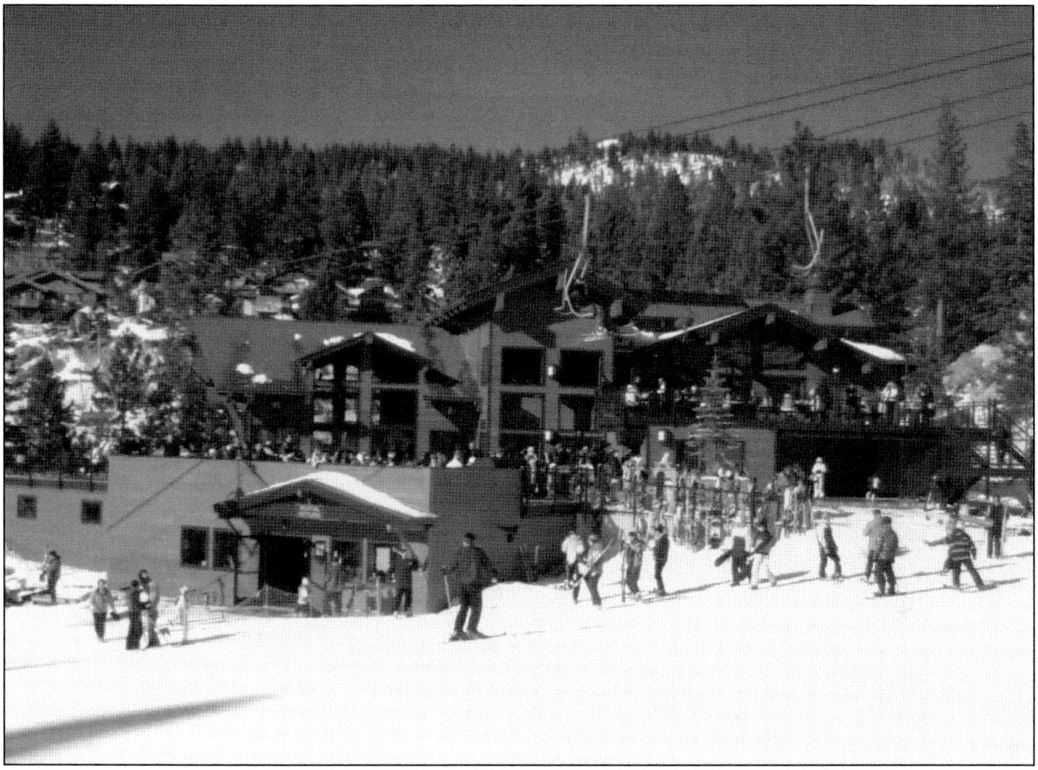

For 30 years after the 1929 stock market crash, Capt. George Whittell, a San Francisco real estate tycoon, owned most of the Nevada side of Lake Tahoe. In 1960, Whittell sold 9,000 acres of land to Art Wood, a developer who built Incline Village, Nevada. The master plan for this vacation resort included a new ski area called Ski Incline. The word "incline" refers to a 19th-century logging operation that hauled lumber up a nearby mountainside. (Courtesy Diamond Peak Ski Resort.)

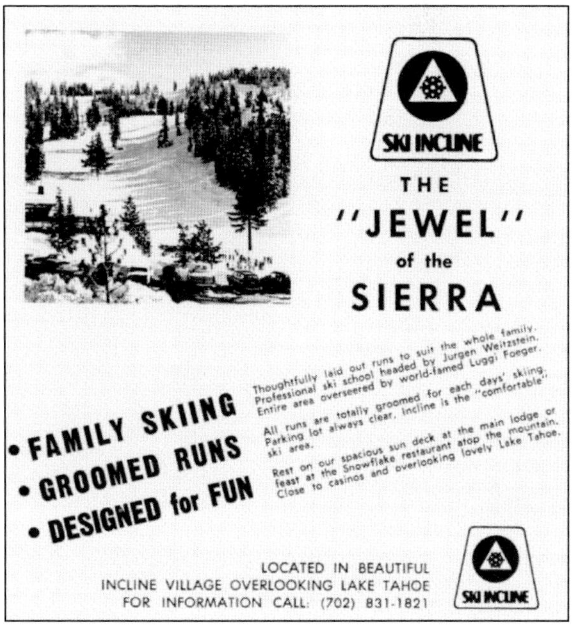


Ski Incline showcases well-groomed ski runs and stunning views of Lake Tahoe. It was fortunate that developer Art Wood hired Luggi Foeger to look over the initial layout of the new ski area, because Foeger told Wood that the location was all wrong from a skier's perspective. Worst of all, the slopes faced south instead of north, which better protected the snow. Foeger found a better location at the present-day site of Diamond Peak. (Courtesy Mark McLaughlin.)

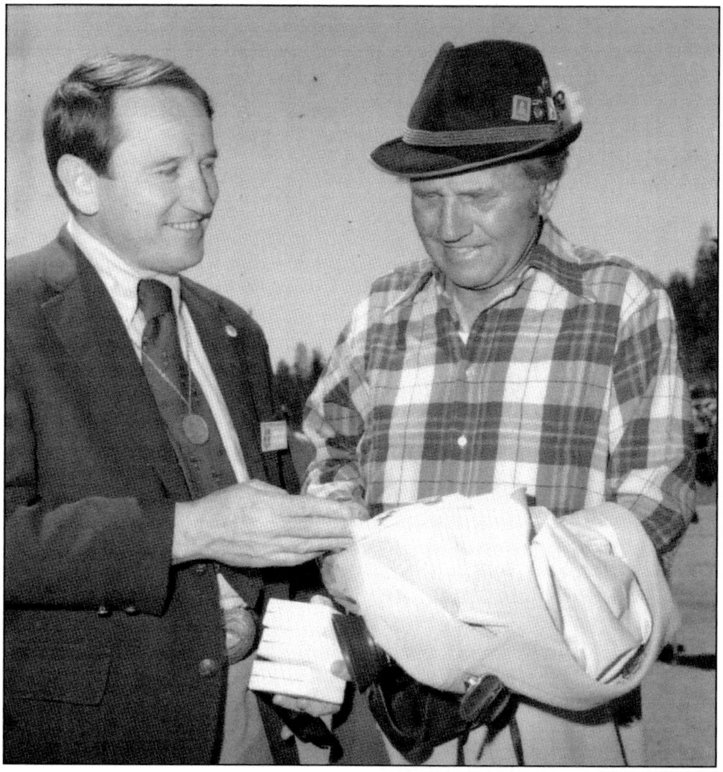

Far West Skiing Association historian John Watson (left) recognized Luggi Foeger's contributions to skiing at the Snowshoe Thompson statue dedication ceremony at the Boreal ski area in 1976. Foeger headed ski schools at Badger Pass, Sugar Bowl, and Alpine Meadows. He also helped design Northstar-at-Tahoe and Diamond Peak. A member of the 10th Mountain Division, Foeger was also elected to the prestigious National Ski Hall of Fame. (Courtesy William B. Berry collection.)

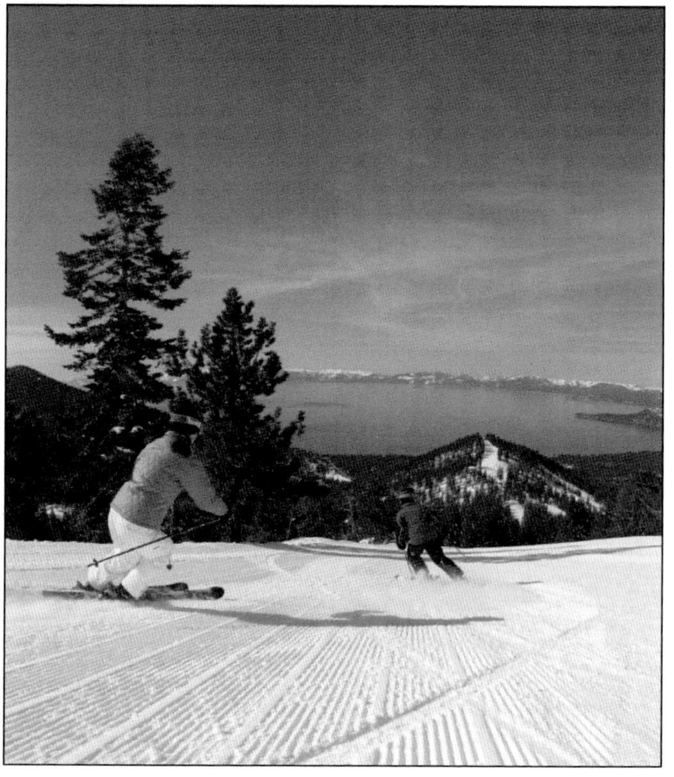

Luggi Foeger designed Ski Incline "to provide a pleasurable experience in the wintertime for the whole family." The resort was the first in the West to utilize a snowmaking system. Future improvements added more chairlifts and expanded snowmaking capability. In 1987, under the direction of ski resort manager Jurgen Wetzstein, the area doubled in size and was renamed Diamond Peak (for the addition of more advanced runs on the new upper mountain). (Courtesy Diamond Peak/ Jeff Engerbretson.)

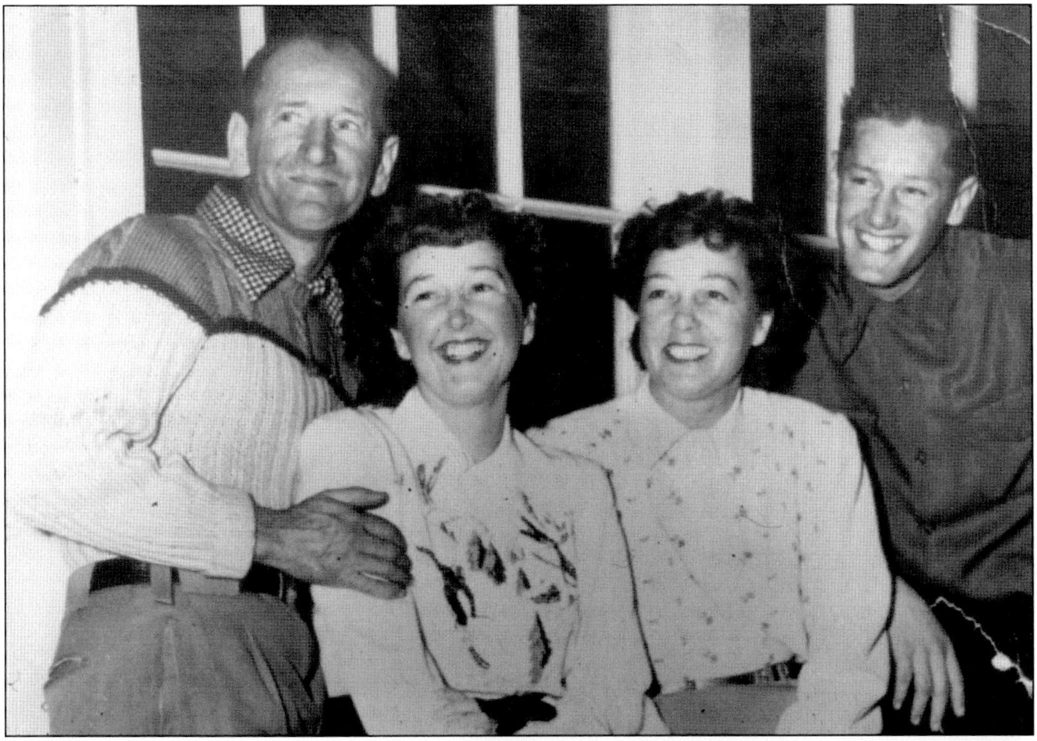

The c. 1950 image above shows the Buek family, an iconic skiing clan from Donner Summit. From left to right are Carl, Gladys, Jean, and Richard ("Dick"). At right, Carl Buek, who ran his own ski school at the Soda Springs ski hill, gets "skewered" by Johnny Fountain (left). Dick Buek, or "Mad Dog of Donner Summit," was one of the most aggressive ski racers in American history. A two-time national downhill champion, he won his second title in 1954, just one year after nearly dying in a motorcycle crash. A member of the 1952 Olympic team, Dick was one of four Olympians to hail from the summit—the others were Hannes Schroll (1932), Dennis Jones (1936), and Jones's niece, Starr Walton (1964). Dick Buek's extreme skiing attracted national attention to Donner Summit. Dick Buek, who died in 1957 when his plane crashed into Donner Lake, was inducted into the US National Ski Hall of Fame in 1974. (Both, courtesy Donner Summit Historical Society/Norm Sayler collection.)

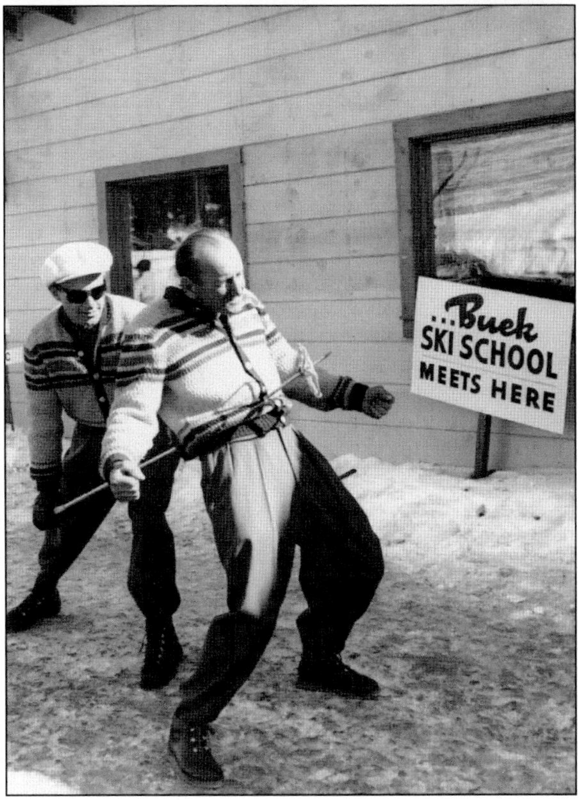

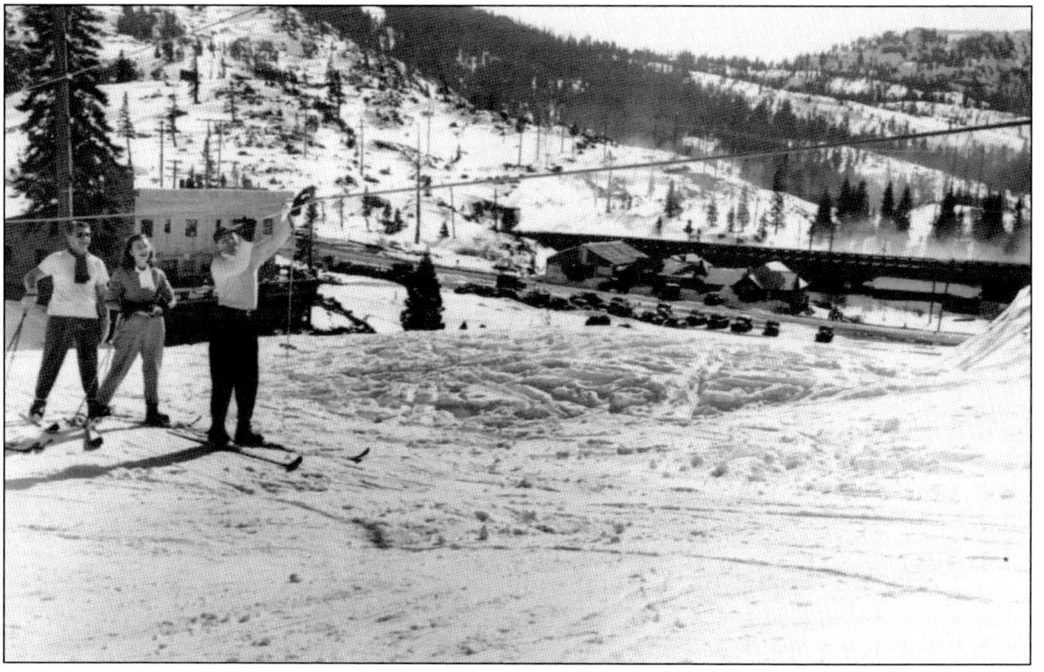

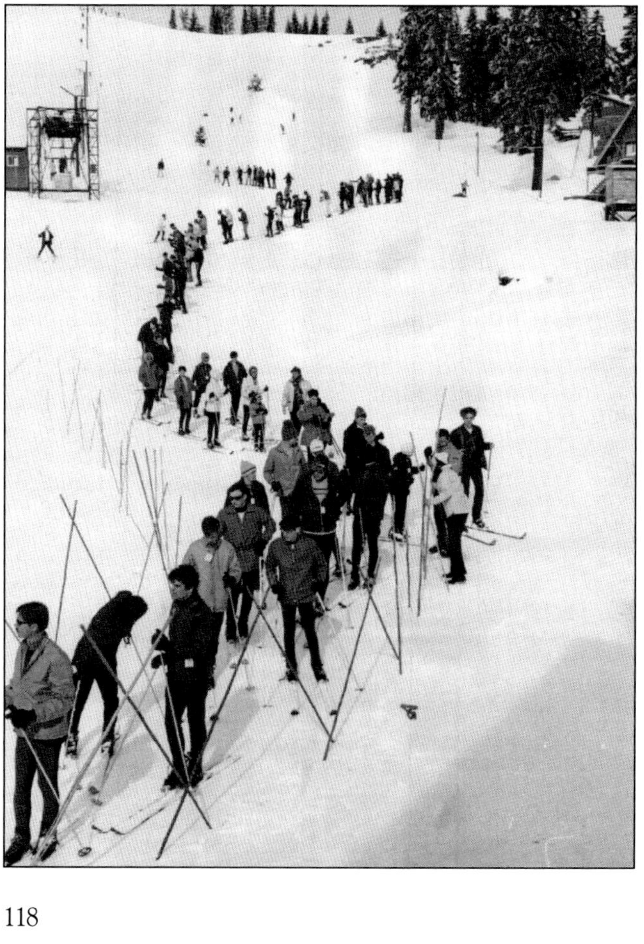

In this c. 1947 image, a Donner Ski Ranch instructor shows students how to use the rope tow grippers on their ski poles to latch onto the moving rope tow. Note the Southern Pacific Railroad wooden snowshed in the middle background, across US Highway 40. The Sugar Bowl ski area is in the far background. (Courtesy Donner Summit Historical Society/Norm Sayler collection.)

Long lift lines like this one at Donner Ski Ranch during the 1960s are the bane of every skier. Fortunately, new chairlift technologies like high-speed detachable chairs, along with larger lift chairs that seat more skiers, now move skiers and snowboarders up the mountain in greater numbers, reducing the wait to ride a lift. (Courtesy Donner Summit Historical Society/Norm Sayler collection.)

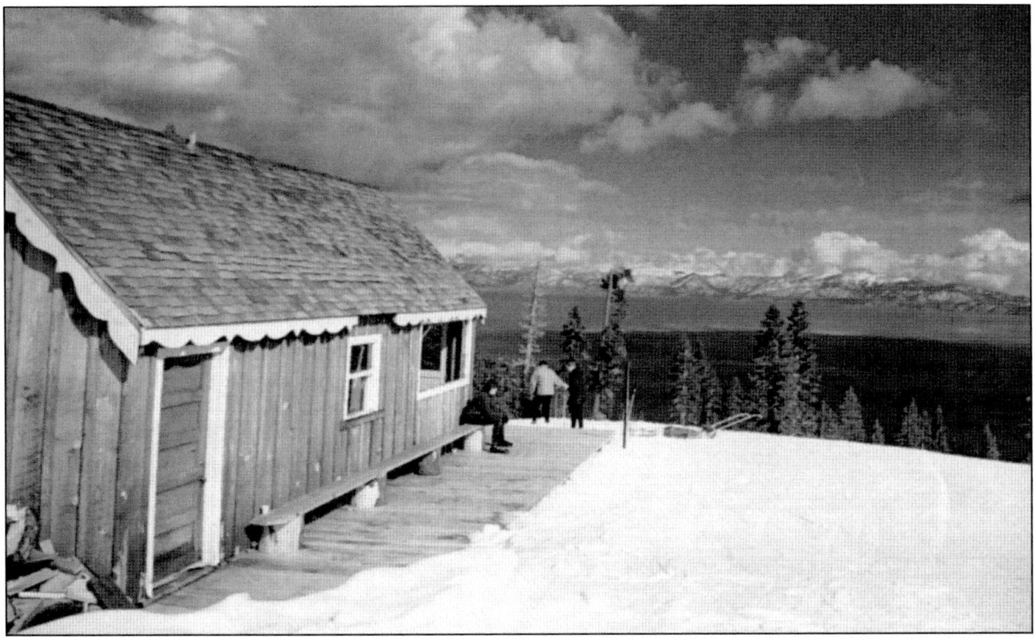

In 1961, Ron Rupp and some friends set up a rope tow in the Homewood neighborhood, on Lake Tahoe's west shore. The following year, Helen Alrich, whose family was invested in a profitable paper company, purchased the ski area and Homewood Hotel. In 1987, Alrich bought the Tahoe Ski Bowl, located a mile south of the Homewood operation, and combined the two areas into Homewood Mountain Resort. (Both, courtesy Homewood Mountain Resort.)

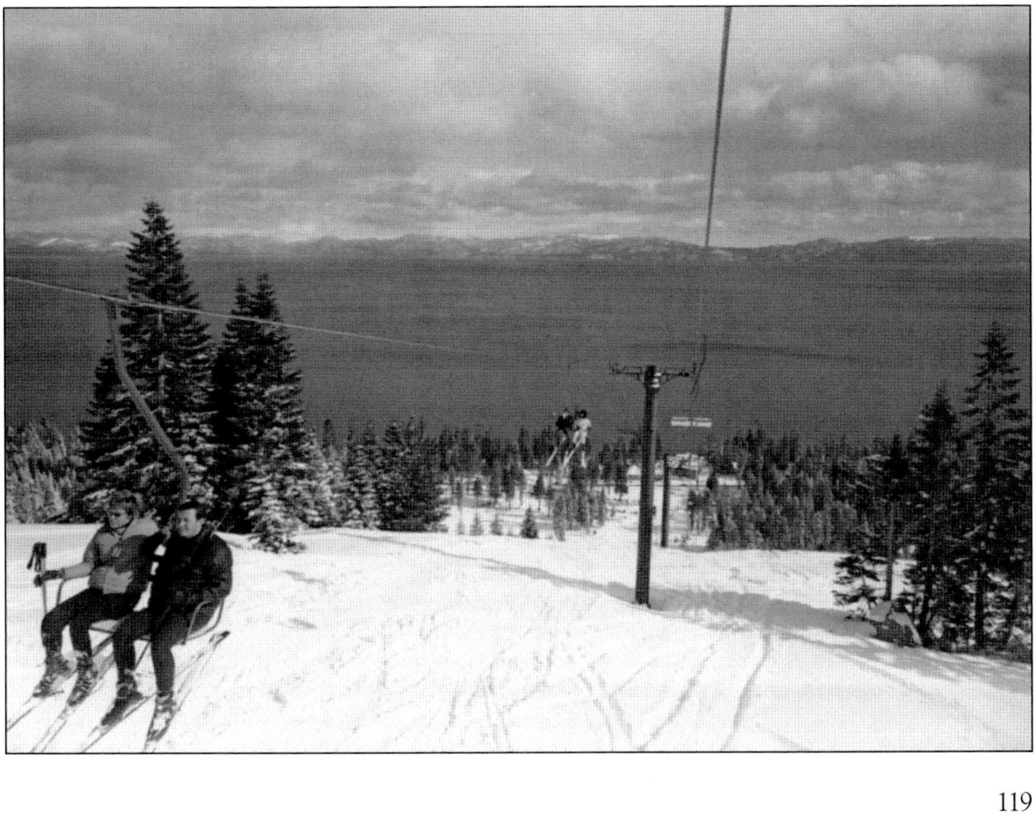

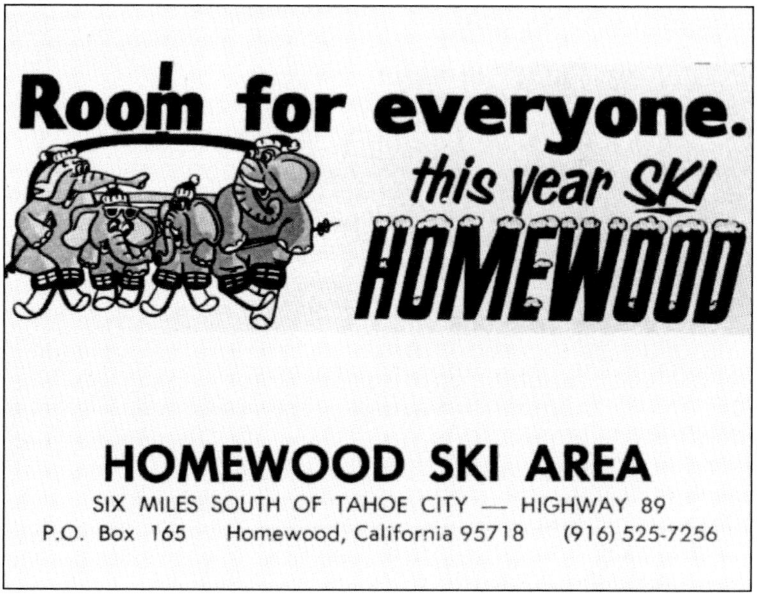


To improve the resort's skiing experience, Homewood added a new quad to its uphill lift system in 1973. Homewood Mountain Resort, a locals' favorite, is often protected from wind during major winter storms and offers some of the best lake views in Tahoe. (Courtesy Mark McLaughlin.)

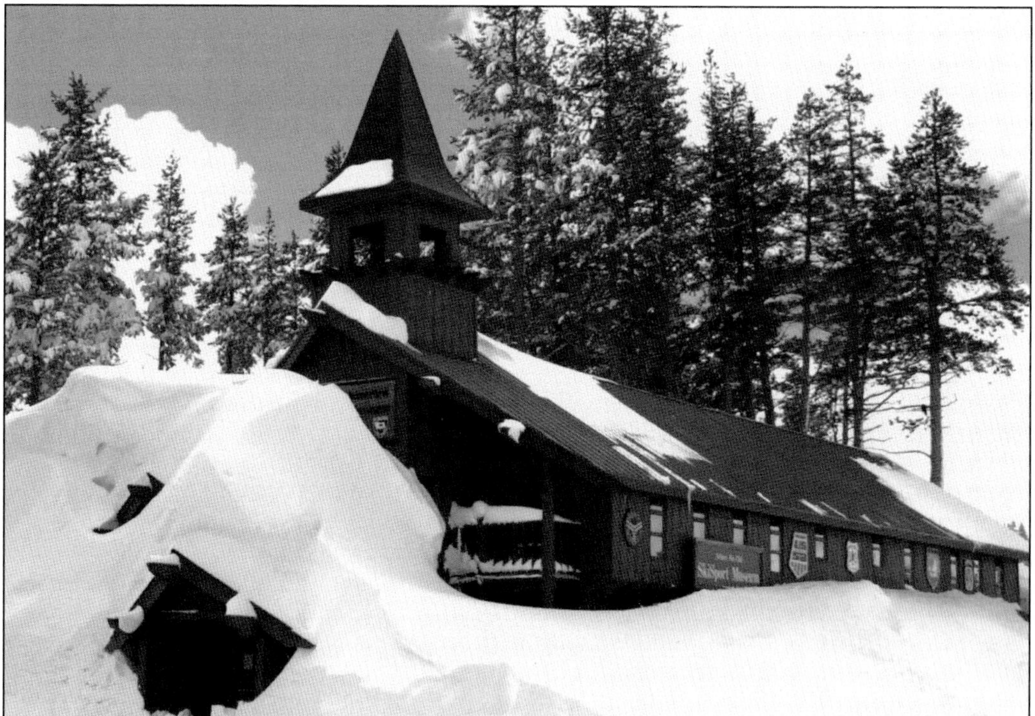


The Western SkiSport Museum is located on Interstate 80 at Boreal Mountain Resort. Founded in 1969 by the Auburn Ski Club, the museum features the collection of ski historian William B. Berry and includes John "Snowshoe" Thompson memorabilia as well as images and artifacts from the longboard racing era, the 10th Mountain Division, and much more. (Courtesy Mark McLaughlin.)

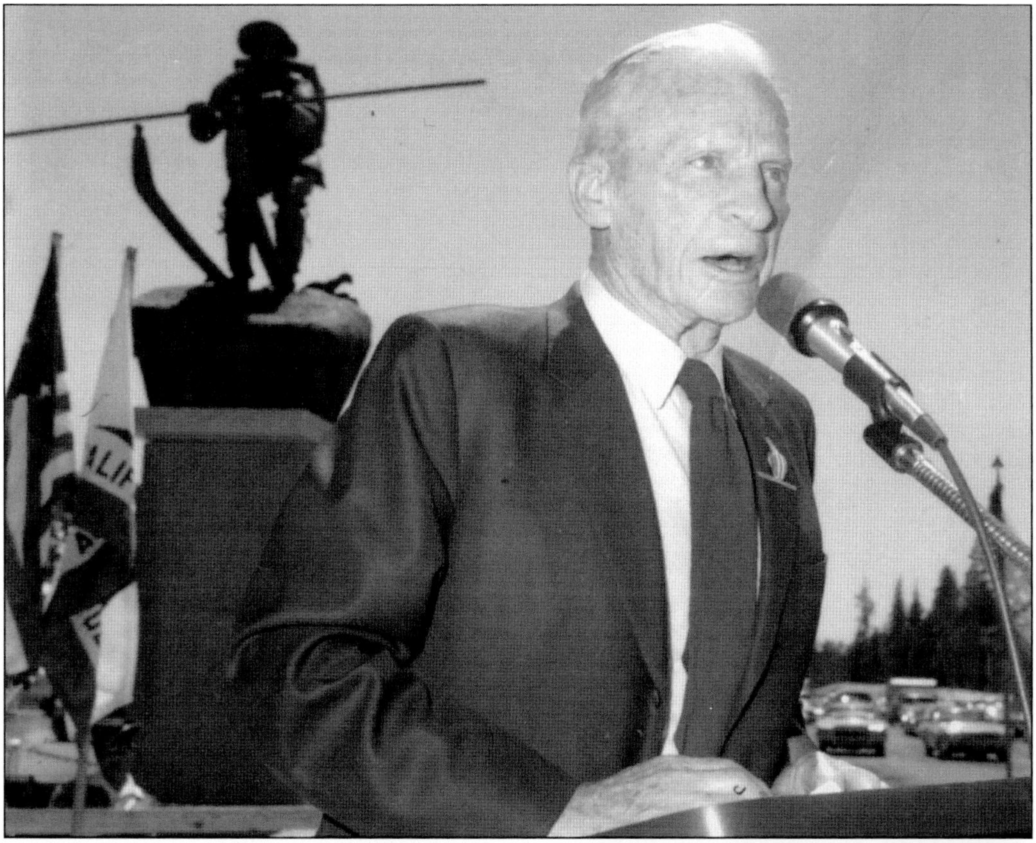

Wendell T. Robie was the driving force behind the Auburn Ski Club's grassroots effort to establish ski clubs, jumps, and warming huts in the central Sierra in the decade before World War II. In 1976, he addressed 1,000 people who gathered at Boreal Mountain Resort to celebrate the dedication of the new Snowshoe Thompson statue. (Courtesy William B. Berry collection.)

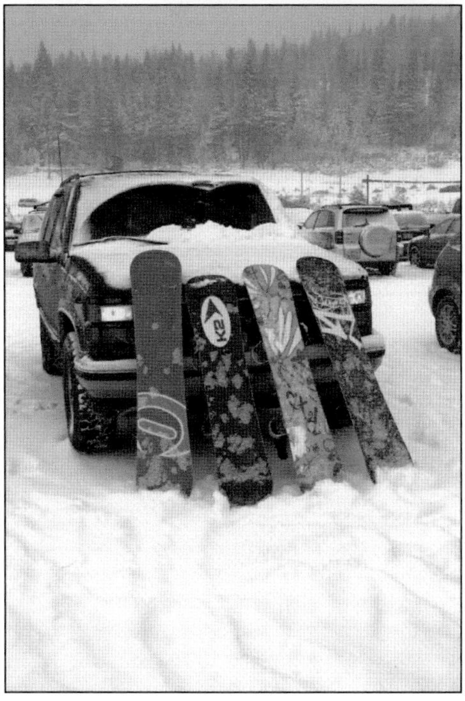

Boreal Mountain Resort was built on land purchased by the Auburn Ski Club after the club's original winter park was destroyed by the construction of Interstate 80. Today, it is a favorite spot for snowboarders, with close and easy access to Sacramento and Reno. Boreal management caters to the young snowboarding set with multiple half-pipes, jumps, rails, and other artificial terrain features. (Courtesy Mark McLaughlin.)

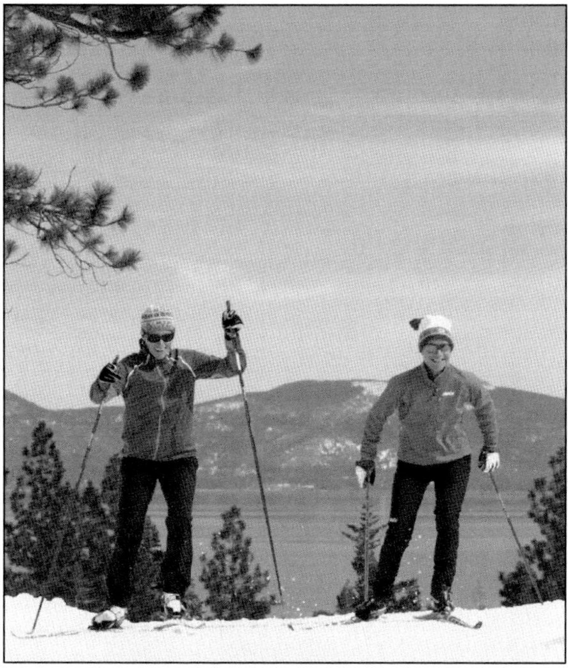

In 1972, Skip Reedy and partner Jerry Smeltzer started a Nordic ski center in Squaw Valley, one of the first cross-country ski areas in the West. They opened Tahoe Nordic on the North Shore in 1976, offering trails that gave skiers views of Lake Tahoe. Today, the Lake Tahoe region is home to one of the greatest concentrations of Nordic facilities in North America. Royal Gorge at Soda Springs is the continent's largest cross-country ski resort. (Courtesy Tahoe Nordic Ski Center/Skip Reedy.)

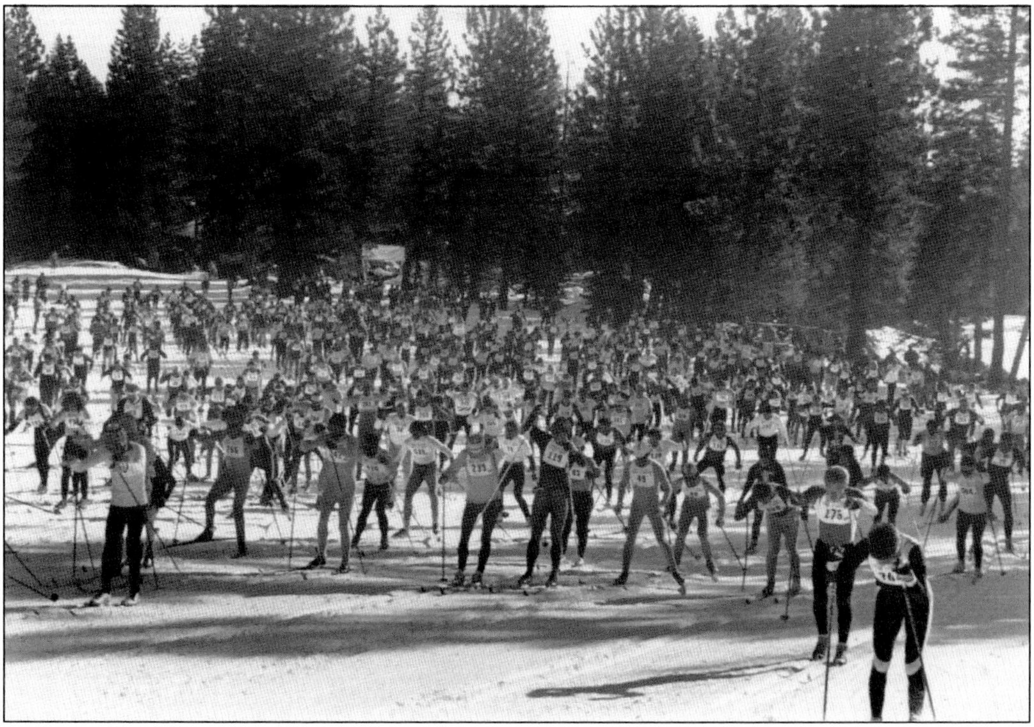

The Great Ski Race starts at Tahoe Cross Country Ski Area and ends at Hilltop in Truckee, a distance of 30 kilometers. The competition, held each March during the North Lake Tahoe Snowfest, attracts hundreds of skiers from around the world. The race is the primary fundraiser for Tahoe Nordic Search and Rescue, a nonprofit, all-volunteer organization. (Courtesy Donner Summit Historical Society/Norm Sayler collection.)

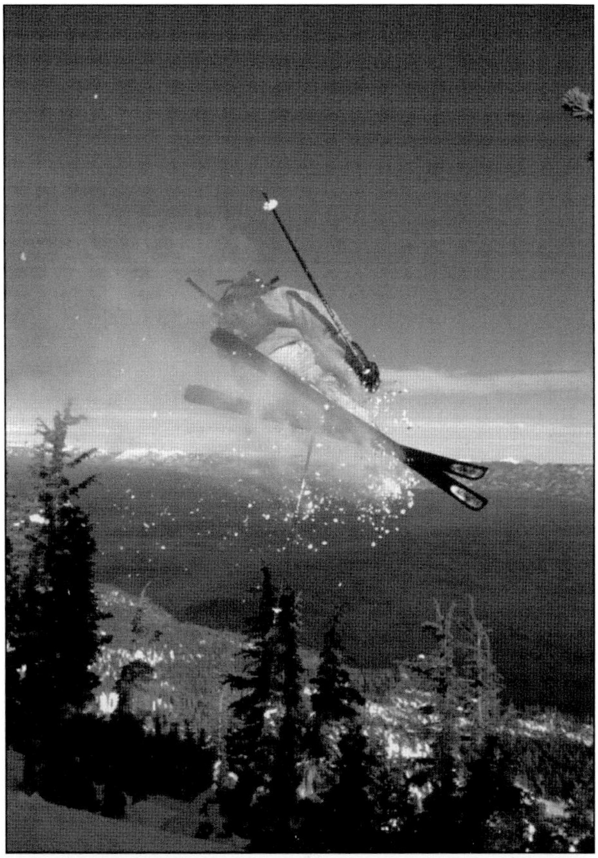

Improvements in backcountry-oriented ski gear have added unlimited terrain to the 22,000 acres of lift-served slopes around the Tahoe Basin. Tahoe is the second deepest alpine lake in the United States, and with an average depth of 1,000 feet, it never freezes, even in the coldest winters. (Both, courtesy David E. Carmazzi/Studio Egidio.)

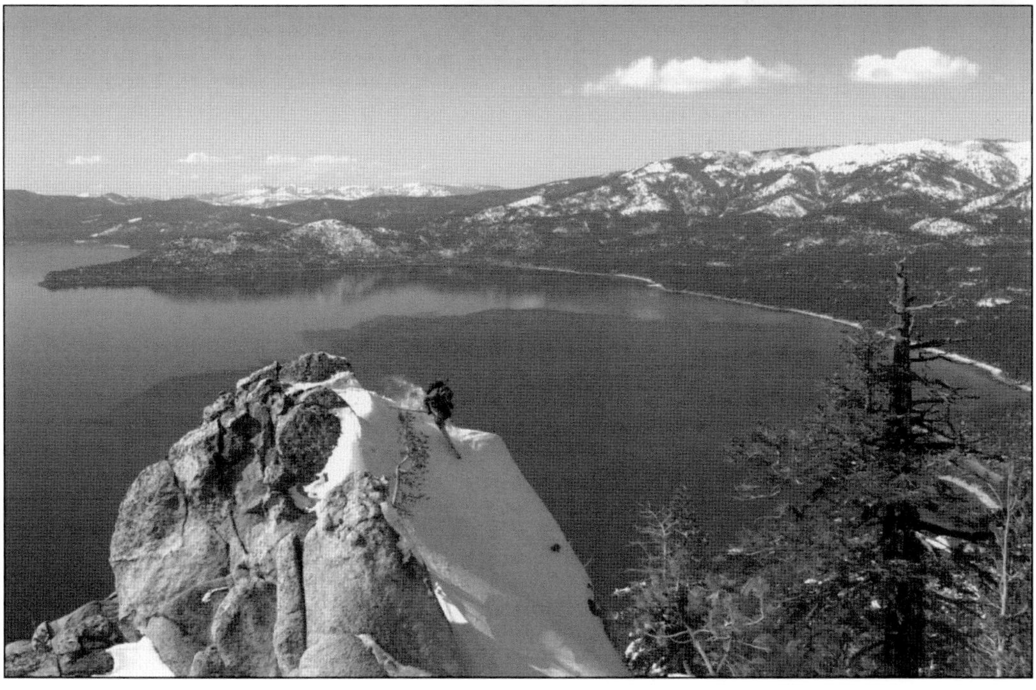

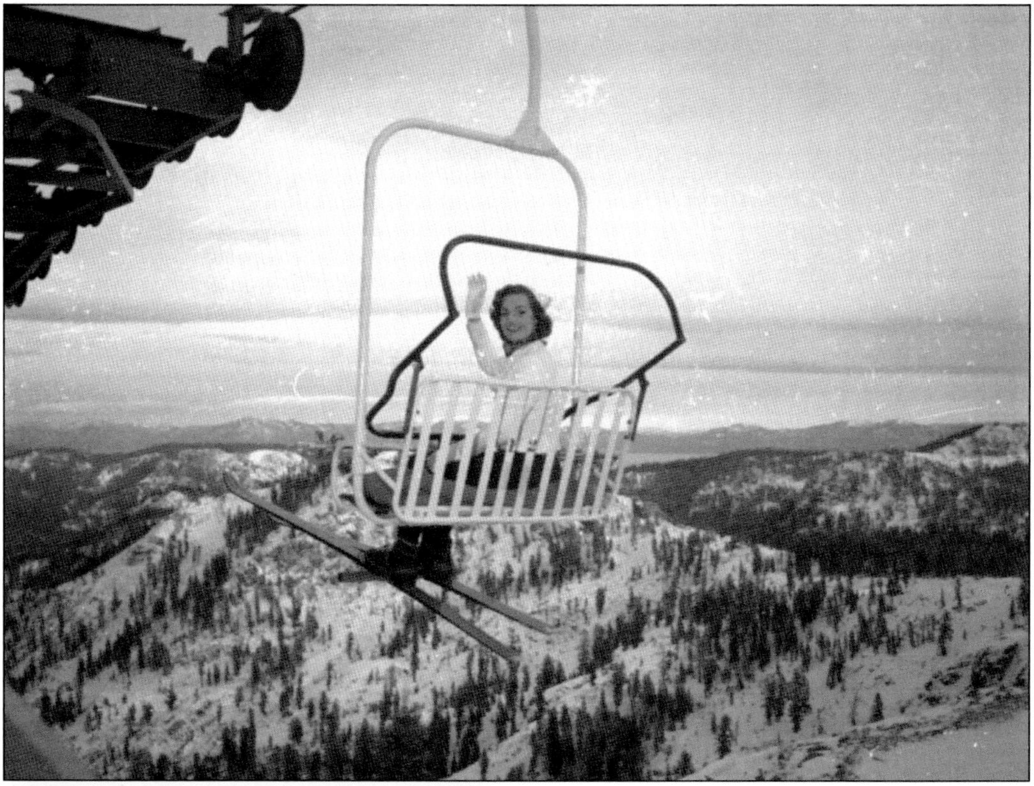

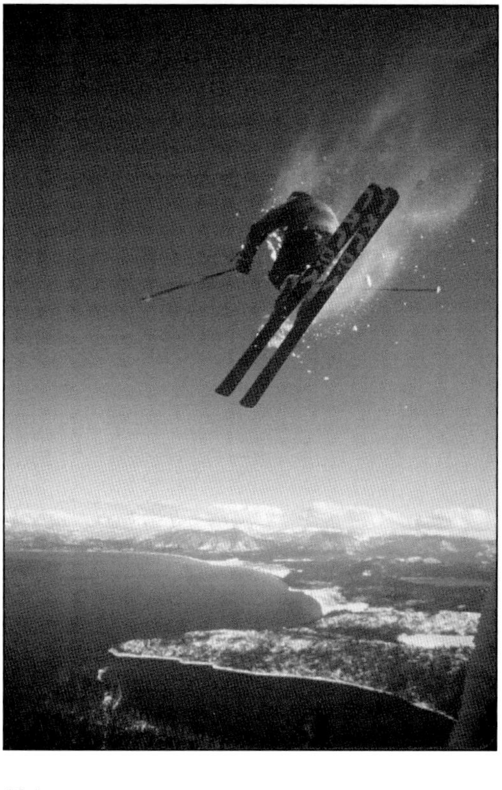

The skiing experience has changed dramatically since this young lady rode a double chair at Squaw Valley in the early 1950s. When combined, Lake Tahoe ski areas form the country's greatest concentration of alpine resorts in one area and make the region one of the most popular ski and snowboard destinations in America. (Courtesy Donner Summit Historical Society/Norm Sayler collection.)

Local skier Scott Hurd launches down Jake's Peak, a popular backcountry descent near Emerald Bay. After a winter storm, skiers and snowboarders scramble to blast fresh powder tracks down steep glades and chutes, all enhanced by the view of "Big Blue" beneath their boards. (Courtesy Keoki Flagg.)

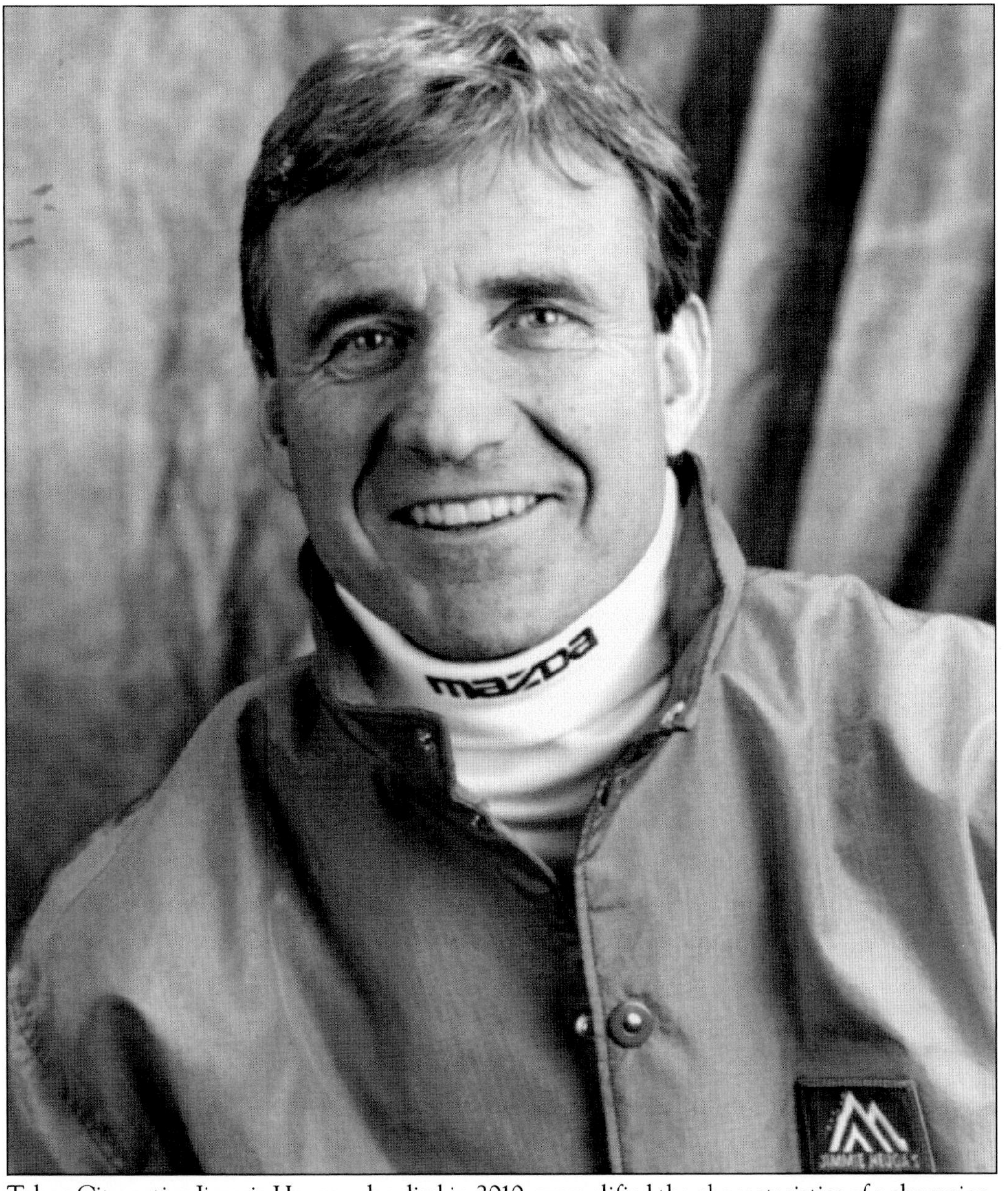


Tahoe City native Jimmie Heuga, who died in 2010, exemplified the characteristics of a champion. One of the first two American men to win an Olympic medal in alpine skiing, Heuga started showing symptoms of multiple sclerosis, a progressive disease that eventually forced him into a wheelchair, in 1968. In 1984, he founded the Heuga Center for Multiple Sclerosis, which has helped thousands afflicted with the disease. For decades, Lake Tahoe has been a launch pad for excellent skiers—and now snowboarders, too. Many have gone on to become national, world, and Olympic champions. These local athletes deserve recognition beyond the ski hill for pushing themselves to be the best and in the process often helping others less able or talented. Many still ski, but some of the best have died; what they all have in common are courage, self-reliance, honesty, and tolerance. These athletes' remarkable stories deserve a book of their own. (Courtesy Donner Summit Historical Society/Robert Frohlich collection.)

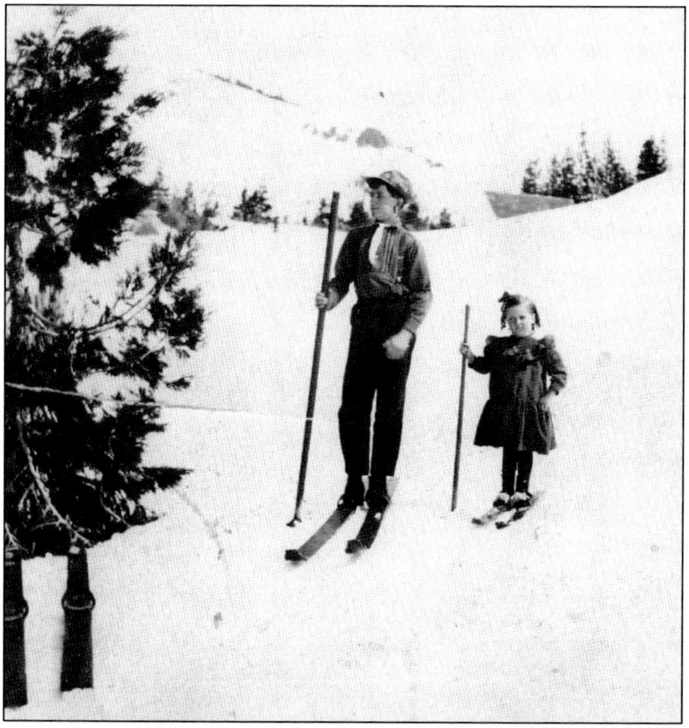

Ski equipment and turning techniques have come a long way since little Ruby Hayes (right) posed on her favorite skis in 1912. Note the simple bindings on the skis at lower left, and the use of one pole to push and steer. (Courtesy William B. Berry collection.)

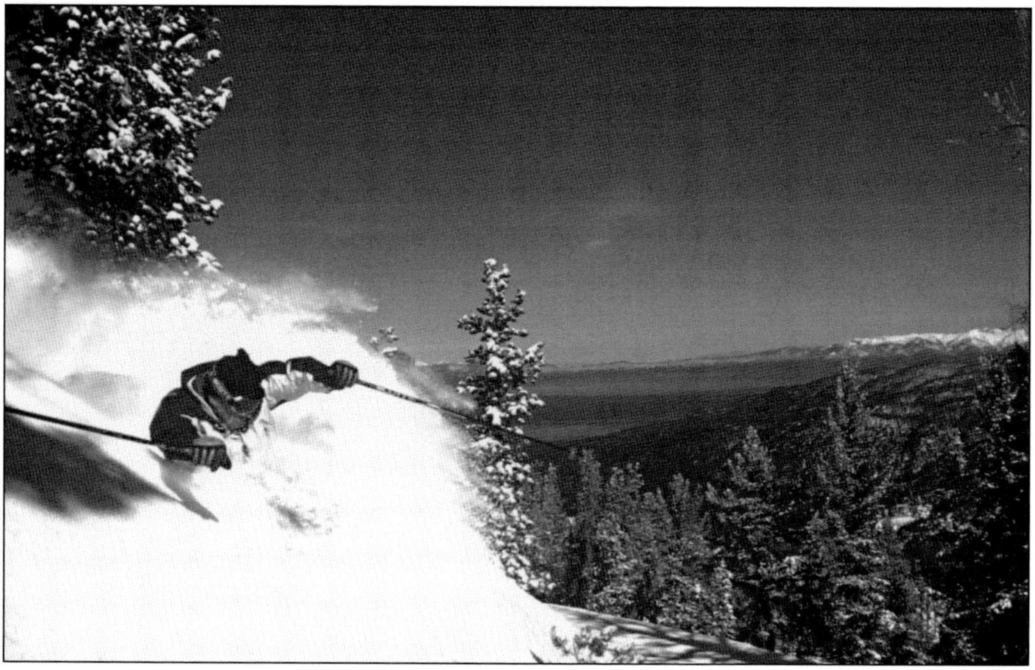

Lake Tahoe boasts some of the best downhill resorts in the nation—extraordinary places like Northstar-at-Tahoe, Heavenly Valley, Sugar Bowl, Squaw Valley USA, Kirkwood, Alpine Meadows, Sierra-at-Tahoe, Homewood, Diamond Peak, and Mount Rose. Cross-country skiing and snowshoeing have also become popular with the advent of better equipment and trail grooming. Tahoe winter sports have a long, rich history, and the future looks bright. (Courtesy Keoki Flagg.)

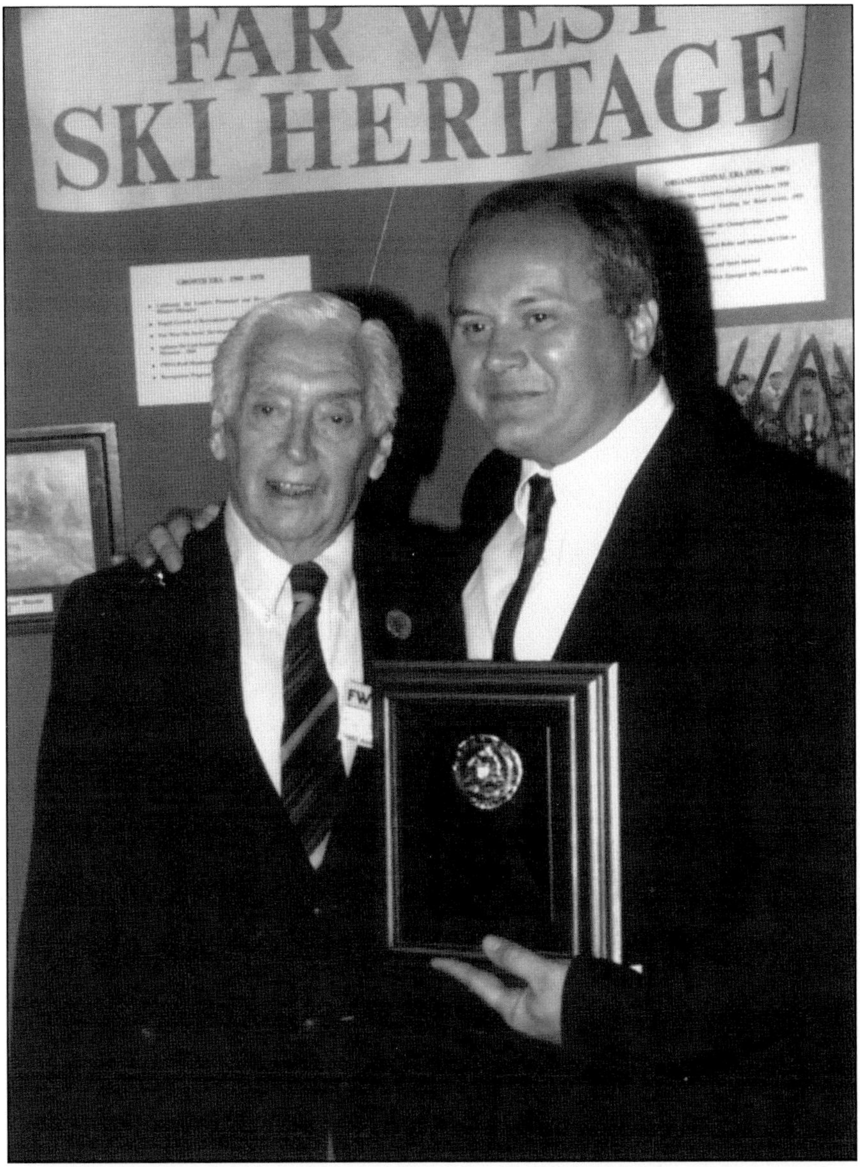


This book is dedicated to the memory of Robert "Fro" Frohlich (right), a longtime North Tahoe resident who died of cancer on October 26, 2010. Fro touched countless lives with his insightful prose about skiing and life's rewards and challenges, as well as with his fundraising efforts for those in need. In 1994, he cofounded Snowtribe Productions, an organization that produces audio-visual shows and other events to benefit local charities. Among his many professional recognitions, Fro accepted the Far West Ski Association's William B. Berry Award for feature writing from Berry himself (left). Frohlich was a respected literary talent who wrote for numerous local and national newspapers and magazines. His 1997 book, *Mountain Dreamers: Visionaries of Sierra Nevada Skiing*, won the prestigious Ullr Award, presented by the International Skiing History Association. Most importantly, Robert Frohlich possessed a boundless zest for life. In his farewell to Frohlich in the *North Lake Tahoe Bonanza*, Bill Jensen wrote, "If, as they say, friends are considered part of the true measure of a man, Fro was as big as the mountains he loved." (Courtesy Donner Summit Historical Society/Robert Frohlich collection.)

Consistent with our mission to preserve history on a local level, this book was printed in South Carolina on American-made paper and manufactured entirely in the United States. Products carrying the accredited Forest Stewardship Council (FSC) label are printed on 100 percent FSC-certified paper.